The Checklist

A K-12 Scope *and* Sequence/Recordkeeper
for Christian Home Educators

by Cindy Downes

The Checklist
A K-12 Scope & Sequence / Recordkeeper for Christian Home Educators

Published by:
C.A.T. Ink
1608 E. Tacoma Street
Broken Arrow, OK 74012

Cover design by N Bishop, Tulsa, Oklahoma

ISBN 0-9765544-0-2

Printed in the United States of America.

Acknowledgements

To my husband, Bill
Thank you, Bill; because, without you, this book wouldn't be written. You made me to keep going when I tried to quit homeschooling and when writing books. You're the best husband in the whole wide world!

To my children Wil and Shelly
Thank you for your patience while I used you as my "guinea pigs" and slowly learned along with you what God really had in store for us all the time!

To all the wonderful homeschool moms who came to my workshops, were part of my homeschool group, and came for consultation: Thank you for letting me be a part of your homeschool, for sharing your ups and downs, what works and what doesn't, and letting me use your stories to help others.

To my best friends in Oklahoma: Linda Cimino, Wendy Curlis, Patty Daugherty, and *Piper Wofford* and *my best friend in Delaware: Carolyn Timmons.* Thank's for being there when I needed you. You are true friends!

Table of Contents

Preface

Is there a desire in your heart to make some changes in your children's educational program? Are your children spending too much time "filling in the blanks" or doing mindless busy work in order to finish the whole textbook by the end of the year? Would you like more time to teach your children the specific skills and character traits needed for them to fulfill God's calling on their lives? Would you like to save money by spending less on textbooks? If you answered yes to any of these questions, then you're a candidate for using The Checklist, A K-12 Scope & Sequence / Recordkeeper for Christian Home Educators.

God created each one of your children for a specific purpose in this generation. Blindly following a mass-produced, school curriculum is not always the best way to get them where God wants them to go. Many teachers (homeschool or regular) make the mistake of overlooking children's God-given gifts and strengths in order to focus on "what every 5th (6th, etc.) grader needs to know" or they assume that all children are called to be engineers, doctors, lawyers, teachers, and the like. But, the real question is: What is the Lord calling them to do?

Your job, as their parent, is to help each of your children find his specific calling, discover what he lacks to pursue it, and then equip him with what he needs to fulfill his calling. My desire in producing *The Checklist* is that it will help you do this *and* fulfill the necessary government requirements as well.

Broken Arrow, Oklahoma   Cindy Downes
February 1, 2005

General Guidelines

In 1994, after my own children had graduated from high school, I began to help other moms with their home education programs. Most of these teacher-moms were struggling with traditional curriculum and found that after spending hours "filling in the blanks," neither they nor their children had the desire or the energy to pursue other desires and interests. I began to encourage them to put aside their traditional curriculum, which was developed for a classroom setting, and select materials that met the specific needs of each of their children. I encouraged them to use more "real" books, add some multi-level unit studies, and make textbooks their servants instead of the other way around. Many of them were afraid that by doing this they wouldn't cover everything that was required by the state, their children wouldn't be able to get into college, or their children's education would somehow be inadequate.

I realized that parents using this nontraditional approach would need a tool that would help them plan their children's educational program and keep track of what has been covered. That's why I began working on The Checklist. By using *The Checklist* in conjunction with your particular state laws, you will have a record showing that your children have covered what is necessary to fulfill requirements and, more importantly, learned the skills needed to fulfill God's call on their lives.

Your children are made up of body, soul (mind), and spirit. (1 Thess, 5:23, "I pray God your whole spirit and soul and body be preserved blameless unto the coming of our Lord Jesus Christ.") Each of these three specific parts needs to be equally fed and nourished in order for your children to fulfill God's call on their lives. Most parents/teachers spend so much time training children's minds and bodies that they have little time left for training the spirit.

Ephesians 4:13 says that a perfect man is one who has attained, "unto the measure of the stature of the fullness of Christ…" This means that Christ, not the world's standards, should be the measuring rod we use to compare our children's physical, spiritual, and academic growth. Jesus, who is our model, matured in all three of these areas as shown in Luke 2:52: "And Jesus increased in wisdom (soul/mind) and stature (body), and in favor with God and man (spirit)." As a Christian, this should be the ultimate goal you have for each of your children.

So how do government requirements for education fit in? God tells us in His Word that Daniel had to learn the language, literature, and knowledge of Babylon, without compromising his faith, in order to fulfill God's plan for his life. (Daniel 1:1-18) Your children must also learn the language, literature, and knowledge of this world, without compromising their faith.

For these reasons, I began *The Checklist* by acquiring a list of "standards" that the government expects your children to master by the twelfth grade. I then combined these "standards" with the skills and character traits Christians need in order to measure up to the standard of Christ. Finally, I arranged this information into outline form based on Luke 2:52 and placed each learning topic into one of four categories as shown on the next page.

- Wisdom, Part I—Acquire knowledge about God. Prov. 9:10, "The fear of the Lord is the beginning of wisdom." (Bible, Church History, World History, U.S. History, State History, Geography, Government, Economics)

    A. Teach them who God is and what His attributes are. (Hebrews 1:1-3)

    B. Teach them about His plan for mankind and how man's acceptance or rejection of Him has or will have affected the world in the past, in the present, and in the future.

    C. Teach them about the unfailing love of God and the difference between the law and grace.

    D. Teach them the basic doctrines of your faith. (Isa. 28:9-10)

    E. Give them role models—people of faith in the Bible and real life.

Wisdom, Part II—Acquire knowledge about God's creation.
(Reading, Literature, Oral and Written Communication, Research Skills, Math, Computer, Science, Art, Music)

    A. Teach them about God's creation.

    B. Teach them to how to subdue and take dominion over all that God has created—Genesis 1:28.

    C. Teach them to read with comprehension, write legibly, communicate effectively, and use basic math skills.

    D. Give them examples of people who have used the knowledge God gave them to take dominion over the earth.

- Stature—Mature physically and chronologically.
(Physical Education, Health, Safety, First Aid, Nutrition, Sex Education)

    A. Physical Development and Exercise

        (1) Help them develop small and large motor skills. Keep in mind that children develop at different paces. (Read *Home Grown Kids* by Dr. Raymond Moore for more information.)

        (2) Keep their physicals, dental and eye checkups, and immunizations current.

        (3) Have them participate in recreational activities, team sports, and physical labor (chores, volunteer work, etc.).

    B. Care of The Temple— Cor. 6:19, "Know ye not that your body is the temple of the Holy Ghost which is in you…therefore glorify God in your body…"

        (1) Teach them proper nutrition, cleanliness, and to dress appropriately.

        (2) Teach them about safety and first aid.

        (3) Teach them the benefits of keeping their bodies under subjection.(1 Cor. 9:27, "But I keep under my body, and bring it into subjection…")

- In Favor With God—Know God personally.

    A. Spiritual Growth—Help them to know God personally and be a person of love, faith, and hope

        (1) Teach them about God's love (John 3:16) and grace (Ephesians 2:8).

        (2) Teach them how to accept salvation.

        (3) Teach them about baptism.

        (4) Help them to make Jesus their Lord, to trust Him in every area of their lives.

        (5) Teach them to pray, read the Word, and praise and worship God.

        (6) Teach them to hate evil. (Psalm 97:10, "Ye that love the Lord, hate evil.")

    B. Doers of the Word—Teach them the benefit of doing what the Word says and the results of neglecting the Word. (James 1:22)

    C. Stewardship—Teach them to be good stewards of their time, talents, personal possessions, and the time and possessions of others.

- In Favor With Man—Teach them how to share the love of God with others and to be a light and an example of Christ to the world. (Matt. 5:14) (Charity, Church Responsibility, Christian Love, Marriage Preparation, Industrial Arts, Home Economics, Sociology [World Customs & Religions, Missions, Foreign Language, Archaeology, Social Work, Social Skills], Psychology [Biblical Counseling, Personality Differences, Crisis Intervention, Respect for Life])

    A. Train them to love and serve the body of Christ.

    B. Train them to love and serve their families.

    C. Train them to love and serve the community around them.

After this basic outline was developed, I then researched each subject area to see what specific topics are normally covered in traditional school curriculums. Because this varies from publisher to publisher, *The Checklist* includes a compilation of many scope and sequences. Therefore, more topics are included in *The Checklist* than any child can cover in twelve years of school. **YOUR CHILD WILL NOT COVER EVERYTHING IN *THE CHECKLIST*!**

What specific topics to cover should be based on your particular state requirements and on each of your children's readiness, abilities, interests, and goals.

Use the analogy of a bank teller to help you decide when to study particular topics. A bank teller is only allowed to touch "real" money during the beginning stages of his training. The idea is that by touching only what is "real", he will be able to recognize what is counterfeit. After he is thoroughly familiar with "real" money, he is given a time of on-the-job training, working with constant supervision. If questions arise regarding the money, the teller is to seek consultation with his trainer. Finally, he is allowed to work on his own without supervision. He is then capable of making sure that only "real" money is exchanged.[1]

In the same way, give your children a sound, Biblically-based education. Everything they read or are taught should reflect the truth of God's Word. The Bible is the final and ultimate authority—the standard

      THE CHECKLIST, Copyright © 2005 by Cindy Downes

by which all ideas are measured and evaluated. As you read and discuss textbooks and other literature, ask "What is the writer trying to say?" Have them compare what they are reading with what the Bible teaches. Help them to evaluate what is being said as it compares to what the Bible teaches. Eventually, they will be able to do this on their own.

During the elementary years, your job is to give them an overall "taste" of all that God has created. Provide a wide variety of literature in all subject areas for them to read or include in your family reading times. Don't be afraid to pursue topics that "spin off" from the one you are currently studying. That's one of the benefits of the *The Checklist*. You can pursue a topic while it's hot and go back later to topics you missed because you have a record of what you have and have not done.

As your children get into junior and senior high, their gifts and specific callings will become more evident. This is the time to expand on those subjects you've already touched on and begin tailoring their studies to suit each of their specific career/ministry needs.

Start working on high school in junior high. There is nothing in the law that says your children must take United States History in junior high and again in senior high even though that is what most schools do. Teach it once, covering it thoroughly even if it takes more than one year. Then write it on their high school transcript. You can print off a sample transcript and a blank transcript from my website (http://www.oklahomahomeschool.com/trans1.html).

At the start of junior high school, obtain copies of admission requirements from any colleges or trade schools your child might be interested in attending, if any. (College catalogs are free for the asking on their websites.) Keep these requirements in mind as you plan your course of study, remembering that these requirements can be fulfilled in many ways. Colleges of all types accept homeschooling students; however, they may have different acceptance policies. Stanford University says in their admissions letter for homeschoolers, "…we do not have a required curriculum or set of courses for applicants to Stanford… Primarily, we want them to be able to demonstrate that they have successfully undertaken a serious, rigorous course of study. They should definitely provide a detailed description of their curriculum when they apply, but it is not necessary to follow a prescribed or approved homeschooling program…the central issue for us is how they have gone about the learning process, not how many hurdles they have jumped."[2]

Don't be overly concerned about a possible inability to teach high school level math and science courses that your children might need to enter college. If you train them in their early years to be independent learners and self-motivated, they will be able to teach themselves what they need to know as long as you get them the necessary materials. If, however, you haven't done a good job in this area, or if you're starting to homeschool later in their academic years, check out other resources for these difficult subjects such as homeschool co-ops, paid tutors, correspondence courses, and courses over the internet. It's also possible for your children to make up missed high school classes during their freshman year of college; however, this can be expensive and time consuming.

Consider apprenticeships for older children. They are not easy to come by, but I have found that with a lot of prayer and by asking questions of people you know, you can find them. A good way to initiate an apprenticeship program is to approach a business owner with the idea of allowing your child to spend one afternoon at their place of business to observe. If that works out for both parties, ask the business owner if the child could come and volunteer on a regular basis. (This means sweeping floors, filing, washing windows, etc. Your child must be willing to do the grunt work!) You will find that over time, if your child is diligent and faithful, he will be welcomed with open arms and slowly given more career-related work.

This volunteer work may eventually lead to a paid position during high school or even a life-time career. Business people are looking for good employees; and when they find someone who has potential, they will do all that they can to help train him. If a degree is necessary, some business owners will even help with funds for education. Even if your child decides from this experience that he does not want to pursue a career in this particular field, think of the time and money you have saved!

Allocate enough time to what is important and limit those things that are not important. No one person can learn everything there is to know! If you have your children try to do everything, they will eventually grow less and less effective in each of their endeavors. Bob Buford in his book, *Game Plan*, says, "Christians are working very hard at things that do not fit their skills, abilities, and interests. One way to counter this is to say no to anything that doesn't maximize these areas in your life, even though it is only five or ten degrees off your mission."[3] John Maxwell in his book, *Developing the Leaders Around You*, says, "A person should be spending 80 percent of his time doing things that require his greatest gifts and abilities."[4] You will need to constantly evaluate and make some tough choices about which school subjects and extracurricular activities are necessary for each of your children. Pray and seek God for wisdom and understanding. As you see their interests and abilities become more evident, have them spend 80% of their time on those things and 20% on the rest.

Expect the best from your children. Look for strengths that others may have missed. Expect them to fulfill God's call on their lives. A study was done by Robert Rosenthal, a Harvard psychologist, and Lenore Jacobson, a San Francisco school principal, to find out if some children perform poorly in school because their teachers expect them to. They administered a learning ability test to a group of 5th graders. The next fall, teachers were given the names of five or six children in their new class who were designated as "spurters" (intellectually gifted) as revealed by this IQ test. The teachers didn't know that the test had been rigged and that these "spurters" were chosen at random. At the end of school year, the children were retested. The supposed "spurters" gained as many as 15 to 27 I.Q. points. The teachers also described these children in more positive terms and said that they had a better chance of success in later life. The only real change was the teacher's attitude towards the child![5] As Goethe said, we should "Treat people as if they were what they ought to be and help them to become what they are capable of being."

Remember Proverbs 29:18, "Where there is no vision, the people perish." Each year, you and your children should set goals for yourselves and write them down. Keep this in front of you all year long and make everything you do line up with your goals! Encourage your children to pursue as many of their goals as possible. This not only tells them that you care about them, but that they need to plan ahead to get what they want. Be willing to incorporate as many of their goals as possible into the goals of your family as a whole. Do everything possible to help them to get where the Lord has called them to go.

Don't assume that your children are lazy or unmotivated. If you gave your children permission to work on favorite hobbies, what would they do? They would display a great deal of motivation as they pursued their interests and abilities. But give the same children, who's reading skills have not developed, reading workbooks and they will sit untouched. Does this mean they are lazy? No, of course not. Children develop different skills at different rates. Skills that develop early in one child may develop years later in another. Talents that develop in one child may never develop in another. Einstein was four before he could speak and seven before he could read. Both Sir Isaac Newton and Thomas Edison were considered poor students in elementary school. But as we know, they eventually discovered their gifts, pursued them, and became the successful people that we know them as today. On the other hand, Mozart was playing the keyboard confidently when only four years of age and composing his first pieces of music at age five. You certainly can't say that Einstein, Newton, and Edison were lazy and Mozart wasn't! Alan McGinnis says in his book, *Bringing Out the Best in People*, "The challenge is not to take lazy people and transform them into industrious types. Rather it is to channel already existing energies into the most worthwhile endeavors. People do not like being lethargic and bored. They will welcome the manager who can teach them to enjoy their work, or the teacher who will impart to them a love of learning that causes the school day to go swiftly."[6] All children have the desire to achieve something, to be somebody, to make their lives count. Your job is to tap into that desire and then watch as they do almost anything to live up to your expectations.

Keep a high standard of excellence. You should allow for individuality but be tough on enforcing standards. Be firm in your standards of excellence even if it makes you temporarily unpopular. Follow undesirable behavior with immediate correction. Be fair. Goals should be both challenging and realistic. Give them clear-cut objectives that are attainable by them. Insist that they do an excellent job on what they are capable of handling rather than a "just-so" job on getting every page done as required by the teacher's manual. Nancy Hanks once said, "My parents always told me that people will never know how long it takes you to do something. They will only know how well it is done."

Teach them that failure is not fatal! As their teacher, be willing to accept some mistakes. Don't be so hard on them that they give up. Everyone needs regular successes. Help them to learn from their mistakes and not to quit. Oliver Goldsmith once said, "Success consists of getting up just one more time than you fall." Encourage them to try new skills and explore different avenues of study. This is especially important during the early years as you are trying to discover their God-given talents. Get them out of their comfort zone occasionally, and you might be surprised what you find out! "The men who try to do something and fail are infinitely better than those who try to do nothing and succeed."[7]

Give them appropriate role models. Tell them about and, if possible, introduce them to successful people in the field in which they are interested. Read biographies of successful people who model behaviors you want them to acquire.

Recognize and applaud achievement. Businesses recognize achievement of their employees by putting pictures of their "Top Salesman" in their company newspaper or giving their "Employee of the Month" special parking privileges. Why not look for signs of positive change in your children, and use their successes as an excuse for celebration? Hang up a picture of your "Student of the Month", along with specifics about what he has accomplished towards his goal. Give tokens of appreciation for a job well done. Be careful, however, not to overdo it to the point that it is meaningless.

Stimulate mild competition. Keep in mind that the goal is not to shame them but to inspire them. The purpose of your competition should be to give them the message that if others can do it, so can they.

Teach them teamwork. Mother Teresa once said, "I can do what you can't do, and you can do what I can't do. Together we can do great things." Reward cooperation. Teach them how to work together to accomplish more. Most people will end up working or ministering where teamwork is essential.

Equip them to get along without you. As you work with your children, "…give them what they need to take care of themselves. Teach them to find resources. Encourage them to get out of their comfort zone on their own. And point them toward additional people who can help them learn and grow. If you can help them to become lifelong learners, you will have given them an incredible gift."[8]

Above all, teach your children God's love and grace. If they don't *experience* the love and grace of God, they will not be able to *give* God's love and grace. My biggest regret regarding my homeschooling years is that I failed in this area. Yes, I was saved and serving God with all my heart, but I hadn't personally experienced the *love* and *grace* of God. Therefore, I was not able to pass this on to my children. They, like me, learned all the rules and regulations of serving God, but not the joy of God's love and His unending grace. Consequently, in spite of all that I taught them, they spent their early adult years running *from God* instead of *to God*. Thanks be to God who *is* love and grace, all of us are now learning to know God's love and grace. My prayer for you is, that not only will you personally experience God's love and grace, but you will pass it on to your children by example. As Paul said, "If I speak in the tongues of men and angels, but have not love (that reasoning, intentional, spiritual devotion such as is inspired by God's love for and in us), I am only a noisy gong or a clanging cymbal. And if I have prophetic powers—that is, the gift of interpreting the divine will and purpose; and understand all the secret truths and mysteries <u>and possess all knowledge</u> (underline mine), and if I have sufficient faith so that I can remove mountains, but have not love (God's love in me), I am nothing—a useless nobody." (Amplified, 1 Corinthians 13:1-2).

Finally, the old saying, "You can lead a horse to water but you can't make them drink." is still valid today. Each child is responsible to work out his own salvation (see Philippians 2:12). Your job is to lead your child to the path of righteousness by teaching and example. You CANNOT make your child walk down the right path. Many homeschool parents, including myself, have had to watch, broken-hearted, as their child made some wrong choices. If that is you, be encouraged that even God, the perfect parent, watched as his children, Adam and Eve, took the wrong path. But God had a plan for them just as he has a plan for us *and* for our children. The Bible says, "...You have heard of the endurance of Job and have seen the outcome of the Lord's dealings, that the Lord is full of compassion and is merciful." (NIV, James 5:11) Remember, God loves your children more than you do and He will do everything in His power to keep them just as He does to keep you. Don't ever give up, "Blessed is the man who perseveres under trial, because when he has stood the test, he will receive the crown of life that God has promised to those who love him." (NIV, James 1:12)

[1] QUINE, DAVID. "A Biblical World View Approach to Classical Education," The Teaching Home, September-October 1997, pp. 44-45.

[2] "HOME SCHOOLING AND THE ADMISSION EVALUATION PROCESS." STANFORD UNIVERSITY. 21 MAY 2004 <HTTP://WWW.STANFORD.EDU/DEPT/UGA/CRITERIA/HOME_SCHOOLING.HTML>.

[3] BUFORD, BOB. Game Plan (Grand Rapids, Zondervan Publishing House, 1997)

[4] MAXWELL, JOHN C. Developing the Leader's Around You (Nashville, Thomas Nelson Publishers, 1995)

[5] ROSENTHAL, ROBERT and LENORE JACOBSON. Pygmalion in the Classroom (New York: Holt, Rinehart and Winston, 1968)

[6] MCGINNIS, ALAN LOY. Bringing Out The Best in People (Minneapolis: Augsburg Publishing House, 1985)

[7] Quoted by LLOYD JONES; Michael Reagan and Bob Phillips, All American Quote Book (Eugene, Harvest House Publishers, 1995)

[8] MAXWELL, JOHN C. and JIM DORNAN, Becoming a Person of Influence (Nashville, Thomas Nelson Publishers, 1997)

Step-by-Step Directions

1. Before you begin planning for next year, read all the way through the instruction pages of this book to get an overall vision for using *The Checklist*.

2. Turn to any page in *The Checklist* and notice the two blank lines before each topical entry. The first line is to be used during preschool and elementary school; the second one is to be used for secondary school. Simply write each child's initials in the appropriate blank line after you cover the material for that topic. Please keep in mind that you will not have a child's initials on every blank for every topic. Some topics will be covered only in elementary school, some only in high school, and some won't be covered at all by a particular child, depending on his specific abilities, interests, and needs. In addition, you may find topics that are not listed in this book that you want to include. Therefore, blank lines and a blank checklist page are included in this book for additional topics. If you prefer to have a separate checklist for each of your children, the purchaser has permission to reproduce *The Checklist* <u>for purchaser's use only</u>. No part of *The Checklist* is reproducible in any format (print, electronic, or any other format) to share, give away, or sell to others.

3. If you have been teaching your children at home for a year or more, take time to initial the topics your children have already covered. Initialing it does not mean that your children have memorized every fact about the topic, but it does mean that you have exposed them to the material in an organized fashion.

4. Obtain a copy of and read your state's home education requirements; and, if you have junior and senior level students, obtain copies of catalogs from colleges your children may want to attend and check the admission requirements. Keep these requirements in mind as you plan your children's course of study.

5. Send off for free home education supply catalogs listed on my website: http://www.oklahomahomeschool.com/textbookpub.html.

6. If you are a new homeschooler, please read through "Getting Started" on my website (http://www.oklahomahomeschool.com/info.html).

7. Before you begin purchasing curriculum, read through "Choosing Curriculum" (http://www.oklahomahomeschool.com/choose.html) and "Choosing Curriculum Based on Learning Styles" (http://www.oklahomahomeschool.com/learnS.html) on my website.

8. Using the "Sample Curriculum Plan" on page 11 of this book or the one on my website (http://www.oklahomahomeschool.com/CPsample.html) as a guide, write down a list of the subjects you want to cover next year for each child. I recommend that you place your child in the grade level he would be according to chronological age even though he may be above or below that level in ability. Children learn in spurts, level off, slow down and speed up all during their growing years. They will catch up and be able to graduate with his peers. For children who are academically advanced, I personally do not recommend graduating them early unless you have a specific reason for doing so. Instead, I recommend having them take college classes concurrently or by correspondence during their high school years. This gives them a head start on their college credits while enabling them to continue to mature under their parents' guidance.

9. Using the reproducible "Yearly Planning Form" on page 181 of the *The Checklist*, write down the specific topics you want to cover for each subject selected. Don't overdo it! Keep your goals attainable. Remember, you will not cover everything in the *The Checklist*, and what you do cover should take you twelve years. Keep each child's individual development, abilities, and goals in mind. Use *The Checklist* as your servant, not your master. Above all, listen to the Holy Spirit.

10. After you have planned the topics for the year, select curriculum and other resources you'll need to teach these topics. Refer to "Recommended Curriculum" on my website (http://www.oklahomahomeschool.com/CurrRec.html) and the curriculum catalogs you received in the mail for resources to teach these topics. There are many more resources available than the ones listed and new ones are being created all the time. Check my website often as I add curriculum recommendations and unit studies on a regular basis. Attend curriculum fairs, go to your local bookstores, and talk with friends to find out what's new. But, <u>always keep in mind the specific needs and abilities of your children</u> before spending valuable dollars on the latest fad in home school resources. Homeschooling has become a lucrative financial market and not all that is being produced is right for your family. I'm amazed at what I'm seeing at curriculum fairs these days. Some of the same reading programs that don't work in public schools are now being marketed to homeschoolers! Check it out for yourself. And even then, be prepared for trial and error. You will not pick out the right product every time. Call it a lesson learned, sell it, and try again. That's part of homeschooling!

11. Plan the first four to six weeks of school before starting school. Integrate unit studies as desired. You can find resources for these on my website at: http://www.oklahomahomeschool.com/unitstudies.html

12. For information on teaching specific subjects, read through "Teaching Homeschool." (http://www.oklahomahomeschool.com/teaching.html)

13. Once your first four to six weeks of school are planned out, it's time to begin. Remember to be flexible! When you go to the library, you may not find the books you are looking for. That's ok! Use books you do find and reserve ones you want to use later. The beauty of this system is that *The Checklist* is a handy record of what you covered, making it easy to spot holes in your child's learning which can be filled in at a later time.

14. Don't let summers and weekends go to waste. If you're going to be studying the American Revolution this year, pick up books at the library related to that topic, have them read them during the summer, and initial the completed topics as you go. You'll be way ahead next September. (Don't forget to document this learning time in your log book.)

15. Continue planning one to two weeks ahead, adjusting your schedule and materials covered as needed. Check off the topics covered in *The Checklist* as you go.

16. For more information on multi-level teaching, read through my web page entitled, "Multi-level Teaching." (http://www.oklahomahomeschool.com/MultiLevel.html).

SAMPLE CURRICULUM PLAN
PRESCHOOL AND KINDERGARTEN

WISDOM

- Art and Music—PreK-K Level Activities Using a Variety of Art Forms and Methods
- Bible Stories and Bible Characters
- Reading, Writing, and Math —Readiness and Beginning Skill Development, Learn to Appreciate Good Literature (Read to Them Daily)
- Science—PreK-K Level Activities Related to God's Creation & Nature Studies

STATURE

- Physical Development—Large and Small Motor Skills (Physical Education, Games, Exercise, and Simple Chores)
- Health—PreK-K Level Health & Nutrition Topics, Medical Checkups
- Safety—PreK-K Level Topics: Stranger Danger, Fire Safety, Home Safety, and First Aid

IN FAVOR WITH GOD (Teach by Example)

- God's Love—Help Your Child to Experience God's Love
- Prayer—Teach Your Child to Talk With God on a Regular Basis
- Obedience—Teach Them Rely on God to Help Them Obey (Philippians 2:13)
- Stewardship—Teach Them Good Stewardship Skills

IN FAVOR WITH MAN

- Charity—Sharing God's Love With Others (Teach by Example)
- Church Attendance (Teach by Example)
- Develop the Fruit of the Spirit (Teach by Example)
- Home Economics—Simple Cooking, Sewing, and Crafts
- Industrial Arts—Simple Chores Around the Home
- Social Studies—Communities, Neighborhoods, and Families Around the World
- Stories of Famous Missionaries and Other Role Models
- Outreach Opportunities (Teach by Example)
- Hospitality (Teach by Example)
- Manners (Teach by Example)

ELEMENTARY SCHOOL

WISDOM

- Art—General Introduction, Beginning Skill Development, and Art Appreciation
- Bible—Bible Stories, Bible Characters, Bible Reading, Basic Church Doctrines, Foundations of Faith, and Introduction to Church History
- Computer—Keyboarding and Basic Computer Skills
- History/Social Studies—Give them a general introduction to history using the *Unit Study Planning Guide for History* on the Oklahoma Homeschool website (http://www.oklahomahomeschool.com/usguideH.html) or the more traditional list below:

  Year 1: Families, Communities Around the World, Famous People, and Map Skills (Home and Neighborhood)
  Year 2: Communities, Local Government, Citizenship, Occupations, and Map Skills (Community)
  Year 3: Early America, Explorers, U.S. Geography, and U.S. Government
  Year 4: Continue American History, State History, U.S. and State Geography, and American Government
  Year 5: World History and World Geography (Eastern Hemisphere)
  Year 6: Continue World History and World Geography (Western Hemisphere)

- Math—Master Basic Math Skills

- Music—General Introduction, Beginning Skill Development, and Music Appreciation
- Oral Communication—Oral Reading, Recite Memory Work/Speech, Drama
- Reading—Master Basic Skills, Develop Fluency, Learn to Appreciate Good Literature (Read to Them Daily), Read to Learn, Read for Enjoyment
- Research Skills—Dictionary, Encyclopedia, Other Reference Books, Library, Internet
- Science—Give them a general introduction to science using the *Unit Study Planning Guide for Science* on the Oklahoma Homeschool website (http://www.oklahomahomeschool.com/usguideS.html) or the list below:

  Two Years of: Earth Sciences (Meteorology, Astronomy, Geology, Oceanography, and Conservation)
  Two Years of: Physical Science and Chemistry
  Two Years of: Life Sciences (Biology, Botany, and Zoology)

- Written Communication—Master Basic Handwriting, Grammar, and Composition Skills

STATURE

- Physical Development—Physical Education, Games, Individual and Team Sports, Exercise, and Chores
- Health—Medical Checkups, Health, Nutrition, Substance Abuse, and Intro to Sex Education
- Safety—First Aid, Home Safety, and Fire Safety

In Favor With God (Teach By Example)

- God's Love—Help Your Child to Experience God's Love
- Prayer—Teach Your Child to Talk With God on a Regular Basis
- Being a Doer of the Word—Teach Them Rely on God to Help Them (Philippians 2:13)
- Stewardship—Teach Them Good Stewardship Skills

In favor With Man

- Charity—Love Your Neighbor as Yourself, Respect for Life (Teach By Example)
- Church Responsibility—As Part of the Body of Christ (Teach By Example)
- Industrial Arts —Occupations*
- Home Economics
- World Customs & Religions—Families*, Communities*, and Communities Around the World*
- Foreign Language—Introduction
- Missions and Famous Missionaries—Famous People*
- Social Work and Charity (Teach By Example)
- Local Government*, Citizenship*
- Social Skills—Manners, Hospitality (Teach By Example)

* Considered Social Studies in traditional curriculum.

Check your state requirements for the minimum number of units needed per year (one unit equals one year of study). Check prospective college or trade-school catalog for specific requirements.

WISDOM

- Bible—Bible Study, Basic Church Doctrines, Foundations of Faith, and Church History

- Computer—Keyboarding, Word Processing, Database, Graphics, Desktop Publishing, Multimedia, Spreadsheet, Website Development, Programming, Repair and Maintenance, CAD.

- Electives—Select as needed to fulfill requirements and according to each child's life goals:

    Art—Art History, Art Appreciation, Famous Painters and Their Works, Art Technique and Skill Development, Architecture, Crafts

    Music—Music History, Music Appreciation, Famous Musicians and Their Music, Music Skill Development

    Economics

    Any high school level subject that is not a requirement can also be used as electives.

- Math—Basic Math Skills, Math History, Computers in Math, Algebra I, Geometry, Business Math, Consumer Math, Christian Stewardship, Logic. College Math, if needed, consisting of Algebra II, Analytical Geometry, Calculus, Trigonometry, Statistics, Math Analysis

- Oral Communication, Speech, Drama

- Reading—Reading to Learn, Reading for Enjoyment, American Literature, and World Literature

- Research Skills, Library Skills, Internet Skills

- History—In most schools, U.S. and World History are taken in junior high school and then again in high school. An option would be to have your children complete the equivalent of a high school level course in each of these subjects one time, taking one to two years to complete them. They may be taken in any order.

    | 1/2-1 Year of: | High School Level State History |
    | 1/2-1 Year of: | High School Level Government |
    | Two Years of: | High School Level U.S. History and Geography |
    | Two Years of: | High School Level World History and Geography |

Another alternative would be to cover all history topics in six years as follows: Government, State History and Geography are integrated into each topic as needed.

> Year 1: Ancient Civilizations: Israel, Egypt, China, India, Japan
> Year 2: Mayan, Incans, Aztec, Ancient Greece, Ancient Rome
> Year 3: Byzantine Empire, Middle Ages, Renaissance, Reformation, Church History
> Year 4: Explorers, US and World History up to 1775
> Year 5: U.S. & World History from 1775-1900.
> Year 6: U.S. and World History through Present (1900-present day)

- Science—Check your high school, college, or trade-school requirements and select as needed and according to each child's goals. Lab work must be included for most colleges. Select from: Physical Science, Biology, Chemistry, Physics, Geology, Astronomy, and Earth Science

- Written Communication—Composition, Grammar as Needed

STATURE

- Physical Development—Physical Education, Individual and Team Sports, Exercise, Chores, and Trades that Involve Physical Labor
- Health—Medical Checkups, Health, Nutrition, Sex Education, and Substance Abuse
- Safety—First Aid, Fire Safety, and Driver's Education

IN FAVOR WITH GOD (Teach By Example)

- God's Love—Help Your Child Experience God's Love

- Prayer—Teach Your Child to Talk With God on a Regular Basis

- Spiritual Growth & Being a Doer of the Word

- Stewardship—Teach Them Good Stewardship Skills

IN FAVOR WITH MAN

- Charity—Love Your Neighbor as Yourself, Respect for Life (Teach By Example)
- Church Responsibility—As Part of the Body of Christ (Teach By Example)
- Marriage Preparation
- Industrial Arts
- Home Economics
- Sociology—World Customs & Religions, Missions, Foreign Language (2 years required for college), Archaeology, Social Work and Charity, Social Skills, Citizenship, Political Science
- Psychology—Biblical Counseling, Personality Differences, Crisis Intervention, Respect for Life

Ten Tips For Teaching More Than One

If you have several children in multiple-grade levels, try some of the tips below.

1. Younger students need daily one-on-one teaching for beginning arithmetic, handwriting, and phonics. Have older children work on subjects they can do without your help while you work one-on-one with your younger. If the older child gets stuck, have him set it aside and go on to something else until you are finished with your one-on-one work.

2. Have your older children correct their own work. Afterwards, go over items they missed and assign new material to reinforce what they just learned.

3. Give older students a daily, weekly, or monthly checklist, letting them decide what to do and when. Have them cross off each item as completed. Allow them free time to pursue other interests after all their daily, weekly, or monthly assignments are completed.

4. Include babies and toddlers in your lessons when possible. As you read aloud, hold them in your lap. When you stop to ask questions, ask them questions also. They may not understand everything they hear but you will be amazed at what they do remember.

5. For your babies and toddlers, check out picture books from the library that are related to the topics you are teaching. Let them "read" these books while you are working with your older children. Then use these books as a read-aloud for your younger children.

6. Set aside special toys for toddlers to be used only during school time (games, puzzles, blocks, art supplies, books, cassette tapes, etc.). Encourage them to play quietly while you are working with your older children.

7. Teach subjects such as Bible, Science, History, Literature, Music, Art, etc. as multi-level units incorporating all your children in the lesson. It is not critical which of these subjects are covered when. Consider your family's interests and goals. Use the same topic for each child but assign different independent reading, hands-on projects, and written work according to each child's abilities and goals. See my website (http://www.oklahomahomeschool.com/MultiLevel.html) for more information.

8. If possible, give the older children specific subjects to teach the younger ones. This will not only help the younger child and you, but it will also help the older children to learn parenting skills for the future and reinforce what they have already learned. I do not recommend this unless the older child is willing and excited about doing it.

9. Consider your circumstances and plan ahead. If you are going to have a new baby or move, plan on less academics during these times. Make up for these times during the summer or on weekends. If you are unable to make it up, don't stress out. Your child WILL catch up if you continue to work hard the other years.

10. Check out this website for more ideas on teaching with little ones: http://www.geocities.com/Athens/Aegean/3446/keeplittleones.html

THE CHECKLIST

Luke 2:52, *"And Jesus increased in wisdom and stature, and in favor with God and man."*

Please note: Dates for events from early history are not consistent in all textbooks and reference materials; therefore, I have chosen to use the dates listed in *Halley's Bible Handbook*. If a date or place of birth is missing, it is because I was not able to obtain this information.

WISDOM, PART I—ACQUIRE KNOWLEDGE ABOUT GOD & HIS STORY

Prov. 9:10, *"The fear of the Lord is the beginning of wisdom and the knowledge of the holy is understanding."*

BIBLE BASICS

Elem	Jr/Sr High	
_____	_____	Major Bible Characters and Events (also see World History)
_____	_____	How the Bible Was Written (also see Church History)
_____	_____	Infallibility of Scriptures
_____	_____	_____
_____	_____	_____
_____	_____	_____
_____	_____	_____
_____	_____	_____
_____	_____	_____
_____	_____	_____
_____	_____	_____

BIBLE STUDY

Elem	Jr/Sr High	
_____	_____	How to Locate the Books of the Bible and/or Memorize Them
_____	_____	How to Study the Bible
_____	_____	How to Read and Write Scripture References
_____	_____	How to Use a Concordance
_____	_____	How to Use a Bible Dictionary
_____	_____	How to Use a Bible Atlas
_____	_____	How to Use a Topical Bible
_____	_____	Symbolism in the Bible
_____	_____	Geography in Bible Times
_____	_____	Memorizes Bible Scriptures
_____	_____	Apologetics (Books by Josh McDowell Recommended)
_____	_____	_____
_____	_____	_____
_____	_____	_____
_____	_____	_____

BASIC CHURCH DOCTRINES

Elem   Jr/Sr High

_____ _____ _____
_____ _____ _____
_____ _____ _____
_____ _____ _____
_____ _____ _____
_____ _____ _____
_____ _____ _____
_____ _____ _____
_____ _____ _____
_____ _____ _____
_____ _____ _____

FOUNDATIONS OF FAITH

Elem   Jr/Sr High

_____ _____ _____
_____ _____ _____
_____ _____ _____
_____ _____ _____
_____ _____ _____
_____ _____ _____
_____ _____ _____
_____ _____ _____
_____ _____ _____
_____ _____ _____
_____ _____ _____

BIBLE TERMINOLOGY

Elem   Jr/Sr High

Elem	Jr/Sr High		Elem	Jr/Sr High	
_____	_____	Anointing	_____	_____	_____
_____	_____	Apologist	_____	_____	_____
_____	_____	Doctrine	_____	_____	_____
_____	_____	Immutability	_____	_____	_____
_____	_____	Omnipotence	_____	_____	_____
_____	_____	Omnipresence	_____	_____	_____
_____	_____	Omniscience	_____	_____	_____
_____	_____	Sanctification	_____	_____	_____
_____	_____	Trinity	_____	_____	_____

CHURCH HISTORY

Elem   Jr/Sr High

MAJOR EVENTS IN CHURCH HISTORY

_____ _____ c. 250 BC, Septuagint Written

_____ _____ c.0-c.30, Jesus' Birth, Baptism, Ministry, Crucifixion and Resurrection

_____ _____ c. 30 Pentecost

_____ _____ c. 30, Church Founded in Roman Empire

_____ _____ c. 34 - 46, Conversion of Paul and His Missionary Journeys

_____ _____ c. 40, Followers of Jesus First Called Christians at Antioch

_____ _____ 54-68, Nero's Reigns—Persecution of Christians

_____ _____ 76, Titus Conquers Jerusalem

_____ _____ 132, Jewish Dispersion

_____ _____ 312, Constantine's Conversion

_____ _____ 325, Council of Nicaea—Nicene Creed

_____ _____ 404, Latin Translation of Bible (Vulgate)—St. Jerome

_____ _____ 432, St. Patrick's Mission to Ireland

_____ _____ 1384, Wycliffe's Translation of Bible

_____ _____ 1517, Martin Luther Nails Theses to Church Door at Wittenburg

_____ _____ 1525, William Tyndale's Bible Translation of New Testament

_____ _____ 1535, Miles Coverdale Produces First Complete English Bible

_____ _____ 1541, John Calvin Founds Church at Geneva

_____ _____ 1549, Book of Common Prayers

_____ _____ 1611, Authorized King James Bible

_____ _____ 1780, Sunday School Founded

_____ _____ NT Canon Fixed

_____ _____ Papal Power

_____ _____ Protestantism and Protestant Persecution

_____ _____ Bible Societies

_____ _____ Modern Missions' Movement

_____ _____ _____

_____ _____ _____

_____ _____ _____

PEOPLE IN CHURCH HISTORY (see also Missionaries, page 177)

Elem   Jr/Sr High

_____ _____ Ananias and Sapphira—Couple Who Lied to Early Church, Acts 5

_____ _____ Ambrose (Italy, 340-397)—Bishop of Milan, Defender of the Faith

_____ _____ Apollos—Preacher at Corinth, Acts 18:24

_____ _____ Aquila and Priscilla—Christian Couple Who Taught Apollos, Acts 18

_____ _____ Aquinas, St. Thomas (Italy, c.1225-1274)—Theologian

_____ _____ Augustine, St. (Algeria, 354-431)—Bishop of Hippo, Confessions, The City of God

_____ _____ Barnabas—Missionary Who Was Commissioned By Paul, Acts 4:36

_____ _____ Bede the Venerable (England, c.673-735)—Father of English Church History

_____ _____ Benedict (England, c.628-689)—Father of Western Monasticism

_____ _____ Boniface (Great Britain, 680-784)—Apostle to Germany

_____ _____ Calvin, John (France, 1509-1564)—Protestant Reformer, Calvinism

_____ _____ Clement of Alexandria (Greece, c.150-c.215)—Church Father

_____ _____ Clement of Rome (d.?101)—One of Apostolic Fathers in Rome

_____ _____ Constantine (Rome, c.274-337)—Roman Emperor, Christian, Nicene Creed

_____ _____ Cornelius—Roman Centurion, Saved While Peter was in Jail, Acts 10

_____ _____ Coverdale, Miles (England, 1488-1568)—Bible Scholar, Published 1st Complete
English Bible

_____ _____ Diocletian (Italy, 284-305)—Roman Emperor, 10 yr. Christian Persecution

_____ _____ Dorcas/Tabitha—Woman Paul Raised From Dead, Acts 9:36

_____ _____ Erasmus, Desiderius (Netherlands, c.1466-1536)—Greek New Testament

_____ _____ Eusebius (Palestine, c.263-339)—Father of Church History

_____ _____ Fox, George (Great Britain, 1624-1691)—Founded the Society of Friends

_____ _____ Gregory the Great (Rome, c.540-604)—Benedictine Monk, Established Temporal
Power of Papacy

_____ _____ Gutenberg, Johann—(German, 1400-1468) Printed the First Bible

_____ _____ Huss, John (Bohemia, 1369-1415)—Religious Reformer

_____ _____ Ignatius (?-c.110)—Bishop of Antioch

_____ _____ Ignatius Loyola, (Spain, 1491-1556)—Founder of Jesuits, I.H.S.

_____ _____ Irenaeus (Asia Minor, c.130-c.200)—Bishop of Lyons

_____ _____ Jerome (Croatia, c.340-420)—Vulgate Version of Bible, Monasticism

_____ _____ Justin Martyr (Greece, c.100-c.165)–Christian Apologist

_____ _____ Knox, John (Scotland, c1505-1572)—Reformer and Founder of Presbyterianism,
Book of Common Prayer

_____ _____ Luther, Martin (German, 1483-1546)—Founder of the Reformation, Hymn Writer,
Bible Translator, Ninety-Five Theses, A Mighty Fortress is Our God

_____ _____ Lydia—Business Woman Converted at Philippi, Acts 16:14

_____ _____ Mark—Companion of Paul, Author of Second Gospel, Acts 12

_____ _____ Matthias—Apostle, Took Place of Judas Iscariot, Acts 1:15

_____ _____ Origen (Greece, c.185-254)—Christian Apologist

_____ _____ Patrick (Great Britain, 390-461)—Apostle of the Irish

_____ _____ Paul of Tarsus/Saul (Rome, 1st Century)—Apostle to the Gentiles

_____ _____ Philemon—Christian Owner of Slave Onesimus, Book of Bible

_____ _____ Polycarp (c.69-c.155)—Disciple of John, Bishop of Church at Smyrna

_____ _____ Stephen—One of Early Deacons of Church, 1st Christian Martyr, Acts 6-7

_____ _____ Tertullian (North Africa, c.150-c.225)—Christian Apologist

_____ _____ Timothy—Paul's Young Fellow Missionary, Wrote Two Books in Bible

_____ _____ Titus—Fellow Missionary With Paul, Book of Bible

_____ _____ Tyndale, William (Great Britain, ?-1536)—Bible Translator, First Printed English
Bible

_____ _____ Wesley, John (Great Britain, 1703-1791)—Founder of Methodism

_____ _____ Whitefield, George (Great Britain, 1714-1770)—Evangelist, The Great Awakening

_____ _____ Williams, Roger (Massachusetts, c.1603-1683)—Separation of Church and State

_____ _____ Wycliffe, John (Great Britain, c.1330-1384)—Reformation, Bible Translator,
Morningstar of the Reformation

_____ _____ Zwingli, Huldreich (Switzerland, 1484-1531)—Reformer

_____ _____ _____

_____ _____ _____
_____ _____ _____
_____ _____ _____
_____ _____ _____
_____ _____ _____
_____ _____ _____
_____ _____ _____
_____ _____ _____
_____ _____ _____
_____ _____ _____
_____ _____ _____
_____ _____ _____
_____ _____ _____
_____ _____ _____
_____ _____ _____
_____ _____ _____
_____ _____ _____

CHURCH HISTORY TERMS

Elem   Jr/Sr High

Elem	Jr/Sr High	Term	Elem	Jr/Sr High	Term
_____	_____	Anabaptists	_____	_____	Monastery
_____	_____	Archbishop	_____	_____	Monasticism
_____	_____	Bishop	_____	_____	Monks
_____	_____	Catacomb	_____	_____	Nicene Creed
_____	_____	Codices	_____	_____	Ninety-Five Theses
_____	_____	Conversion	_____	_____	Ottomans Rule
_____	_____	Council of Trent	_____	_____	Papacy States
_____	_____	Crusade	_____	_____	Persecution
_____	_____	Deacon	_____	_____	Reformation
_____	_____	Dead Sea Scrolls	_____	_____	Translation
_____	_____	Diet of Worms	_____	_____	_____
_____	_____	Gnosticism	_____	_____	_____
_____	_____	Great Schism	_____	_____	_____
_____	_____	Heresy	_____	_____	_____
_____	_____	Hermit	_____	_____	_____
_____	_____	Holy Roman Empire	_____	_____	_____
_____	_____	Indulgences	_____	_____	_____
_____	_____	Jesuits	_____	_____	_____
_____	_____	Inquisition	_____	_____	_____
_____	_____	Lutherans	_____	_____	_____
_____	_____	Martyr	_____	_____	_____
_____	_____	Methodists	_____	_____	_____
_____	_____	Mohammed	_____	_____	_____

WORLD HISTORY

ARCHAEOLOGY AND THE BIBLE*

_____ _____	Biblical Archaeology (1 Tim.6:20-21)
_____ _____	Careers in Archaeology
_____ _____	Tools of Archaeologist
_____ _____	Underwater Archaeology (see also Oceanography, page 148)
_____ _____	Space-Age Archaeology (see also Astronomy, page 150)

_____ _____
_____ _____
_____ _____
_____ _____
_____ _____
_____ _____
_____ _____

FAMOUS ARCHAEOLOGISTS

_____ _____ Bingham, Hiram (Hawaii, 1875-1956) - Archaeologist - noted for Discovering the Inca Ruins

_____ _____ Carter, Howard (England, 1874-1939), British Archaeologist who discovered Tutankhamun's tomb.

_____ _____ Jefferson, Thomas, (Virginia, 1743-1826) - 3rd president of the U.S. Dug up and studied a Native American grave site in Virginia.

_____ _____ Kenyon, Kathleen (England, 1906-1978) - Archaeologist, noted for excavations in Jericho.

_____ _____ Leakey, Mary (England, 1913 -) - Archaeologist in Kenya, noted for finding fossilized hominid footprints.

_____ _____ Petrie, Sir W. M. Flinders (England, 1853-1942) - Archaeologist. Noted for excavations in Egypt and Palestine.

_____ _____ Pitt-Rivers, Augustus (England, 1827-1900) - Archaeologist. Developed new scientific approach to excavation which became a model for later workers.

_____ _____ Schliemann, Heinrich (Germany, 1822-1890) - Archaeologist, noted for excavations at Troy, Mycenae, and Tiryns.

_____ _____ Woolley, Sir Leonard (England, 1880-1960) - Archaeologist, noted for excavations at Ur in Mesopotamia.

_____ _____ Yadin, Yigael (Israel, 1917-1984) - Archaeologist, noted for excavations in Israel including Dead Sea Caves, Hazor, and Masada.

_____ _____
_____ _____
_____ _____
_____ _____
_____ _____

TERMS

_____ _____	Absolute Age	
_____ _____	A.D. or C.E.	
_____ _____	Amphora	
_____ _____	Antiquity	
_____ _____	Archaeology	
_____ _____	Archaeological Site	
_____ _____	Archaeologist	
_____ _____	Aristotle's Dictum	
_____ _____	Artifact	
_____ _____	B.C.E.	
_____ _____	Balk	
_____ _____	Bibliographic Test	
_____ _____	Carbon 14	
_____ _____	Catalogue	
_____ _____	Cenozoic	
_____ _____	Ceramic Technologist	
_____ _____	Chronology	
_____ _____	Coprolites	
_____ _____	Culture	
_____ _____	Dendrochronologist	
_____ _____	Digs	
_____ _____	Evolution	
_____ _____	Extinct	
_____ _____	Excavate	
_____ _____	External Test	
_____ _____	Forensic Archaeologist	
_____ _____	Fossils	
_____ _____	Geiger Counter	
_____ _____	Geological Column	
_____ _____	Geologic Time Scale	
_____ _____	Glyphs	
_____ _____	Half-life	
_____ _____	*Homo Erectus*	
_____ _____	*Homo Habilis*	
_____ _____	Ice Age	
_____ _____	In Situ	
_____ _____	Index Fossils	
_____ _____	Internal Test	
_____ _____	Known Age	

_____ _____	Locus
_____ _____	Locus Sheet
_____ _____	Mesozoic
_____ _____	Midden
_____ _____	"Missing" Link
_____ _____	Neanderthal
_____ _____	Numismatist
_____ _____	Oral Tradition
_____ _____	Paleobotanist
_____ _____	Paleographer
_____ _____	Paleozoic
_____ _____	Petrifaction
_____ _____	Petrographs
_____ _____	Potassium-Argon Dating
_____ _____	Pothunters
_____ _____	Potsherd
_____ _____	Precambrian
_____ _____	Primary Sources
_____ _____	Prehistory
_____ _____	Quipu
_____ _____	Radiocarbon Dating
_____ _____	Radioactive Decay
_____ _____	Reconstruct
_____ _____	Relative Age
_____ _____	Resin
_____ _____	Sieve
_____ _____	Site Map
_____ _____	Square
_____ _____	Stone Age
_____ _____	Strata
_____ _____	Surface Survey
_____ _____	Tel
_____ _____	Test Trench
_____ _____	Thermoluminescence
_____ _____	Tree Trunks
_____ _____	Trowel
_____ _____	Uranium Dating
_____ _____	_____
_____ _____	_____

SEE ALSO DINOSAURS AND THE BIBLE, PAGE 156.

* NOTE: An excellent resource for this topic is *Exploring Ancient Cities of the Bible* by Michael and Caroline Carroll. 2001.

CREATION THROUGH THE FLOOD

For help with this topic, check this website: http://www.christiananswers.net/archaeology/home.html

Elem   Jr/Sr High

MAJOR EVENTS

_____ _____ Creation vs. Evolutionary Theory (See also Archaeology, page 22)
_____ _____ Purpose of God's Creation
_____ _____ Sin and the Fall of Man
_____ _____ Results of the Fall
_____ _____ The Flood

PEOPLE (GENESIS, JOB)

_____ _____ Adam and Eve   _____ _____ Noah
_____ _____ Abel   _____ _____ Satan (Lucifer)
_____ _____ Cain   _____ _____ Seth
_____ _____ Enoch   _____ _____ Shem
_____ _____ Japheth   _____ _____ _____
_____ _____ Job*   _____ _____ _____
_____ _____ Ham   _____ _____ _____
_____ _____ Methuselah   _____ _____ _____

PLACES

_____ _____ Euphrates River   _____ _____ Tigris River
_____ _____ Fertile Crescent   _____ _____ _____
_____ _____ Garden of Eden   _____ _____ _____
_____ _____ Mesopotamia   _____ _____ _____
_____ _____ Mount Ararat   _____ _____ _____

TERMS

_____ _____ Ark   _____ _____ _____
_____ _____ Epic of Gilgamesh   _____ _____ _____
_____ _____ Evolutionary Theory   _____ _____ _____
_____ _____ Rainbow   _____ _____ _____
_____ _____ Sacrifice   _____ _____ _____
_____ _____ Theocracy   _____ _____ _____
_____ _____ _____   _____ _____ _____

Note: * Job is thought by some to be Jobab mentioned in Genesis 10:29, 3rd in descent from Eber. Descendants Of Noah are generally thought to have migrated to the following areas: Japheth—Europe and Asia; Ham—Egypt, Africa, Arabia, Mediterranean Shores; Shem—Israel.

ANCIENT MESOPOTAMIA TO C. 1400 BC

Elem   Jr/Sr High

MAJOR EVENTS

Elem	Jr/Sr High	
_____	_____	Tower of Babel is Built by Nimrod
_____	_____	Confusion of Languages
_____	_____	The Dispersion
_____	_____	c. 5000 BC, Early Sumerians Begin to Farm in Southern Mesopotamia (Iraq)
_____	_____	c. 2000 BC, City of Ur Destroyed by Elamites. End of Sumerian Civilization
_____	_____	c.1894 BC, Amorite People Establish Minor Kingdom of Babylon in Mesopotamia
_____	_____	c.1792-1750 BC, Reign of King Hammurabi, Babylon First Rises to Power
_____	_____	c.1595 BC, Babylon is Plundered by the Hittites
_____	_____	The Call of Abraham
_____	_____	Abraham's Sojourn in Egypt (Middle Kingdom)
_____	_____	Abraham and Lot Separate
_____	_____	The Destruction of Sodom and Gomorrah
_____	_____	The Birth of Ishmael and Isaac
_____	_____	Beginning of the Arab Line
_____	_____	Birth of Jacob and Esau
_____	_____	Jacob Obtains Abraham's Blessing
_____	_____	Jacob's Vision at Bethel (Ladder)
_____	_____	The Birth of the Twelve Patriarchs
_____	_____	Jacob's Return to Canaan
_____	_____	Joseph Sold As Slave Into Egypt (See Ancient Egypt-page 28)
_____	_____	_____
_____	_____	_____
_____	_____	_____

PEOPLE

Elem	Jr/Sr High	
_____	_____	Abraham
_____	_____	Asher
_____	_____	Benjamin
_____	_____	Dan
_____	_____	Elamites
_____	_____	Esau
_____	_____	Gad
_____	_____	Gilgamesh
_____	_____	Hagar
_____	_____	Hammurabi—King of Babylon, Famous for Hammurabi's Code
_____	_____	Isaac
_____	_____	Ishmael
_____	_____	Issachar
_____	_____	Jacob
_____	_____	Joseph
_____	_____	Judah

_____ _____ King Nebuchadnezzar II
_____ _____ Laban
_____ _____ Leah
_____ _____ Levi
_____ _____ Lot
_____ _____ Melchizedek
_____ _____ Nahor
_____ _____ Naphtali
_____ _____ Nimrod—Grandson of Ham, Founder of Babylon
_____ _____ Rachel
_____ _____ Rebekah
_____ _____ Reuben
_____ _____ Sarah
_____ _____ Simeon
_____ _____ Sumerians
_____ _____ Sargon (c.2370 BC)—Babylonian Ruler
_____ _____ Terah—Father of Abraham
_____ _____ Zebulun

_____ _____ _____
_____ _____ _____
_____ _____ _____
_____ _____ _____
_____ _____ _____
_____ _____ _____
_____ _____ _____
_____ _____ _____
_____ _____ _____
_____ _____ _____
_____ _____ _____
_____ _____ _____
_____ _____ _____

PLACES

_____ _____ Akkad (Accad)   _____ _____ _____
_____ _____ Babylon   _____ _____ _____
_____ _____ Bethel   _____ _____ _____
_____ _____ Dead Sea   _____ _____ _____
_____ _____ Gomorrah   _____ _____ _____
_____ _____ Haran   _____ _____ _____
_____ _____ Hebron   _____ _____ _____
_____ _____ Ishtar Gate   _____ _____ _____
_____ _____ Royal Tombs at Ur   _____ _____ _____
_____ _____ Sodom   _____ _____ _____
_____ _____ Ur   _____ _____ _____

TERMS

_____ _____	Akkadia	_____ _____ Idolatry
_____ _____	Amalekites	_____ _____ Iron Age
_____ _____	Ammonites	_____ _____ Immortals (Persian Army)
_____ _____	Amorites	_____ _____ Marduk
_____ _____	Artisans	_____ _____ _____
_____ _____	Astrology (Babel)	_____ _____ _____
_____ _____	Chaldean	_____ _____ _____
_____ _____	City-States	_____ _____ _____
_____ _____	Edomites	_____ _____ _____
_____ _____	Hittites	_____ _____ _____

DISCOVERIES/ACCOMPLISHMENTS

_____ _____	Abacus	_____ _____ Precious Stones
_____ _____	Arch (in Building) (3000 BC)	_____ _____ Reed Houses
_____ _____	Code of Hammurabi	_____ _____ System of Weights
_____ _____	Cuneiform Writing (2700 BC)	_____ _____ Wheel, c. 3500 BC
_____ _____	Hanging Garden of Babylon	_____ _____ Writing c. 3500 BC
_____ _____	Horse Drawn Carriage	_____ _____ Ziggurat
_____ _____	Maps-Oldest World Map: Babylon at Center	_____ _____ _____
_____ _____	Musical Instruments	_____ _____ _____
_____ _____	Pictographic Writing (3200 BC)	_____ _____ _____
_____ _____	Pottery Wheel	_____ _____ _____

CULTURE STUDY: _____ (SUMERIANS OR BABYLONIANS)

_____ _____	Family Life	_____ _____ Arts & Crafts
_____ _____	Homes	_____ _____ Music
_____ _____	Food and Agriculture	_____ _____ Oral and Written Language
_____ _____	Clothing	_____ _____ Government, Military and Weapons of Warfare
_____ _____	Occupations	
_____ _____	Religion	_____ _____ Economy, Technology, Manufacturing, & Trade
_____ _____	Health & Medicine	
_____ _____	Recreation & Entertainment	_____ _____ _____
_____ _____	Education	_____ _____ _____

ANCIENT EGYPT (& AFRICA)

MAJOR EVENTS

_____ _____ c. 3100 BC, Egyptian Dynasties Begin

_____ _____ _____

_____ _____ _____

_____ _____ _____

_____ _____ _____

_____ _____ c. 2680 BC, Old Kingdom

_____ _____ _____

_____ _____ _____

_____ _____ _____

_____ _____ _____

_____ _____ 1991 BC, Middle Kingdom Begins

_____ _____ _____

_____ _____ _____

_____ _____ _____

_____ _____ Joseph Imprisoned

_____ _____ Joseph Becomes Ruler in Egypt

_____ _____ Israel Settles in Egypt (The New Kingdom)

_____ _____ Israel's Slavery in Egypt (400 Years)

_____ _____ Moses Born and Raised by Pharaoh's Daughter

_____ _____ Moses' 40 Years in Wilderness

_____ _____ The Burning Bush

_____ _____ Moses Confronts Pharaoh

_____ _____ The Ten Plagues

_____ _____ The Passover

_____ _____ Cloud by Day and Pillar of Fire by Night

_____ _____ The Exodus (Crossing the Red Sea)

_____ _____ _____

_____ _____ 1552 BC - 30 BC, New Kingdom

_____ _____ 1360 BC, Amenhotep IV Establishes Sun God Worship

_____ _____ 1175 BC, Upper and Lower Kingdoms

_____ _____ 671 BC, Assyrian Conquest of Egypt

_____ _____ 51 BC, Cleopatra Becomes Queen of Egypt

_____ _____ _____

_____ _____ _____

_____ _____ _____

_____ _____ _____

PEOPLE

_____ _____ Aaron—Moses' Brother
_____ _____ Cheops (Builder of Great Pyramid)
_____ _____ Cleopatra (Egypt, 69 BC -30 BC), Queen of Egypt
_____ _____ Imhotep—Architect, Doctor, Scribe, Priest, Vizier
_____ _____ Jethro—Moses' Father
_____ _____ Khufu—King of Egypt c. 2589 - 2566 BC
_____ _____ Menes (Historically-1st Ruler of Egypt), c.3100 BC
_____ _____ Miriam—Moses' Sister
_____ _____ Mizraim, Son of Ham, Founder of Egypt
_____ _____ Moses
_____ _____ Nefertiti
_____ _____ Queen Hatshepsut—Thought to be the Princess Who Raised Moses
_____ _____ Rameses II, King of Egypt, c. 1289 - 1224 BC
_____ _____ Seti
_____ _____ Tutankhamun, King of Egypt, c. 1347 - 1337 BC
_____ _____ Tuthmosis III, King of Egypt, c.1479 - 1425 BC
_____ _____ Zipporah—Moses' Wife

_____ _____ _____
_____ _____ _____
_____ _____ _____
_____ _____ _____
_____ _____ _____
_____ _____ _____
_____ _____ _____
_____ _____ _____

PLACES

_____ _____ Canaan
_____ _____ Carthage
_____ _____ Congo River
_____ _____ Giza
_____ _____ Gold Coast
_____ _____ Goshen
_____ _____ Great Rift Valley
_____ _____ Kalahari Desert
_____ _____ Lower Egypt
_____ _____ Midian
_____ _____ Mount Sinai
_____ _____ Nile River
_____ _____ Nineveh
_____ _____ Phoenicia
_____ _____ Red Sea

_____ _____ Sahara Desert
_____ _____ Senegal River
_____ _____ Upper Egypt
_____ _____ _____
_____ _____ _____
_____ _____ _____
_____ _____ _____
_____ _____ _____
_____ _____ _____
_____ _____ _____
_____ _____ _____
_____ _____ _____

TERMS

_____ _____	Archaeology	_____ _____ Polytheism
_____ _____	Artifacts	_____ _____ Prophets
_____ _____	Book of the Covenant	_____ _____ Sabbath
_____ _____	Camel Caravans	_____ _____ Sacrifice
_____ _____	Cartouche	_____ _____ Savannah
_____ _____	Consecration	_____ _____ Ships of the Desert
_____ _____	Dark Continent	_____ _____ Ten Commandments
_____ _____	Delta	_____ _____ Tithe
_____ _____	Dynasty	_____ _____ Torah
_____ _____	Egyptian gods	_____ _____ Viziers
_____ _____	Exile	
_____ _____	Exodus	
_____ _____	Gold	
_____ _____	Hebrews	
_____ _____	Hieroglyphics	
_____ _____	Kohl	
_____ _____	Lower Egypt	
_____ _____	Manna	
_____ _____	Midianites	
_____ _____	Moabites	
_____ _____	Monotheism	
_____ _____	Mummy	
_____ _____	Oasis	
_____ _____	Offerings	
_____ _____	Passover	
_____ _____	Pharaoh	

DISCOVERIES/ACCOMPLISHMENTS

_____ _____	Canopic Jar	_____ _____ Pyramids
_____ _____	Ebony	_____ _____ Rosetta Stone
_____ _____	Embalming	_____ _____ Sphinx
_____ _____	Furniture	_____ _____ Sundial
_____ _____	Geometry	_____ _____ Turquoise Mine
_____ _____	Hieroglyphics (page 127)	_____ _____ Water Clock
_____ _____	Ivory	
_____ _____	Jewelry	
_____ _____	Mummy	
_____ _____	Obelisk	
_____ _____	Papyrus	
_____ _____	Postal System	

CULTURE STUDY: ANCIENT EGYPT

_____ _____	Family Life	_____ _____ Music
_____ _____	Homes	_____ _____ Oral and Written Language
_____ _____	Food and Agriculture	_____ _____ Government, Military and
_____ _____	Clothing	Weapons of Warfare
_____ _____	Occupations	_____ _____ Economy, Technology,
_____ _____	Religion	Manufacturing, and Trade
_____ _____	Health & Medicine	_____ _____ _____
_____ _____	Recreation & Entertainment	_____ _____ _____
_____ _____	Education	
_____ _____	Arts & Crafts	

CULTURE STUDY: _____

(Modern Egypt, Ghana, Kenya, Ivory Coast, Nambia, Swaziland, Tanzania, Uganda, and Zimbabwe)

_____ _____	Family Life	_____ _____ Music
_____ _____	Homes	_____ _____ Oral and Written Language
_____ _____	Food and Agriculture	_____ _____ Government, Military and
_____ _____	Clothing	Weapons of Warfare
_____ _____	Occupations	_____ _____ Economy, Technology,
_____ _____	Religion	Manufacturing, and Trade
_____ _____	Health & Medicine	_____ _____ _____
_____ _____	Recreation & Entertainment	_____ _____ _____
_____ _____	Education	
_____ _____	Arts & Crafts	

Also see: African American History, Page 96.

EARLY NORTH AND SOUTH AMERICAN CIVILIZATIONS

Elem   Jr/Sr High

MAJOR EVENTS

_____ _____ First Americans Cross the Bering Strait (Land Bridge)

_____ _____ c. 1150 BC, Olmec Civilization in Southern Mexico

_____ _____ c. AD 250 to 900, Height of Mayan Civilization (Begins c. 2500 BC)

_____ _____ c. AD 500, Mississippi Mound Builders Appear

_____ _____ c. AD 986, Eric the Red Colonizes Greenland

_____ _____ c. AD 1000, Lief Ericson Explores American Coast (1000)

_____ _____ c. AD 1250 - 1521, Height of Aztec Civilization

_____ _____ c. AD 1438 - 1532, Height of Inca Civilization

_____ _____ c. AD ? , Inuit Civilization

_____ _____ _____

_____ _____ _____

_____ _____ _____

PEOPLE

_____ _____ Aztecs   _____ _____ _____

_____ _____ Incas   _____ _____ _____

_____ _____ Inuit & Eskimos (Arctic &   _____ _____ _____
                  Alaska)   _____ _____ _____

_____ _____ Mayas   _____ _____ _____

PLACES

_____ _____ Alaska   _____ _____ _____

_____ _____ Aleutian Islands   _____ _____ _____

_____ _____ Andes Mountains   _____ _____ _____

_____ _____ Antarctic   _____ _____ _____

_____ _____ Arctic   _____ _____ _____

_____ _____ Bering Strait   _____ _____ _____

_____ _____ Teotihuacån   _____ _____ _____

TERMS

_____ _____ Burial Mounds   _____ _____ Pit Houses

_____ _____ Eskimo   _____ _____ Yucatan

_____ _____ Ice Age   _____ _____ _____

_____ _____ Land Bridge   _____ _____ _____

_____ _____ Llama   _____ _____ _____

_____ _____ Maize   _____ _____ _____

_____ _____ Mound Builders   _____ _____ _____

THE CHECKLIST, Copyright © 2005 by Cindy Downes

ACCOMPLISHMENTS

_____ _____ _____   _____ _____ _____
_____ _____ _____   _____ _____ _____
_____ _____ _____   _____ _____ _____
_____ _____ _____   _____ _____ _____
_____ _____ _____   _____ _____ _____
_____ _____ _____   _____ _____ _____
_____ _____ _____   _____ _____ _____

CULTURE STUDY: MAYANS

_____ _____ Family Life   _____ _____ Music
_____ _____ Homes   _____ _____ Oral and Written Language
_____ _____ Food and Agriculture   _____ _____ Government, Military and
_____ _____ Clothing   Weapons of Warfare
_____ _____ Occupations   _____ _____ Economy, Technology,
_____ _____ Religion   Manufacturing, and Trade
_____ _____ Health & Medicine
_____ _____ Recreation & Entertainment   _____ _____ _____
_____ _____ Education   _____ _____ _____
_____ _____ Arts & Crafts

CULTURE STUDY: INCAS

_____ _____ Family Life   _____ _____ Music
_____ _____ Homes   _____ _____ Oral and Written Language
_____ _____ Food and Agriculture   _____ _____ Government, Military and
_____ _____ Clothing   Weapons of Warfare
_____ _____ Occupations   _____ _____ Economy, Technology,
_____ _____ Religion   Manufacturing, and Trade
_____ _____ Health & Medicine
_____ _____ Recreation & Entertainment   _____ _____ _____
_____ _____ Education   _____ _____ _____
_____ _____ Arts & Crafts

CULTURE STUDY: AZTECS

_____ _____ Family Life   _____ _____ Arts & Crafts
_____ _____ Homes   _____ _____ Music
_____ _____ Food and Agriculture   _____ _____ Oral and Written Language
_____ _____ Clothing   _____ _____ Government, Military and
_____ _____ Occupations   Weapons of Warfare
_____ _____ Religion   _____ _____ Economy, Technology,
_____ _____ Health & Medicine   Manufacturing, and Trade
_____ _____ Recreation & Entertainment
_____ _____ Education   _____ _____ _____
                                                 _____ _____ _____

INDUS CIVILIZATIONS

Elem   Jr/Sr High

MAJOR EVENTS

_____	_____	c. 2000 - C. 1800 BC Harappa Civilization
_____	_____	c. 1500 BC Aryan migration in Indus Valley
_____	_____	c. 530 BC, Buddha's enlightenment
_____	_____	521 BC, Persian Army annexed Indus Valley
_____	_____	326 BC, Alexander the Great's army crossed into the Indus Valley
_____	_____	322 BC, Chandragupta Maurya comes to power with Mauryan Empire
_____	_____	268-232 BC, Ashoka is Emperor of Mauryan Empire
_____	_____	180 BC, Mauryan Empire falls
_____	_____	AD 320, Chandragupta Maurya founds Gupta Empire
_____	_____	AD 480 - 550, Huns conquer Gupta Empire
_____	_____	1100, Muslim rule begins

_____ _____ _____

_____ _____ _____

_____ _____ _____

_____ _____ _____

_____ _____ _____

PEOPLE

_____ _____ Aryans

_____ _____ Ashoka Maurya, Emperor of Mauryan Empire

_____ _____ Chandragupta Maurya, (c. 322 BC), Founder of Mauryan Empire

_____ _____ Chandragupta I, (c. AD 320), Founder of Gupta Empire

_____ _____ Dravidians

_____ _____ Kalidasa, South India poet of Gupta period (5th century AD)

_____ _____ Siddartha Gautama - known as Buddha (c.563-c.483 BC)—Indian Philosopher and
              Founder of Buddhism.

_____ _____ Veddahs

_____ _____ _____

_____ _____ _____

_____ _____ _____

PLACES

_____	_____	Genges River	_____	_____	Pakistan
_____	_____	Gobi Desert	_____	_____	Punjab
_____	_____	Harappa	_____	_____	Yangtze River
_____	_____	Himalaya Mountains	_____	_____	Yellow River
_____	_____	India	_____	_____	Sri Lanka
_____	_____	Indus River	_____	_____	_____
_____	_____	Mohenjo-Daro	_____	_____	_____
_____	_____	Nepal	_____	_____	_____

TERMS

_____ _____	Brahmans	_____ _____ Sanskrit
_____ _____	Caste System	_____ _____ Shintoism
_____ _____	Dharma	_____ _____ Stupa
_____ _____	Enlightenment	_____ _____ Vedas
_____ _____	Gupta Period	_____ _____ _____
_____ _____	Guru	_____ _____ _____
_____ _____	Hinduism	_____ _____ _____
_____ _____	Karma	_____ _____ _____
_____ _____	Mandarin	_____ _____ _____
_____ _____	Mantra	_____ _____ _____
_____ _____	Punjab	_____ _____ _____
_____ _____	Reincarnation	_____ _____ _____

DISCOVERIES/ACCOMPLISHMENTS

_____ _____	Arabic Numbers	_____ _____ Smallpox Inoculations
_____ _____	Astronomy & Physics	_____ _____ Zero, the Number
_____ _____	Cotton Cloth	_____ _____ _____
_____ _____	Citadels	_____ _____ _____
_____ _____	Granaries	_____ _____ _____
_____ _____	Libraries	_____ _____ _____

CULTURE STUDY: MODERN INDIA

_____ _____	Family Life	_____ _____ Music
_____ _____	Homes	_____ _____ Oral and Written Language
_____ _____	Food and Agriculture	_____ _____ Government, Military and
_____ _____	Clothing	Weapons of Warfare
_____ _____	Occupations	_____ _____ Economy, Technology,
_____ _____	Religion	Manufacturing, and Trade
_____ _____	Health & Medicine	
_____ _____	Recreation & Entertainment	_____ _____ _____
_____ _____	Education	_____ _____ _____
_____ _____	Arts & Crafts	

ANCIENT CHINA

(Includes History of China to 1900s)

Elem   Jr/Sr High

MAJOR EVENTS

_____	_____	c. 1500 - 1050 BC, Shang Dynasty
_____	_____	c. 1050 - 249 BC, Zhou (Chou) Dynasty
_____	_____	c. 221 - 206 BC, Qin (Ch'in) Dynasty
_____	_____	c. 202 BC - AD 200, Han Dynasty
_____	_____	AD 215 - Great Wall of China is Started to Keep Out Invaders
_____	_____	AD 618-907, Age of Tang
_____	_____	AD 624, Buddhism Become State Religion in China
_____	_____	AD 751, Arab Muslims Crush Chinese Armies, Islam Spreads Through Central Asia
_____	_____	AD 1215, Ghengis Khan Invades China
_____	_____	AD 1260, Khubilai Khan Becomes Emperor of China, First Foreigner to Rule
_____	_____	AD 1368 - 1644, Ming Dynasty Rules
_____	_____	AD 1644-1911, Manchus Overthrow Ming Dynasty and Ch'ing Dynasty Rules
_____	_____	1900, Boxer Rebellion
_____	_____	1911, Sun Yat-Sen Establishes New Republican Government
_____	_____	1934-1935, Mao Tse-Tung and The Long March, 6,000 Mile March Across China
_____	_____	1949, People's Republic of China Proclaimed with Mao Tse-Tung as Chairman
_____	_____	1950-1953, Korean War, Mao Tse-Tung's Role
_____	_____	1960s-1976, Gang of Four
_____	_____	1989, March on Tiananmen Square, China's Struggles for Democracy
_____	_____	_____
_____	_____	_____
_____	_____	_____
_____	_____	_____
_____	_____	_____

PEOPLE

_____	_____	Genghis Khan (1162-1227)—Mongol Conqueror and Emperor
_____	_____	Khubilai Khan (1214-1294)—Mongol Emperor, Founded Peking
_____	_____	Kung Fuzi, know as Confucius (China, c 550-479 BC)—Chinese Philosopher
_____	_____	Mao Tse-Tung (Mao Zedong), 1893-1976, Chinese Communist Party
_____	_____	Marco Polo (Italy, c.1254-1324)—Adventurer, Served Khubilai Khan for 17 Years
_____	_____	Shi Huangdi (Shi Huang Ti), c. 246 BC —First Ruler of Qin (Ch'in) Dynasty
_____	_____	Sun Yat-Sen (Sun Yixian), 1866-1925, Founder & Leader of Nationalist Party
_____	_____	Zhu Yuanzhang (Chu Yuan-Chang), Ruler of Ming Dynasty (AD 1368-
_____	_____	_____
_____	_____	_____
_____	_____	_____
_____	_____	_____
_____	_____	_____

PLACES

___ ___	Anyang	___ ___ Vietnam
___ ___	Beijing	___ ___ Yangtze River
___ ___	Burma	___ ___ Yellow River
___ ___	Forbidden City	
___ ___	Ganges River	
___ ___	Great Wall of China	
___ ___	Korea	
___ ___	Luminous Hall	
___ ___	Manchuria	
___ ___	Mongolia	
___ ___	Nanjing	
___ ___	Silk Road	
___ ___	Tiananmen Square (1989)	
___ ___	Tibet	

TERMS

___ ___	Daoism	
___ ___	Emperor	
___ ___	Kamikaze	
___ ___	Kimono	
___ ___	Land of the Rising Sun	
___ ___	Legalists	
___ ___	Mandarin	
___ ___	Mongols	
___ ___	Pagoda	
___ ___	Panda	
___ ___	Red Guards	
___ ___	Shamans	
___ ___	Shogun	
___ ___	Sumarai	
___ ___	Taoism	
___ ___	White Lotus Society	
___ ___	Yin and Yang	

DISCOVERIES/ACCOMPLISHMENTS

_____	_____	Astronomic Observatories	_____	_____	Silk
_____	_____	Bronze Making	_____	_____	Standardized System of
_____	_____	Canals			Weights
_____	_____	Chinese Writing	_____	_____	Star Maps
_____	_____	Civil Service Exam	_____	_____	Sun Dials
_____	_____	Copper Coins	_____	_____	Water Clock
_____	_____	Crossbow	_____	_____	Winnowing Machine
_____	_____	Fireworks	_____	_____	_____
_____	_____	Gun Powder	_____	_____	_____
_____	_____	Junk	_____	_____	_____
_____	_____	Libraries	_____	_____	_____
_____	_____	Magnetic Compass	_____	_____	_____
_____	_____	Movable Type	_____	_____	_____
_____	_____	Paper From Rags	_____	_____	_____
_____	_____	Porcelain China	_____	_____	_____
_____	_____	Sewer Systems	_____	_____	_____

CULTURE STUDY: ANCIENT CHINA

_____	_____	Family Life	_____	_____	Music
_____	_____	Homes	_____	_____	Oral and Written Language
_____	_____	Food and Agriculture	_____	_____	Government, Military and
_____	_____	Clothing			Weapons of Warfare
_____	_____	Occupations	_____	_____	Economy, Technology,
_____	_____	Religion			Manufacturing, and Trade
_____	_____	Health & Medicine	_____	_____	_____
_____	_____	Recreation & Entertainment	_____	_____	_____
_____	_____	Education			
_____	_____	Arts & Crafts			

CULTURE STUDY: MODERN CHINA

_____	_____	Family Life	_____	_____	Music
_____	_____	Homes	_____	_____	Oral and Written Language
_____	_____	Food and Agriculture	_____	_____	Government, Military and
_____	_____	Clothing			Weapons of Warfare
_____	_____	Occupations	_____	_____	Economy, Technology,
_____	_____	Religion			Manufacturing, and Trade
_____	_____	Health & Medicine	_____	_____	_____
_____	_____	Recreation & Entertainment	_____	_____	_____
_____	_____	Education			
_____	_____	Arts & Crafts			

ANCIENT JAPAN

(Includes History to Present-Day)

Elem   Jr/Sr High

MAJOR EVENTS

_____ _____ c. 300 BC, First Japanese Civilization Appears

_____ _____ c. AD 200 - 646, Yamato Period

_____ _____ 1182, Minamoto Yoritomo Becomes Shogun of Japan

_____ _____ 1274, Samurai Drive Off Mongols

_____ _____ 1542, First Europeans Visits Japan, Portuguese Sailors and Catholic Missionaries

_____ _____ 1597, Persecution of Japanese Christians Begins

_____ _____ 1853, Commodore Matthew Perry Sails into Tokyo Bay Opening Japan to US Trade

_____ _____ 1889, Constitutional Democracy Agreed to on Paper, not Fact

_____ _____ 1941, Japanese Bombers Attack Pearl Harbor, WWII Begins

_____ _____ 1952, End of US Occupation of Japan

_____ _____ _____

_____ _____ _____

_____ _____ _____

_____ _____ _____

_____ _____ _____

_____ _____ _____

PEOPLE

_____ _____ Himiko, Ruler of Japan (c. AD 167)

_____ _____ Jesuit Francis Xavier, Catholic Missionary to Japan (1500s)

_____ _____ Minamto Yoritomo (1147-1199), First Shogun of Japan

_____ _____ Oda Nobunaga (1534-1582), First Unifier of Japan

_____ _____ Toyotomi Hideyoshi (1536-1598), Second Unifier of Japan

_____ _____ _____

_____ _____ _____

_____ _____ _____

_____ _____ _____

PLACES

_____ _____ Golden Pavilion (1397)   _____ _____ _____

_____ _____ Heian-Kyo (794)   _____ _____ _____

_____ _____ Hokkaido   _____ _____ _____

_____ _____ Honshu   _____ _____ _____

_____ _____ Kyushu   _____ _____ _____

_____ _____ Shikoku

_____ _____ _____   _____ _____ _____

TERMS

_____ _____ Bushido

_____ _____ Daimyo

_____ _____ Diet (1889)

_____ _____ Haiku

_____ _____ Judo

_____ _____ Kamikaze

_____ _____ Karate

_____ _____ Kimono

_____ _____ Nippon

_____ _____ No Play

_____ _____ Origami

_____ _____ Pagoda

_____ _____ Samurai

_____ _____ Shinto

_____ _____ Shrine

_____ _____ _____

_____ _____ _____

_____ _____ _____

_____ _____ _____

_____ _____ _____

_____ _____ _____

DISCOVERIES/ACCOMPLISHMENTS

_____ _____ Abacus

_____ _____ Bookbinding by Sewing

_____ _____ Kana System of Writing

_____ _____ Martial Arts

_____ _____ _____

_____ _____ _____

_____ _____ _____

_____ _____ _____

_____ _____ _____

_____ _____ _____

_____ _____ _____

_____ _____ _____

CULTURE STUDY: JAPAN

_____ _____ Family Life

_____ _____ Homes

_____ _____ Food and Agriculture

_____ _____ Clothing

_____ _____ Occupations

_____ _____ Religion

_____ _____ Health & Medicine

_____ _____ Recreation & Entertainment

_____ _____ Education

_____ _____ Arts & Crafts

_____ _____ Music

_____ _____ Oral and Written Language

_____ _____ Government, Military and Weapons of Warfare

_____ _____ Economy, Technology, Manufacturing, and Trade

_____ _____ _____

_____ _____ _____

CONQUEST OF CANAAN, PERIOD OF JUDGES, KINGDOM YEARS
c.1400 BC - c. 1000 BC

Elem   Jr/Sr High

MAJOR EVENTS

Elem	Jr/Sr High	
_____	_____	Manna and Quail
_____	_____	Mount Sinai and the Ten Commandments
_____	_____	Idolatry and the Golden Calf
_____	_____	The Tabernacle is Built
_____	_____	The Levitical Priesthood is Established
_____	_____	Vows and Tithes
_____	_____	The Mosaic Laws are Given
_____	_____	Twelve Spies Sent to Canaan
_____	_____	Forty Years in the Wilderness
_____	_____	The Death of Moses
_____	_____	Joshua Replaces Moses
_____	_____	The Two Spies and Rahab
_____	_____	The Fall of Jericho
_____	_____	The Day the Sun Stood Still
_____	_____	The Rule of Judges
_____	_____	Samson and Delilah
_____	_____	Ruth Marries Boaz
_____	_____	Samuel's Call
_____	_____	Ark Captured by the Philistines
_____	_____	Saul Becomes King
_____	_____	David Becomes King
_____	_____	Solomon's Reign
_____	_____	The Temple is Built (c.1000 BC)

PEOPLE

_____ _____	Ahab (c.869-850 BC)	_____ _____ Jesse (David's Father)
_____ _____	Ahaz (741-726 BC)	_____ _____ Jezebel (Ahab's Wife)
_____ _____	Amos (835-765 BC)	_____ _____ Jonathan
_____ _____	Baal	_____ _____ Joshua
_____ _____	Balaam	_____ _____ Josiah
_____ _____	Bathsheba	_____ _____ Naaman
_____ _____	Boaz	_____ _____ Naomi
_____ _____	Caleb	_____ _____ Obed
_____ _____	David	_____ _____ Rahab
_____ _____	Deborah	_____ _____ Ruth
_____ _____	Delilah	_____ _____ Samson
_____ _____	Eli	_____ _____ Samuel
_____ _____	Elijah	_____ _____ Saul
_____ _____	Elisha	_____ _____ Solomon
_____ _____	Gideon	_____ _____ _____
_____ _____	Goliath (Philistine)	_____ _____ _____
_____ _____	Hannah	_____ _____ _____

PLACES

_____ _____	Jericho	_____ _____ _____
_____ _____	Jerusalem (City of David)	_____ _____ _____
_____ _____	Jordan River	_____ _____ _____
_____ _____	Moab	_____ _____ _____
_____ _____	Sidon	_____ _____ _____
_____ _____	Tyre	_____ _____ _____

TERMS

_____ _____	Judges	_____ _____ _____
_____ _____	Moloch	_____ _____ _____
_____ _____	Murex Shellfish	_____ _____ _____
_____ _____	Philistines	_____ _____ _____
_____ _____	Temple	_____ _____ _____
_____ _____ _____		_____ _____ _____
_____ _____ _____		_____ _____ _____
_____ _____ _____		_____ _____ _____
_____ _____ _____		_____ _____ _____

PARTS OF THE TABERNACLE

_____ _____	Altar of Incense	_____ _____ Laver
_____ _____	Altar of Burnt Offering	_____ _____ Table of Shewbread
_____ _____	Ark	_____ _____ Tent
_____ _____	Candlestick	_____ _____ Veil
_____ _____	Court	_____ _____ _____
_____ _____	Holy of Holies	_____ _____ _____
_____ _____	Holy Place	

OFFERINGS/SACRIFICES

_____ _____	Burnt Offering	_____ _____ Sin Offering (Trespass)
_____ _____	Drink Offering	_____ _____ Wave Offering
_____ _____	Heave Offering	_____ _____ _____
_____ _____	Meal Offering	_____ _____ _____
_____ _____	Peace Offering	

FEASTS (For more info, read *The Feasts of the Lord* by Ron Cantrell)

_____ _____ Feast of Passover (Feast of Unleavened Bread)

_____ _____ Pentecost (Shavuot, Feast of Weeks or First Fruits)

_____ _____ Feast of Tabernacles (Sukkot)

_____ _____ Day of Atonement (Yom Kippur)

_____ _____ Feast of Trumpets (Rosh Hashana, Ushered in Civil Year)

_____ _____ Feast of Dedication (Hanukkah)

_____ _____ Festival of Purim

_____ _____ _____

_____ _____ _____

_____ _____ _____

CULTURE STUDY: THE JEWISH PEOPLE

_____ _____	Family Life	_____ _____ Music
_____ _____	Homes	_____ _____ Oral and Written Language
_____ _____	Food and Agriculture	_____ _____ Government, Military and
_____ _____	Clothing	Weapons of Warfare
_____ _____	Occupations	_____ _____ Economy, Technology,
_____ _____	Religion	Manufacturing, and Trade
_____ _____	Health & Medicine	_____ _____ _____
_____ _____	Recreation & Entertainment	_____ _____ _____
_____ _____	Education	
_____ _____	Arts & Crafts	

THE DIVIDED KINGDOM, CAPTIVITY, EXILE, RETURN & THE PERSIAN EMPIRE

Elem   Jr/Sr High

MAJOR EVENTS

_____ _____ c.1126-1105 BC, Reign of King Nebuchadnezzar I

_____ _____ c.933 BC, Kingdom Divides: Rehoboam, King of Judah and Jeroboam, King of Israel

_____ _____ c. 731-626 BC, Assyrians and Chaldeans Fight for Control of Babylon

_____ _____ c. 721 BC, Israel Taken Captive by Assyrians

_____ _____ c. 626-605 BC, King Nabopolassar Defeats Assyrians, Rules Babylon

_____ _____ c. 606 BC, Judah Taken Captive by Babylonians

_____ _____ c. 605 BC - 562 BC, King Nebuchadnezzar II Rules

_____ _____ c. 539 BC, Babylon is Conquered by Persians

_____ _____ 536 BC, Persian Empire Begins

_____ _____ 536 BC, Return from Captivity Permitted by Persians

_____ _____ 516 BC, Temple Completed

_____ _____ 478 BC, Esther Becomes Queen of Persia

_____ _____ 444 BC, Nehemiah Rebuilds Wall

_____ _____ 331 BC, Persian Empire Ends

_____ _____ _____

_____ _____ _____

_____ _____ _____

PEOPLE

_____ _____ Artaxerxes I (485-465 BC)

_____ _____ Ashurbanipal—King of Assyria (669-640 BC)

_____ _____ Cyrus (538-529BC)

_____ _____ Daniel (606-534 BC)

_____ _____ Darius I (521-485 BC)

_____ _____ Darius III (335-331 BC)

_____ _____ Esther

_____ _____ Ezekiel (592-570 BC)

_____ _____ Ezra (457 BC)

_____ _____ Herodotus (c.490-c.425 BC)

_____ _____ Hezekiah (726-697 BC)

_____ _____ Hosea (760-721 BC)

_____ _____ Isaiah (745-695 BC)

_____ _____ Jeroboam I (933-911 BC)

_____ _____ Jeremiah (626-586 BC)

_____ _____ Joel (?840-830 BC)

_____ _____ Jonah (790-770 BC)

_____ _____ Malachi (450-400 BC)

_____ _____ Meshach, Shadrach, and Abednego

_____ _____ Micah (735-665 BC)

_____ _____ Nahum (630-610 BC)

_____ _____ Nebuchadnezzar

_____ _____ Nehemiah (444 BC)

_____ _____ Sennacherib

_____ _____ Tiglathpileser III -King, of Assyrians, conquered Israel (c.745-727 BC)

_____ _____ Zachariah (520-516 BC)

_____ _____ Zephaniah (639-608 BC)

_____ _____ Zerubbabel (536 BC)

_____ _____ Zoroaster (c.630-c.553 BC)

_____ _____ _____

_____ _____ _____

_____ _____ _____

PLACES

_____ _____	Ashur	_____ _____ Sidon
_____ _____	Ishtar Gate	_____ _____ Tyre
_____ _____	Nimrud	_____ _____ _____
_____ _____	Nineveh	_____ _____ _____
_____ _____	Persepolis	_____ _____ _____

TERMS

_____ _____	Alphabet	_____ _____ Prophet
_____ _____	Assyrians	_____ _____ Sailor
_____ _____	Bitumen	_____ _____ Shipbuilder
_____ _____	Chaldeans	_____ _____ Yahweh
_____ _____	Clay Tablet	_____ _____ _____
_____ _____	Judaism	_____ _____ _____
_____ _____	Medes	_____ _____ _____
_____ _____	Minted Coins	_____ _____ _____
_____ _____	Persians	_____ _____ _____
_____ _____	Phoenicians	_____ _____ _____

DISCOVERIES/ACCOMPLISHMENTS

_____ _____	Alphabet of 22 Letters	_____ _____ Purple-dyed Cloth
_____ _____	Carved Ivory	_____ _____ Ships (see page 148)
_____ _____	Cedar Wood	_____ _____ _____
_____ _____	Glassware	_____ _____ _____
_____ _____	Metal Work	_____ _____ _____

CULTURE STUDY: ANCIENT PERSIA

_____ _____	Family Life	_____ _____ Music
_____ _____	Homes	_____ _____ Oral and Written Language
_____ _____	Food and Agriculture	_____ _____ Government, Military and
_____ _____	Clothing	Weapons of Warfare
_____ _____	Occupations	_____ _____ Economy, Technology,
_____ _____	Religion	Manufacturing, and Trade
_____ _____	Health & Medicine	_____ _____ _____
_____ _____	Recreation & Entertainment	_____ _____ _____
_____ _____	Education	
_____ _____	Arts & Crafts	

ANCIENT GREECE

Elem   Jr/Sr High

MAJOR EVENTS

_____ _____ c.2000 BC - c.1450 BC, Minoan Civilization in Crete
_____ _____ c.1600 BC, Mycenae Civilization
_____ _____ c.1260 BC, Trojan War—War Between Greek Invaders and Defenders of Troy
_____ _____ 800 BC, Homer Composes Iliad and Odyssey—also see Literature
_____ _____ 776 BC, First Olympic Games
_____ _____ 494 BC - 479 BC, Persian Wars
_____ _____ c.460 BC, Temple of Zeus Erected at Olympia
_____ _____ 433 BC, Parthenon Built at Athens
_____ _____ 431-404 BC, Peloponnesian Wars—War Between Athens and Sparta
_____ _____ c.370 BC, Plato Opens Academy in Athens
_____ _____ 336-323 BC, Empire of Alexander the Great
_____ _____ 323-30 BC, Hellenistic Age
_____ _____ c. 290 BC Library of Alexandria Founded

_____ _____ _____
_____ _____ _____
_____ _____ _____
_____ _____ _____
_____ _____ _____

PEOPLE

_____ _____ Alexander the Great
_____ _____ Aristophanes
_____ _____ Homer
_____ _____ Pericles
_____ _____ Philip II
_____ _____ Plato

_____ _____ Sophocles
_____ _____ Xerxes
_____ _____ _____
_____ _____ _____
_____ _____ _____
_____ _____ _____

PLACES

_____ _____ Aegean Sea
_____ _____ Acropolis
_____ _____ Asia Minor
_____ _____ Athens
_____ _____ Black Sea
_____ _____ Corinth
_____ _____ Crete (Minoan)
_____ _____ Cyprus
_____ _____ Ionia (Samos, Miletus, Ephesus)

_____ _____ Macedonia
_____ _____ Malta
_____ _____ Parthenon
_____ _____ Petra
_____ _____ Sicily
_____ _____ Sparta
_____ _____ Troy
_____ _____ _____
_____ _____ _____

TERMS

___ ___	Abacus	___ ___ Parthenon
___ ___	Citadel	___ ___ Pharos Lighthouse
___ ___	Drama	___ ___ Polytheism
___ ___	Epicureans	___ ___ Stoics
___ ___	Frescoe	___ ___ Symposium
___ ___	Frieze	___ ___ Trojan Horse
___ ___	Greek Gods and Goddesses	___ ___ _____
___ ___	Gymnasium	___ ___ _____
___ ___	Mythology	___ ___ _____

DISCOVERIES/ACCOMPLISHMENTS

___ ___ Astronomy (See Scientists/Inventors)

___ ___ Columns (Doric, Ionic, Corinthian)

___ ___ Democratic Form of Government (See Government)

___ ___ Education (See Math: Pythagoras, Euclid, Archimedes)

___ ___ Greek Alphabet

___ ___ Greek Architecture (See Art History and Appreciation)

___ ___ Jury System (See Government)

___ ___ Libraries

___ ___ Lighthouses

___ ___ Literature (See Literature: Sophocles, Homer, Aristophanes)

___ ___ Medicine (See Scientist/Inventors: Hippocrates)

___ ___ Mime

___ ___ Mosaic Floors

___ ___ Olympic Games

___ ___ Philosophy (See Literature: Socrates, Plato, Aristotle)

___ ___ Sculpture (See Art)

___ ___ Shorthand

___ ___ _____

___ ___ _____

CULTURE STUDY: ANCIENT GREECE

___ ___	Family Life	___ ___ Music
___ ___	Homes	___ ___ Oral and Written Language
___ ___	Food and Agriculture	___ ___ Government, Military and
___ ___	Clothing	Weapons of Warfare
___ ___	Occupations	___ ___ Economy, Technology,
___ ___	Religion	Manufacturing, and Trade
___ ___	Health & Medicine	___ ___ _____
___ ___	Recreation & Entertainment	___ ___ _____
___ ___	Education	
___ ___	Arts & Crafts	

ANCIENT ROME

Elem   Jr/Sr High

MAJOR EVENTS

Elem	Jr/Sr High	Event
_____	_____	753 BC, Founding of Rome
_____	_____	509 BC, Roman Republic Begins
_____	_____	312 BC, First Roman Highway Build
_____	_____	300 BC, Circus Maximus Begun
_____	_____	264 BC, Punic Wars Begin, Wars Between Rome and Carthage
_____	_____	218 BC, Hannibal Crosses Alps, 2nd Punic War
_____	_____	73 BC, Spartacus Leads Revolt
_____	_____	60 BC, First Triumvirate Rules Rome
_____	_____	47 BC, Julius Caesar, Dictator of Rome
_____	_____	46 BC, Caesar Meets Cleopatra
_____	_____	46 BC, Julian Calendar
_____	_____	44 BC, Ides of March, Caesar Assassinated
_____	_____	27 BC, Augustus (Octavian) Rules Rome, Pax Romana Begins
_____	_____	c. AD 0 The Birth and Childhood of Jesus
_____	_____	c. AD 26, Pontius Pilate Made Procurator of Judaea
_____	_____	c. AD 30, Jesus' Baptism
_____	_____	Jesus' Temptation in the Wilderness
_____	_____	Jesus Calls and Trains His Disciples
_____	_____	Sermon on the Mount and Beatitudes
_____	_____	Parables of Jesus
_____	_____	Miracles of Jesus
_____	_____	Other Teachings and Ministry of Jesus
_____	_____	The Triumphal Entry and the Last Supper
_____	_____	Jesus' Trial Before Pilate
_____	_____	c. AD 33 AD, Jesus' Crucifixion, Burial, and Resurrection (c.33-36 AD)
_____	_____	The Great Commission
_____	_____	Jesus' Ascension into Heaven
_____	_____	AD 43, Roman Invasion of Britain
_____	_____	AD 64, Nero Burns Rome
_____	_____	c.AD 60-62, Paul in Roman Prison
_____	_____	AD 64, Great Fire of Rome
_____	_____	AD 70, Titus Destroys Temple
_____	_____	AD 73, Seige of Masada
_____	_____	AD 79, Pompeii Destroyed by Vesuvius Eruption
_____	_____	AD 80, Colosseum Completed
_____	_____	AD 121, Hadrian Wall Built to Keep Out Barbarians
_____	_____	AD 124, Pantheon Completed
_____	_____	AD 230, Persian Wars Begin
_____	_____	AD 303, Great Persecution of Christians Begins
_____	_____	AD 324, Constantine Rules Empire
_____	_____	AD 325, Nicene Creed Written
_____	_____	AD 330, Capital of Roman Empire Moves to Constantinople

_____	_____	AD 337, Constantine Baptized as Christian
_____	_____	AD 380, Theodosius Establishes Christianity as Roman State Religion
_____	_____	AD 395, Rome Split into Two Empires - Eastern and Western
_____	_____	AD 410, Visigoths Sack Rome
_____	_____	AD 455, Vandals Sack Rome
_____	_____	AD 447, Attila the Hun Attacks Rome
_____	_____	AD 476, End of Roman Empire, Middle Ages Begin

_____ _____
_____ _____
_____ _____
_____ _____
_____ _____
_____ _____
_____ _____
_____ _____
_____ _____
_____ _____
_____ _____
_____ _____
_____ _____

PEOPLE

_____ _____ Apostles—Peter, James, John, Andrew, Simon, Philip, Thomas, Bartholomew, Matthew, James son of Alphaeus, Simon Zealot, Judas son of James—Thaddaeus, Judas Iscariot

_____ _____ Attila the Hun (c.406-453)—King of the Huns: Attacked Roman Empire

_____ _____ Augustus, Octavius (63 BC-AD 14)—First Roman Emperor: Ordered Census, Luke 2:1

_____ _____ Barabbas—Robber: Matt. 27

_____ _____ Bartimaeus—Blind Man Jesus Healed, Mark 10:46

_____ _____ Caesar, Julius (Rome, c.100-44 BC)—Emperor of Rome

_____ _____ Caiaphas—High Priest During Jesus's Trial: Matt. 26:3

_____ _____ Constantine (c.274-337)—Roman Emperor: Promoted Christianity

_____ _____ Elizabeth—Mother of John the Baptist: Luke 1

_____ _____ Gabriel—Angel Sent to Mary, Mother of Jesus: Luke 1:19

_____ _____ Hadrian

_____ _____ Hannibal (247-182 BC)—General of Carthage

_____ _____ Herod—Ruler During Time of Jesus: Matt. 2

_____ _____ Jairus—Synagogue Ruler Whose Daughter Jesus Healed: Mark 5:1

_____ _____ Jesus (?3-33 AD)—The Savior of the World

_____ _____ John the Baptist—Forerunner of the Messiah: Luke 1:3

_____ _____ Nero (37-68)—Roman Emperor: Christian Persecution

_____ _____ Nicodemus—Jewish Leader Who Came Secretly to Jesus: John 3:7

_____ _____ Paul/Saul (1st cent., d. c.65)—Apostle (also see Church History)

_____ _____ Romulus and Remus

_____ _____ Spartacus (d. 71 BC)—Roman Slave and Gladiator

_____ _____ Theodosius I

_____ _____ Titus

_____ _____ Zacharias—Father of John the Baptist: Luke 1

_____ _____ _____

_____ _____ _____

_____ _____ _____

_____ _____ _____

_____ _____ _____

_____ _____ _____

PLACES

_____ _____ Black Sea	_____ _____ Rome
_____ _____ Capernaum	_____ _____ Samaria
_____ _____ Cappadocia	_____ _____ Sardinia
_____ _____ Carthage	_____ _____ Sicily
_____ _____ Corsica	_____ _____ Tiber River
_____ _____ Galatia	_____ _____ _____
_____ _____ Judea	_____ _____ _____
_____ _____ Macedonia	_____ _____ _____
_____ _____ Mediterranean Sea	_____ _____ _____
_____ _____ Mt. Vesuvius	_____ _____ _____
_____ _____ Palestine	_____ _____ _____
_____ _____ Pompeii	_____ _____ _____

TERMS

_____ _____ Aqueduct	_____ _____ Pantheon
_____ _____ Circus Maximus	_____ _____ Pax Romana
_____ _____ Citizenship	_____ _____ Pharisee
_____ _____ Civil War	_____ _____ Republic
_____ _____ Colosseum	_____ _____ Samaritans
_____ _____ Crucifixion	_____ _____ Senate
_____ _____ Dictator	_____ _____ Scribe
_____ _____ Emperor	_____ _____ Stylus
_____ _____ Etruscans	_____ _____ Triumvirate
_____ _____ Gladiator	_____ _____ Volcano
_____ _____ Roman Gods and Goddesses	_____ _____ _____
_____ _____ Ides of March	_____ _____ _____
_____ _____ International Law	_____ _____ _____
_____ _____ Latin	_____ _____ _____
_____ _____ Mosaic	_____ _____ _____

DISCOVERIES/ACCOMPLISHMENTS

_____ _____	Aqueduct	_____ _____ Roman Numerals
_____ _____	Atrium	_____ _____ Spread of Christianity
_____ _____	Central Heating	_____ _____ State Supported Schools
_____ _____	Circus	_____ _____ Stone Bridges
_____ _____	Colosseum	_____ _____ Trade
_____ _____	Education System	_____ _____ Water system
_____ _____	Julian Calendar	_____ _____ _____
_____ _____	Justinian Code	_____ _____ _____
_____ _____	Money, Coins (700 BC)	_____ _____ _____
_____ _____	Newspapers	_____ _____ _____
_____ _____	Road building	_____ _____ _____

CULTURE STUDY: ANCIENT ROME

_____ _____	Family Life	_____ _____ Music
_____ _____	Homes	_____ _____ Oral and Written Language
_____ _____	Food and Agriculture	_____ _____ Government, Military and
_____ _____	Clothing	Weapons of Warfare
_____ _____	Occupations	_____ _____ Economy, Technology,
_____ _____	Religion	Manufacturing, and Trade
_____ _____	Health & Medicine	_____ _____ _____
_____ _____	Recreation & Entertainment	_____ _____ _____
_____ _____	Education	_____ _____ _____
_____ _____	Arts & Crafts	_____ _____ _____

CULTURE STUDY: MODERN ITALY

_____ _____	Family Life	_____ _____ Music
_____ _____	Homes	_____ _____ Oral and Written Language
_____ _____	Food and Agriculture	_____ _____ Government, Military and
_____ _____	Clothing	Weapons of Warfare
_____ _____	Occupations	_____ _____ Economy, Technology,
_____ _____	Religion	Manufacturing, and Trade
_____ _____	Health & Medicine	_____ _____ _____
_____ _____	Recreation & Entertainment	_____ _____ _____
_____ _____	Education	_____ _____ _____
_____ _____	Arts & Crafts	_____ _____ _____

THE BYZANTINE EMPIRE & ISLAM
(OTTOMAN EMPIRE)
See also Medieval England

Elem   Jr/Sr High

MAJOR EVENTS

_____ _____ 658 BC, Constantinople Founded

_____ _____ AD 334, Constantine Makes Constantinople the Capital of the Roman Empire

_____ _____ AD 379-392, Emperor Theodosius rules Roman empire, Establishes Christianity as Roman State Religion

_____ _____ AD 395, Rome Split into Two Empires - Eastern and Western.

_____ _____ AD 625, Mohammed Dictates Koran

_____ _____ AD 641, Arabs Begin Conquest of North Africa

_____ _____ 1096, Crusades Begin (See Medieval Ages)

_____ _____ c.1300, Ottoman Empire Begins

_____ _____ 1453, End of Byzantine Empire, Constantinople is renamed Istanbul which means "City of Islam". Istanbul Becomes Muslim

_____ _____ _____

_____ _____ _____

_____ _____ _____

_____ _____ _____

PEOPLE

_____ _____ Constantine (c.274-337)—Roman Emperor.

_____ _____ Emperor Justinian (AD 527-565), Roman Emperor

_____ _____ Gregory the Great, Pope of Roman Catholic Church, 590 - 604 A.D

_____ _____ Ishmael (Genesis 16:15, 17:20)

_____ _____ Mohammed (Mecca, c.570-632)—Founder of Islam, Arab Prophet

_____ _____ Theodosius (346?-395), Eastern Roman Emperor

_____ _____ _____

_____ _____ _____

_____ _____ _____

_____ _____ _____

PLACES

_____ _____ Byzantium

_____ _____ Constantinople

_____ _____ Damascus

_____ _____ Istanbul

_____ _____ Magog

_____ _____ Mecca

_____ _____ Mosque

_____ _____ Turkish Empire

_____ _____ Turkey

_____ _____ _____

_____ _____ _____

_____ _____ _____

_____ _____ _____

TERMS

_____ _____	Alchemy	_____ _____ Mosque
_____ _____	Allah	_____ _____ Muslim
_____ _____	Arabesques	_____ _____ Pilgrimage
_____ _____	Arabian Nights, The	_____ _____ Sultan
_____ _____	Arabs	_____ _____ _____
_____ _____	Bedouin	_____ _____ _____
_____ _____	Caliph	_____ _____ _____
_____ _____	Five Pillars	_____ _____ _____
_____ _____	Jihad	_____ _____ _____
_____ _____	Islam	_____ _____ _____
_____ _____	Koran	_____ _____ _____

DISCOVERIES/ACCOMPLISHMENTS

_____ _____	Arabic Number System	_____ _____ _____
_____ _____	Geometry	_____ _____ _____
_____ _____	Persian Rugs	_____ _____ _____
_____ _____	Oil	_____ _____ _____
_____ _____	Rotation of Crops	_____ _____ _____
_____ _____	Trigonometry	_____ _____ _____
_____ _____	_____	_____ _____ _____

CULTURE STUDY: _____
(IRAQ, SAUDI ARABIA, SYRIA, JORDAN, OR IRAN)

_____ _____	Family Life	_____ _____ Music
_____ _____	Homes	_____ _____ Oral and Written Language
_____ _____	Food and Agriculture	_____ _____ Government, Military and Weapons of Warfare
_____ _____	Clothing	
_____ _____	Occupations	_____ _____ Economy, Technology, Manufacturing, and Trade
_____ _____	Religion	
_____ _____	Health & Medicine	_____ _____ _____
_____ _____	Recreation & Entertainment	_____ _____ _____
_____ _____	Education	
_____ _____	Arts & Crafts	

MIDDLE AGES
ENGLAND, SCOTLAND, IRELAND, WALES
SCANDINAVIA (DENMARK, NORWAY AND SWEDEN)
(See also Byzantine Empire & Islam)

Elem   Jr/Sr High

MAJOR EVENTS

_____ _____ c.2900 BC, Stonehenge Built

_____ _____ c.AD 370, Hunnish Invasion of Europe

_____ _____ AD 449, Anglos, Saxons, and Jutes Invade Britain

_____ _____ c.AD 515, St. Benedict Institutes Monastic Rule

_____ _____ AD 534, Justinian's Legal Code

_____ _____ AD 732, Muslims Defeated—Battle of Tours

_____ _____ AD 771, Charlemagne Crowned King of Franks

_____ _____ AD 787, Viking Raids on Britain Begin

_____ _____ AD 800, Charlemagne Crowned Emperor of Rome

_____ _____ AD 871, King Alfred the Great Becomes King of England

_____ _____ 1054, Christian Church Divides

_____ _____ 1066, Norman Conquest of England

_____ _____ 1066, Battle of Hastings—Fought Between Harold II, Saxon King of England and William, Duke of Normandy

_____ _____ 1086, Domesday Book Completed

_____ _____ 1096-1291, Crusades

_____ _____ 1163, Notre Dame Built in Paris

_____ _____ 1170, Assassination of Thomas à Becket—Archbishop of Canterbury

_____ _____ 1215, Magna Carta—Signed by King John of England for English Barons

_____ _____ 1297, William Wallace defeat the English

_____ _____ 1306, Scots Revolt Under Robert Bruce, King of Scotland

_____ _____ 1314, Bannockburn—Battle Between Scottish and English Armies During Scottish War of Independence

_____ _____ 1337-1453, Hundred Years' War—Series of Wars Between England and France

_____ _____ 1339, Kremlin Built at Moscow

_____ _____ 1347-1351, Black Death

PEOPLE

_____ _____ Alfred the Great (England, c.849-c.900)—Anglo-Saxon King of Wessex

_____ _____ Augustine, Saint (Algeria, 345-430) Bishop of Hippo, Theologian

_____ _____ Bede the Venerable (England, c.672-735)—Historian and Scholar, Monk

_____ _____ Bruce, Robert (Scotland, 1274-1329)—Liberator and King of Scotland

_____ _____ Charlemagne (Europe, 747-814)—Anglo-Saxon Ruler

_____ _____ King Clovis (Europe, c. 466-511), Frankish King

_____ _____ King Edward I (England, 1239-1307), King of England 1272, Jewish persecution

_____ _____ King John (England, 1167-1216)—King, Magna Carta, Character in Ivanhoe

_____ _____ Richard the Lionhearted (England, 1157-1199)—King, Third Crusade

_____ _____ Vikings

_____ _____ Wallace, William (Scotland, c. 1270-1305), Scotland's National Hero

_____ _____ William the Conqueror (England, c.1027-1087)—King, Battle of Hastings, Norman Conquest

_____ _____ _____

_____ _____ _____

_____ _____ _____

_____ _____ _____

_____ _____ _____

_____ _____ _____

_____ _____ _____

_____ _____ _____

_____ _____ _____

_____ _____ _____

_____ _____ _____

_____ _____ _____

_____ _____ _____

_____ _____ _____

PLACES

_____ _____ Balkans

_____ _____ Britannia

_____ _____ Canterbury

_____ _____ Cordoba

_____ _____ Danube Mountains

_____ _____ Edinburgh

_____ _____ England

_____ _____ Ireland

_____ _____ Louvre

_____ _____ London Bridge

_____ _____ Monte Cassino

_____ _____ Ravenna

_____ _____ Scotland

_____ _____ Spain

_____ _____ Stirling Castle

_____ _____ Stonehenge

_____ _____ Wales

_____ _____ _____

_____ _____ _____

_____ _____ _____

_____ _____ _____

_____ _____ _____

_____ _____ _____

_____ _____ _____

_____ _____ _____

_____ _____ _____

_____ _____ _____

_____ _____ _____

_____ _____ _____

TERMS

_____ _____	Accolade	_____ _____ Mongols
_____ _____	Age of Chivalry	_____ _____ Moors
_____ _____	Anglo-Saxon	_____ _____ Mosaics
_____ _____	Apprentice	_____ _____ Normans
_____ _____	Armor	_____ _____ Norseman
_____ _____	Black Death	_____ _____ Papal Bull
_____ _____	Castles	_____ _____ Parliament
_____ _____	Celtic	_____ _____ Roman Catholic Church
_____ _____	Chivalry	_____ _____ Sacrament
_____ _____	Coat of Arms	_____ _____ Saracens
_____ _____	Common Law	_____ _____ Saxons
_____ _____	Convent	_____ _____ Squire
_____ _____	Crusades	_____ _____ Tourneys
_____ _____	Czar	_____ _____ Tudors
_____ _____	Druids	_____ _____ Turks
_____ _____	Excommunication	_____ _____ Vassal
_____ _____	Fealty	
_____ _____	Fief	
_____ _____	Fjords	
_____ _____	Feudalism	
_____ _____	Great Council	
_____ _____	Guilds	
_____ _____	Herald	
_____ _____	Heresy	
_____ _____	Hill Forts	
_____ _____	Holy Lands	
_____ _____	Icons	
_____ _____	Inquisition	
_____ _____	Journeyman	
_____ _____	Knight	
_____ _____	Knight's Templar	
_____ _____	Lombards	
_____ _____	Manor	
_____ _____	Master Craftsman	
_____ _____	Middle Ages	
_____ _____	Monastery	

DISCOVERIES/ACCOMPLISHMENTS

_____ _____	Archery	_____ _____ _____
_____ _____	Eyeglasses (1280)	_____ _____ _____
_____ _____	Lute, Harp, Flute	_____ _____ _____
_____ _____	Parliament	_____ _____ _____
_____ _____ _____		_____ _____ _____
_____ _____ _____		_____ _____ _____
_____ _____ _____		_____ _____ _____
_____ _____ _____		_____ _____ _____

CULTURE STUDY: MEDIEVAL ENGLAND

_____ _____ Family Life

_____ _____ Homes

_____ _____ Food and Agriculture

_____ _____ Clothing

_____ _____ Occupations

_____ _____ Religion

_____ _____ Health & Medicine

_____ _____ Recreation & Entertainment

_____ _____ Education

_____ _____ Arts & Crafts

_____ _____ Music

_____ _____ Oral and Written Language

_____ _____ Government, Military and Weapons of Warfare

_____ _____ Economy, Technology, Manufacturing, and Trade

_____ _____ _____

_____ _____ _____

CULTURE STUDY: MODERN ENGLAND

_____ _____ Family Life

_____ _____ Homes

_____ _____ Food and Agriculture

_____ _____ Clothing

_____ _____ Occupations

_____ _____ Religion

_____ _____ Health & Medicine

_____ _____ Recreation & Entertainment

_____ _____ Education

_____ _____ Arts & Crafts

_____ _____ Music

_____ _____ Oral and Written Language

_____ _____ Government, Military and Weapons of Warfare

_____ _____ Economy, Technology, Manufacturing, and Trade

_____ _____ _____

_____ _____ _____

CULTURE STUDY: _____ (Scotland, Ireland, Wales)

_____ _____ Family Life	_____ _____ Music
_____ _____ Homes	_____ _____ Oral and Written Language
_____ _____ Food and Agriculture	_____ _____ Government, Military and
_____ _____ Clothing	Weapons of Warfare
_____ _____ Occupations	_____ _____ Economy, Technology,
_____ _____ Religion	Manufacturing, and Trade
_____ _____ Health & Medicine	_____ _____ _____
_____ _____ Recreation & Entertainment	_____ _____ _____
_____ _____ Education	
_____ _____ Arts & Crafts	

CULTURE STUDY: _____ (Denmark, Norway, Sweden)

_____ _____ Family Life	_____ _____ Music
_____ _____ Homes	_____ _____ Oral and Written Language
_____ _____ Food and Agriculture	_____ _____ Government, Military and
_____ _____ Clothing	Weapons of Warfare
_____ _____ Occupations	_____ _____ Economy, Technology,
_____ _____ Religion	Manufacturing, and Trade
_____ _____ Health & Medicine	_____ _____ _____
_____ _____ Recreation & Entertainment	_____ _____ _____
_____ _____ Education	
_____ _____ Arts & Crafts	

RENAISSANCE AND REFORMATION (1350-1600)

Elem   Jr/Sr High

MAJOR EVENTS

_____ _____ 1350, Renaissance Begins in Italy

_____ _____ 1429, Joan of Arc Leads French Army Against England

_____ _____ 1431, Joan of Arc Burned at Stake

_____ _____ 1450-1763, European Exploration and Colonization—See U.S. History

_____ _____ 1455-1485 Wars of the Roses—Civil War in England Between House of Plantagenet (White Rose) and Lancaster (Red Rose)

_____ _____ 1469, Ferdinand and Isabella Marry, Uniting Spain

_____ _____ 1492, Jews Expelled from Spain

_____ _____ 1517, Reformation—16th Century Religious Revolution Which Begins When Martin Luther Publishes His "95 Theses" and Ends with the Formation of the Protestant Churches, See Church History

_____ _____ 1533, Ivan the Terrible (Russia, 1530-1584)—Became Czar of Russian at Age Three

_____ _____ 1534, Ignatius Loyola (Spain, 1491-1556)—Founded Jesuits

_____ _____ 1534, Henry VIII Breaks with Rome and Establishes Church of England

_____ _____ 1558 - 1603, Elizabethan Age (The Tudor Years)

_____ _____ 1587, Mary, Queen of Scots (Scotland, 1541-1587)—Executed (1587)

_____ _____ 1588, Spanish Armada—Failed Attempt to Invade England by King Philip of Spain

_____ _____ 1608, Quebec Founded by the French

_____ _____ 1618-1648, Thirty Years' War—Power Struggle Between Kings of France and Habsburg Rulers of Holy Roman Empire and Spain (Catholics vs. Protestants)

_____ _____ 1640, Stage Coaches Introduced in England

_____ _____ 1651, Oliver Cromwell Unites England, Scotland, and Ireland

_____ _____ 1660, Restoration of Monarchy in England

_____ _____ 1661, Louis XIV Assumes Absolute Power in France

_____ _____ 1666, Great Fire in London

PEOPLE

_____ _____ Charles V (1500-1558)—Holy Roman Emperor
_____ _____ Cromwell, Oliver (England, 1599-1658)—Unites England, Scotland, and Ireland
_____ _____ Drake, Sir Francis (England, 1540?-1596)—Explorer, Spanish Armada
_____ _____ Elizabeth I (England, 1533-1603)—Queen of England
_____ _____ Ferdinand (Spain, 1451-1504) and Isabella (?)—Funded Columbus' Voyage
_____ _____ Henry VIII (England, 1491-1547)—Tudor King
_____ _____ Joan of Arc (France, c.1412-1431)—Patriot and Martyr
_____ _____ Louis XIV (France, 1638-1715)—King of France
_____ _____ Mary, Queen of Scots (Scotland, 1541-1587)
_____ _____ More, Sir Thomas (England, 1478-1535)—Statesman
_____ _____ Pizarro, Francisco (Spain, c.1478-1541)—Conquistador: Conquered Incas of Peru
_____ _____ Pope Leo X (Germany, 1475-1521)—Declared Luther a Heretic

PLACES

_____ _____ London
_____ _____ Wittenbury

TERMS

_____ _____ Alliance
_____ _____ Book of Common Prayer
_____ _____ Edict of Worms
_____ _____ Education
_____ _____ Elizabethan Age
_____ _____ Heresy
_____ _____ Heliocentric
_____ _____ Mercenaries
_____ _____ Monarchs
_____ _____ Protestant
_____ _____ Wittenberg

DISCOVERIES/ACCOMPLISHMENTS

_____ _____	Printing Press	_____ _____ _____
_____ _____	Movable Type	_____ _____ _____
_____ _____	Bookmaking	_____ _____ _____
_____ _____	Plays	_____ _____ _____
_____ _____	_____	_____ _____ _____
_____ _____	_____	_____ _____ _____
_____ _____	_____	_____ _____ _____
_____ _____	_____	_____ _____ _____
_____ _____	_____	_____ _____ _____
_____ _____	_____	_____ _____ _____
_____ _____	_____	_____ _____ _____
_____ _____	_____	_____ _____ _____

CULTURE STUDY: THE ELIZABETHAN AGE (1558-1603)

_____ _____	Family Life	_____ _____ Arts & Crafts
_____ _____	Homes	_____ _____ Music
_____ _____	Food and Agriculture	_____ _____ Oral and Written Language
_____ _____	Clothing	_____ _____ Government, Military and
_____ _____	Occupations	Weapons of Warfare
_____ _____	Religion	_____ _____ Economy, Technology,
_____ _____	Health & Medicine	Manufacturing, and Trade
_____ _____	Recreation & Entertainment	_____ _____ _____
_____ _____	Education	_____ _____ _____

THE AGE OF ENLIGHTENMENT & THE EIGHTEENTH CENTURY
(1700's)
(Also see U.S. History)

Elem   Jr/Sr High

MAJOR EVENTS

_____ _____ 1700-1950, Industrial Revolution—The Shift from an Agriculturally-Based
Economy to One Based on Mechanized Production of Manufactured Goods.

_____ _____ 1701-1714, War of Spanish Succession—War Fought Over Succession to the
Spanish Throne

_____ _____ 1740-1748, War of Austrian Succession—Struggle for Mastery of German States
Between Prussia and Austria

_____ _____ 1756-1763, Seven Years War—World-Wide Conflict Over Control of Germany and
Colonial Struggle Between Britain and France in the New World and the Far
East (also see French and Indian War)

_____ _____ 1770-1850, Industrial Revolution Begins in England

_____ _____ 1774, Marie Antoinette Becomes Queen of France

_____ _____ 1775-1783, American War of Independence

_____ _____ 1789-1799, French Revolutionary Wars—War Between France and Neighboring
Europe Merging Ultimately with the Napoleonic Wars

_____ _____ 1793, The Reign of Terror Begins

_____ _____ 1799, Napoleon Bonaparte seizes control of the government ending the Revolution.

_____ _____ _____
_____ _____ _____
_____ _____ _____
_____ _____ _____
_____ _____ _____
_____ _____ _____
_____ _____ _____
_____ _____ _____
_____ _____ _____
_____ _____ _____
_____ _____ _____
_____ _____ _____
_____ _____ _____
_____ _____ _____

PEOPLE

_____ _____ Antoinette, Marie (France, 1755-1793), Queen of France

_____ _____ Bacon, Frances (England, 1561–1626), Philosopher

_____ _____ Bayle, Pierre (France,1647-1706), Philosopher.

_____ _____ Bonaparte, Napoleon (Corsica, 1769-1821), Emperor of France

_____ _____ de Montesquieu,Baron (France, 1689–1755), Jurist and political philosopher

_____ _____ Descartes, René (France,1596–1650), French philosopher, mathematician, and
scientist

_____ _____ Diderot, Denis (France, 1713–84), Encyclopedist, philosopher of materialism, and critic of art and literature

_____ _____ Jefferson, Thomas (Virginia, 1743–1826), Third President of the United States

_____ _____ Kant, Immanuel (Germany, 1724–1804), Metaphysician and philosopher

_____ _____ Locke, John (England, 1632–1704), Philosopher

_____ _____ Louis XVI, (France, 1754-1793) King of France during French Revolution

_____ _____ Newton, Sir Isaac (England, 1642–1727) Mathematician and natural philosopher

_____ _____ Paine, Thomas (England, 1737–1809) Anglo-American political theorist and writer

_____ _____ Pascal, Blaise (France, 1623-1662) Mathematician and Theologian. Used the analytic logic of the Enlightenment to prove Christianity.

_____ _____ Robespierre, Maximilien (France, 1758-1794), Leader of the French Revolution.

_____ _____ Rousseau, Jean Jacques (Switzerland, 1712–1778), Philosopher, author, political theorist, and composer

_____ _____ Smith, Adam (Scotland, 1723–90), Economist

_____ _____ Voltaire, François Marie Arouet de (France, 1694–1778), Philosopher and author

_____ _____ Wesley, John (England, 1707-1788), preacher and founder of the Methodist Church

_____ _____ _____
_____ _____ _____
_____ _____ _____
_____ _____ _____
_____ _____ _____
_____ _____ _____
_____ _____ _____
_____ _____ _____
_____ _____ _____
_____ _____ _____

PLACES

_____ _____ Austria
_____ _____ France
_____ _____ Holland
_____ _____ Russia

_____ _____ Sweden
_____ _____ Versailles
_____ _____ _____
_____ _____ _____

TERMS

_____ _____ Aristocracy
_____ _____ Bourgeoisie
_____ _____ Enlightenment
_____ _____ French Revolution
_____ _____ Masons
_____ _____ Reign of Terror
_____ _____ _____
_____ _____ _____

_____ _____ _____
_____ _____ _____
_____ _____ _____
_____ _____ _____
_____ _____ _____
_____ _____ _____

DISCOVERIES/ACCOMPLISHMENTS

_____ _____ _____   _____ _____ _____
_____ _____ _____   _____ _____ _____
_____ _____ _____   _____ _____ _____
_____ _____ _____   _____ _____ _____
_____ _____ _____   _____ _____ _____
_____ _____ _____   _____ _____ _____
_____ _____ _____   _____ _____ _____
_____ _____ _____   _____ _____ _____
_____ _____ _____   _____ _____ _____
_____ _____ _____   _____ _____ _____
_____ _____ _____   _____ _____ _____

CULTURE STUDY: FRANCE

_____ _____ Family Life

_____ _____ Homes

_____ _____ Food and Agriculture

_____ _____ Clothing

_____ _____ Occupations

_____ _____ Religion

_____ _____ Health & Medicine

_____ _____ Recreation & Entertainment

_____ _____ Education

_____ _____ Arts & Crafts

_____ _____ Music

_____ _____ Oral and Written Language

_____ _____ Government, Military and Weapons of Warfare

_____ _____ Economy, Technology, Manufacturing, and Trade

_____ _____ _____

_____ _____ _____

NINETEENTH CENTURY, (1800's)
(Also see U.S. History)

Elem   Jr/Sr High

_____ _____ 1803-1815, The Napoleonic Wars—Series of Wars Between France and a Number of European Nations to Restore the French Monarchy

_____ _____ 1807, Abolishment of Slave Trade in British Empire

_____ _____ 1812, Napoleon Bonaparte Invades Russia

_____ _____ 1815, Battle of Waterloo—Ended Napoleonic Wars

_____ _____ 1825, Erie Canal Opens

_____ _____ 1840, Marriage of Queen Victoria and Prince Albert

_____ _____ 1848, Marx, Karl Publishes The Communist Manifesto

_____ _____ 1853-1856, Crimean War—Military Conflict Between Russia, Great Britain, and the Ottoman Empire

_____ _____ 1864, Red Cross Founded at Geneva Convention

_____ _____ 1861-1865, American Civil War—Conflict Between the United States and Eleven Secessionist Southern States over Slavery and Political and Economic Issues. Also Known as The War Between the States

_____ _____ 1866, Mendel's Laws Published, Modern Hereditary Theory

_____ _____ 1867, Dominion of Canada Established

_____ _____ 1867, Karl Marx Publishes Das Kapital

_____ _____ 1869, Suez Canal Opened

_____ _____ 1870-1871, Franco-Prussian War—War Between France and Prussia

_____ _____ 1878, William and Catherine Booth Form the Salvation Army

_____ _____ _____

_____ _____ _____

_____ _____ _____

_____ _____ _____

_____ _____ _____

PEOPLE

_____ _____ Bolivar, Simon (Venezuela, 1783-1830)—Revolutionary Leader

_____ _____ Bonaparte, Napoleon (France, 1769-1821)—Emperor of France

_____ _____ Booth, William and Catherine, Founders of the Salvation Army (see page 177)

_____ _____ Marx, Karl (Germany, 1818-1883)—German Socialist, author of *The Communist Manifesto*

_____ _____ Nightingale, Florence (Italy, 1820-1910)—British Nurse, Hospital Reformer, and Humanitarian

_____ _____ Victoria, Alexandrina (England, 1819-1901), Queen of England

_____ _____ _____

_____ _____ _____

_____ _____ _____

_____ _____ _____

_____ _____ _____

PLACES

___	___	___	___	___	___
___	___	___	___	___	___
___	___	___	___	___	___
___	___	___	___	___	___
___	___	___	___	___	___
___	___	___	___	___	___
___	___	___	___	___	___

TERMS

___	___	___	___	___	___
___	___	___	___	___	___
___	___	___	___	___	___
___	___	___	___	___	___
___	___	___	___	___	___
___	___	___	___	___	___
___	___	___	___	___	___
___	___	___	___	___	___

DISCOVERIES/ACCOMPLISHMENTS

___	___	___	___	___	___
___	___	___	___	___	___
___	___	___	___	___	___
___	___	___	___	___	___
___	___	___	___	___	___
___	___	___	___	___	___
___	___	___	___	___	___
___	___	___	___	___	___

CULTURE STUDY: THE VICTORIAN AGE (1832 - 1901)

___ ___	Family Life		___ ___	Health & Medicine
___ ___	Homes		___ ___	Recreation & Entertainment
___ ___	Food and Agriculture		___ ___	Education
___ ___	Clothing		___ ___	Arts & Crafts
___ ___	Occupations		___ ___	Music
___ ___	Religion			

TWENTIETH CENTURY: TO 1950

(Also see U.S. History)

Elem   Jr/Sr High

_____ _____ 1911, Chinese Revolution

_____ _____ 1912-1913, Balkan Wars—Fought Among Countries in Balkan Peninsula for
                Possession of European Territories Held by Ottoman Empire

_____ _____ 1912, SS Titanic Sinks

_____ _____ 1912, Chiang Kai-shek Establishes the Republic of China

_____ _____ 1914, Opening of Panama Canal

_____ _____ 1914-1918, War World I—War Involving 32 Nations Which Began with the
                Assassination of Archduke Franz Ferdinand and Reaction to Ambition of
                German Empire

_____ _____ 1917-1922, Irish Rebellion

_____ _____ 1917-1921, The Russian Revolution

_____ _____ 1917, Balfour Declaration Promises Jews a Home in Palestine

_____ _____ 1919, Treaty of Versailles

_____ _____ 1920, League of Nations Established

_____ _____ 1922, Benito Mussolini Comes to Power in Italy

_____ _____ 1922, Tutankhamun's Tomb Discovered in Egypt

_____ _____ 1925, Publication of Adolf Hitler's Mein Kampf

_____ _____ 1933, Hitler Forms Third Reich in Germany

_____ _____ 1936, Arab Revolt in Palestine

_____ _____ 1936-1939, Spanish Civil War

_____ _____ 1939, Great Purge in Soviet Union

_____ _____ 1939-1945, World War II

_____ _____ 1945, Nuremberg War Crimes Tribunal

_____ _____ 1945, United Nations Established

_____ _____ 1947, Dead Sea Scrolls Found in Palestine

_____ _____ 1947, Marshall Plan for European Reconstruction

_____ _____ 1948, State of Israel Established

_____ _____ 1948, Creation of the World Council of Churches

_____ _____ 1948, First Arab-Israeli War

_____ _____ 1948, Hindu Nationalist Leader Mahatma Gandhi Assassinated

_____ _____ 1948, Apartheid Policy Begins in South Africa

_____ _____ 1949, Creation of West and East Germany

_____ _____ _____

_____ _____ _____

_____ _____ _____

_____ _____ _____

_____ _____ _____

_____ _____ _____

PEOPLE

_____ _____ Chiang Kai-shek (China, 1887-1975)—Revolutionary Leader of China
_____ _____ Mussolini, Benito (Italy, 1883-1945)—
_____ _____ Gandhi, Mahatma (India, 1869-1948)
_____ _____ Hitler, Adolf (Germany,)
_____ _____ Peron, Juan (Argentina, 1895-1974)—President of Argentina (1946)

_____ _____ _____
_____ _____ _____
_____ _____ _____
_____ _____ _____
_____ _____ _____

PLACES

_____ _____ Berlin
_____ _____ Ottoman Empire
_____ _____ Panama

TERMS

_____ _____ Apartheid
_____ _____ Assassination
_____ _____ Canal (see page 148)
_____ _____ Scroll
_____ _____ Tribunal

DISCOVERIES/ACCOMPLISHMENTS

_____ _____ Air Conditioner (1902)   _____ _____ Zipper (1913)
_____ _____ Bandaid (1920)
_____ _____ Cellophane (1908)
_____ _____ Crayons (1903)
_____ _____ Lie Detector (1902)
_____ _____ Model T (1908)
_____ _____ Radios (1916)
_____ _____ Safety Razor (1901)
_____ _____ Talking Motion Picture (1910)
_____ _____ Windshield Wipers (1905)

MODERN WORLD: 1950'S TO PRESENT

(Also see U.S. History)

Elem   Jr/Sr High

MAJOR EVENTS

_____ _____ 1950-1953, Korean War—War Which Started with the Invasion of South Korea by North Korea

_____ _____ 1952, Detonation of the First Hydrogen Bomb

_____ _____ 1955, Warsaw Pact

_____ _____ 1956, Suez War—Britain and France, Allied with Israel, Against Egypt to Regain Control of the Suez Canal

_____ _____ 1961-1973, Vietnam War—War Between Communist North Vietnam and Non-Communist South Vietnam

_____ _____ 1957, Soviet Union Launches Sputnik

_____ _____ 1959, Castro, Fidel (Cuba, 1927-)— Takes Power in Cuba

_____ _____ 1960, Organization of the Petroleum Exporting Countries (OPEC) Formed

_____ _____ 1961, Berlin Wall Built

_____ _____ 1961, Gagarin, Yuri (Russia, 1934-1968) —Becomes First Man in Space

_____ _____ 1964, Palestine Liberation Organization (PLO) Founded

_____ _____ 1966, Chinese Cultural Revolution

_____ _____ 1967, Six-Day War

_____ _____ 1973, Major Famine in Ethiopia

_____ _____ 1977, Panama Canal Treaty

_____ _____ 1979, Civil War in Nicaragua

_____ _____ 1979, Islamic Republic Established in Iran Under Ayatollah Khomeini

_____ _____ 1979, Invasion of Afghanistan by USSR

_____ _____ 1979, Hussein, Saddam (Iraq, 1937-)—President of Iraq

_____ _____ 1979, Thatcher, Margaret (England, 1925-)—Britain's Prime Minister

_____ _____ 1980-1988, Iran-Iraq War—Battle Between Iran and Iraq

_____ _____ 1982, Falklands War—Britain Against Argentina

_____ _____ 1985, Gorbachev, Mikhail (Russia, 1931-)— Takes Power in Soviet Union

_____ _____ 1986, Chernobyl Nuclear Power Disaster

_____ _____ 1987, World Population Passes Five Thousand Million

_____ _____ 1989, Opening of Berlin Wall

_____ _____ 1989, Demonstration at Tiananmen Square and Massacre in Beijing

_____ _____ 1989, Collapse of Soviet Domination of Eastern Europe

_____ _____ 1989, Hirohito (Japan, 1901-1989)—Emperor of Japan Dies

_____ _____ 1990, Germany is Unified

_____ _____ 1990, Walesa, Lech (Poland, 1943-)— Becomes President of Poland

_____ _____ 1990, Persian Gulf War—War Between Iraq and U.S. Led Allies Over the Invasion of Kuwait by Iraq

_____ _____ 1990, F. W. de Klerk (South Africa, 1936-)—Begins Dismantling of South African Apartheid

_____ _____ 1991, Soviet Union Disbanded (Commonwealth of Independent States)

_____ _____ 1991-1995, Yugoslavian Civil War—Confrontation by Croatia and Serb-dominated National Army

_____ _____ 1992, Independence of Bosnia and Herzegovina

_____ _____ 1993, Israel Peace Agreement with PLO

_____ _____ 1994, Mandela, Nelson (South Africa, 1918-)— Becomes South African President

_____ _____ 1994, Opening of Channel Tunnel

_____ _____ 1994, Russian Forces Invade Chechenya

_____ _____ 1994, Cease Fire in Northern Ireland

_____ _____ 1995, Assassination of Israeli Prime Minister Yitzhak Rabin

_____ _____ 1995, Bosnia Peace Agreement

_____ _____ _____

_____ _____ _____

_____ _____ _____

_____ _____ _____

_____ _____ _____

_____ _____ _____

_____ _____ _____

PEOPLE

_____ _____ Gandhi, Indira (India, 1917-1984)—Prime Minister of India

_____ _____ Khomeini, Ayatollah (Iran, 1900-1989)—Iranian Political and Religious Leader

_____ _____ Khrushchev, Nikita (Russia, 1894-1971)—Prime Minister of Russia

_____ _____ Minh, Ho Chi (Vietnam, 1890-1969)—Vietnam Communist Leader

_____ _____ Sakharov, Andrei (Russia, 1921-1989)—Physicist, Nuclear Weapons

_____ _____ Tutu, Desmond (South Africa, 1931-)—Clergyman, Opposed Apartheid

_____ _____ _____

_____ _____ _____

_____ _____ _____

_____ _____ _____

_____ _____ _____

_____ _____ _____

PLACES

_____ _____ Bangladesh   _____ _____ _____

_____ _____ Berlin   _____ _____ _____

_____ _____ Persian Gulf   _____ _____ _____

_____ _____ Suez Canal (see page 148)   _____ _____ _____

_____ _____ West Bank   _____ _____ _____

_____ _____ _____   _____ _____ _____

_____ _____ _____   _____ _____ _____

TERMS

_____ _____ _____   _____ _____ _____
_____ _____ _____   _____ _____ _____
_____ _____ _____   _____ _____ _____
_____ _____ _____   _____ _____ _____
_____ _____ _____   _____ _____ _____

CULTURE STUDY: RUSSIA

_____ _____	Family Life	_____ _____ Music
_____ _____	Homes	_____ _____ Oral and Written Language
_____ _____	Food and Agriculture	_____ _____ Government, Military and
_____ _____	Clothing	Weapons of Warfare
_____ _____	Occupations	_____ _____ Economy, Technology,
_____ _____	Religion	Manufacturing, and Trade
_____ _____	Health & Medicine	
_____ _____	Recreation & Entertainment	_____ _____ _____
_____ _____	Education	_____ _____ _____
_____ _____	Arts & Crafts	

_____ _____ **CURRENT EVENTS** (Weekly)

FAMOUS WORLD LANDMARKS
(also see Landmarks of the U.S., page 113)

Elem   Jr/Sr High

_____ _____ _____   _____ _____ _____
_____ _____ _____   _____ _____ _____
_____ _____ _____   _____ _____ _____
_____ _____ _____   _____ _____ _____
_____ _____ _____   _____ _____ _____

THE FUTURE

Elem   Jr/Sr High

_____ _____ The Lord's Second Coming (Rev. 4,5)
_____ _____ Battle of Armageddon (Rev. 19:11-21, Zech. 14)
_____ _____ The New Heaven and Earth (Rev. 21,22)
_____ _____ _____
_____ _____ _____
_____ _____ _____
_____ _____ _____
_____ _____ _____

GEOGRAPHY

Elem   Jr/Sr High

_____ _____ Identify and Locate all Fifty States and Capitals of America

_____ _____ Identify and Locate all Seven Continents of the World

(Africa, Antarctica, Asia, Australia, Europe, North America, South America)

_____ _____ Identify and Locate all the Major Countries of the World

_____ _____ Identify and Locate all the Major Waterways of the World

_____ _____ Identify and Locate all the Major Cities of the World

_____ _____ Identify and Locate all the Major Mountains of the World

_____ _____ _____

_____ _____ _____

_____ _____ _____

_____ _____ _____

_____ _____ _____

_____ _____ _____

_____ _____ _____

_____ _____ _____

_____ _____ _____

_____ _____ _____

_____ _____ _____

_____ _____ _____

_____ _____ _____

_____ _____ _____

MAP READING

_____ _____ Conic Projection

_____ _____ Contour Lines and Intervals

_____ _____ Directions

_____ _____ Distance Scale

_____ _____ Elevation and Depressions

_____ _____ How to Fold and Unfold a Map

_____ _____ Legend (Map Symbols)

_____ _____ Locator Key

_____ _____ Longitude and Latitude

_____ _____ Mercator Projection

_____ _____ Meridian

_____ _____ Parallels

_____ _____ Prime Meridian

_____ _____ Using a Compass

_____ _____ _____

_____ _____ _____

_____ _____ _____

_____ _____ _____

_____ _____ _____

_____ _____ _____

TYPES OF MAPS

_____	_____	Political Maps
_____	_____	Physical Maps
_____	_____	Typographical Maps
_____	_____	_____
_____	_____	_____
_____	_____	_____

PEOPLE IN GEOGRAPHY

_____	_____	Peleg (Genesis 10:25)—Alive When the Earth Divided
_____	_____	Mercator, Gerardus (Belgium, 1512-1594)—Mapmaker: Atlas (1585), Mercator's Projection

MAP MAKING

_____	_____	Mapping Home	_____	_____	Flat Maps
_____	_____	Mapping Neighborhood	_____	_____	Globes
_____	_____	Mapping City/Town	_____	_____	3-D (Salt Dough) Maps
_____	_____	Mapping State	_____	_____	_____
_____	_____	Mapping United States	_____	_____	_____
_____	_____	Mapping World	_____	_____	_____

CULTURE STUDIES: (other countries are included throughout history section)

CULTURE STUDY: CANADA

_____	_____	Family Life	_____	_____	Music
_____	_____	Homes	_____	_____	Oral and Written Language
_____	_____	Food and Agriculture	_____	_____	Government, Military and Weapons of Warfare
_____	_____	Clothing			
_____	_____	Occupations	_____	_____	Economy, Technology, Manufacturing, and Trade
_____	_____	Religion			
_____	_____	Health & Medicine	_____	_____	_____
_____	_____	Recreation & Entertainment	_____	_____	_____
_____	_____	Education			
_____	_____	Arts & Crafts			

CULTURE STUDY: SWITZERLAND

_____ _____	Family Life	_____ _____ Music
_____ _____	Homes	_____ _____ Oral and Written Language
_____ _____	Food and Agriculture	_____ _____ Government, Military and
_____ _____	Clothing	Weapons of Warfare
_____ _____	Occupations	_____ _____ Economy, Technology,
_____ _____	Religion	Manufacturing, and Trade
_____ _____	Health & Medicine	_____ _____ _____
_____ _____	Recreation & Entertainment	_____ _____ _____
_____ _____	Education	
_____ _____	Arts & Crafts	

CULTURE STUDY: AUSTRALIA

_____ _____	Family Life	_____ _____ Music
_____ _____	Homes	_____ _____ Oral and Written Language
_____ _____	Food and Agriculture	_____ _____ Government, Military and
_____ _____	Clothing	Weapons of Warfare
_____ _____	Occupations	_____ _____ Economy, Technology,
_____ _____	Religion	Manufacturing, and Trade
_____ _____	Health & Medicine	_____ _____ _____
_____ _____	Recreation & Entertainment	_____ _____ _____
_____ _____	Education	
_____ _____	Arts & Crafts	

CULTURE STUDY: _____

_____ _____	Family Life	_____ _____ Music
_____ _____	Homes	_____ _____ Oral and Written Language
_____ _____	Food and Agriculture	_____ _____ Government, Military and
_____ _____	Clothing	Weapons of Warfare
_____ _____	Occupations	_____ _____ Economy, Technology,
_____ _____	Religion	Manufacturing, and Trade
_____ _____	Health & Medicine	_____ _____ _____
_____ _____	Recreation & Entertainment	_____ _____ _____
_____ _____	Education	
_____ _____	Arts & Crafts	

COUNTRIES OF THE WORLD—MAJOR RELIGIONS

Elem	Jr/Sr High		Elem	Jr/Sr High	
_____	_____	Afghanistan—Muslim			
_____	_____	Albania—Muslim			
_____	_____	Algeria—Muslim			
_____	_____	Andorra—R. Catholic			
_____	_____	Angola—R. Catholic			
_____	_____	Argentina—R. Catholic			
_____	_____	Armenia—Christian			
_____	_____	Australia—Christian			
_____	_____	Austria—R. Catholic			
_____	_____	Bangladesh—Muslim			
_____	_____	Belgium—R. Catholic			
_____	_____	Belize—R. Catholic			
_____	_____	Bolivia—R. Catholic			
_____	_____	Boznia—Muslim			
_____	_____	Brazil—R. Catholic			
_____	_____	Bulgaria—Other			
_____	_____	Burundi-R. Catholic			
_____	_____	Cambodia—Buddhist			
_____	_____	Cameroon—Christian			
_____	_____	Canada—R. Catholic			
_____	_____	Chad—Muslim			
_____	_____	Chile—R. Catholic			
_____	_____	China—Atheist			
_____	_____	Colombia—R. Catholic			
_____	_____	Congo—R. Catholic			
_____	_____	Costa Rica—R. Catholic			
_____	_____	Croatia—R. Catholic			
_____	_____	Cuba—R. Catholic			
_____	_____	Cyprus—Greek Orthodox			
_____	_____	Czech Republic—R. Catholic			
_____	_____	Denmark—Lutheran			
_____	_____	Dominican Republic— R.Catholic			
_____	_____	Ecuador—R. Catholic			
_____	_____	Egypt—Muslim			
_____	_____	El Salvador—R. Catholic			
_____	_____	Ethiopia—Muslim			
_____	_____	Finland—Lutheran			
_____	_____	France—R. Catholic			
_____	_____	Germany—Lutheran			
_____	_____	Ghana—Christian			

Elem	Jr/Sr High	
_____	_____	Greece—Christian
_____	_____	Greenland—Lutheran
_____	_____	Grenada—R. Catholic
_____	_____	Guatemala—R. Catholic
_____	_____	Guinea—Muslim
_____	_____	Guyana—Christian
_____	_____	Haiti—R. Catholic
_____	_____	Honduras—R. Catholic
_____	_____	Hungary—R. Catholic
_____	_____	Iceland—Lutheran
_____	_____	India—Hindu
_____	_____	Indonesia—Muslim
_____	_____	Iran—Muslim
_____	_____	Iraq—Muslim
_____	_____	Ireland—R. Catholic
_____	_____	Israel—Jewish
_____	_____	Italy—R. Catholic
_____	_____	Jamaica—Christian
_____	_____	Japan—Shintoist
_____	_____	Jordan—Muslim
_____	_____	Kazakhstan—Muslim
_____	_____	Kenya—Christian
_____	_____	Korea, North—Atheist
_____	_____	Korea, South—Protestant
_____	_____	Kuwait—Muslim
_____	_____	Laos—Buddhist
_____	_____	Latvia—Lutheran
_____	_____	Lebanon—Muslim
_____	_____	Liberia—Animist
_____	_____	Libya—Muslim
_____	_____	Lithuania—R. Catholic
_____	_____	Luxembourg—R. Catholic
_____	_____	Macedonia—Christian
_____	_____	Madagascar—Animist
_____	_____	Malawi—Protestant
_____	_____	Malaysia—Muslim
_____	_____	Mali—Muslim
_____	_____	Malta—R. Catholic
_____	_____	Mexico—R. Catholic
_____	_____	Moldova—Christian
_____	_____	Monaco—R. Catholic

Elem	Jr/Sr High		Elem	Jr/Sr High	
_____	_____	Mongolia—Buddhist	_____	_____	Swaziland—Christian and Animist
_____	_____	Morocco—Muslim	_____	_____	Sweden—Lutheran
_____	_____	Mozambique—Animist	_____	_____	Switzerland—R. Catholic and Protestant
_____	_____	Myanmar (Burma)—Buddhist	_____	_____	Syria—Muslim
_____	_____	Namibia—Christian	_____	_____	Taiwan—Taoist
_____	_____	Nepal—Hindu	_____	_____	Tajikistan—Muslim
_____	_____	Netherlands—R. Catholic	_____	_____	Tanzania—Christian, Muslim, and Animist
_____	_____	New Zealand—Christian	_____	_____	Thailand—Buddhist
_____	_____	Nicaragua—R. Catholic	_____	_____	Togo—Animist
_____	_____	Niger—Muslim	_____	_____	Trinidad—R. Catholic and Protestant
_____	_____	Nigeria—Muslim	_____	_____	Tunisia—Muslim
_____	_____	Norway—Lutheran	_____	_____	Turkey—Muslim
_____	_____	Oman—Muslim	_____	_____	Uganda—R. Catholic and Protestant
_____	_____	Pakistan—Muslim	_____	_____	Ukraine—Orthodox
_____	_____	Panama—R. Catholic	_____	_____	United Arab Emirates—Muslim
_____	_____	Papua New Guinea—Protestant	_____	_____	United Kingdom (England, Scotland, Wales, Northern Ireland)—Christian
_____	_____	Paraguay—R. Catholic	_____	_____	United States—Christian
_____	_____	Peru—R. Catholic	_____	_____	Uruguay—R. Catholic
_____	_____	Philippines—R. Catholic	_____	_____	Uzbekistan—Muslim
_____	_____	Poland—R. Catholic	_____	_____	Venezuela—R. Catholic
_____	_____	Portugal—R. Catholic	_____	_____	Vietnam—Buddhist
_____	_____	Qatar—Muslim	_____	_____	Western Samoa—Christian
_____	_____	Romania—Eastern Orthodox Christian	_____	_____	Yemen—Muslim
_____	_____	Russia (Russian Federation)—Atheist	_____	_____	Yugoslavia—Serbian Orthodox
_____	_____	Rwanda—Christian	_____	_____	Zaire—R. Catholic
_____	_____	Saudi Arabia—Muslim	_____	_____	Zambia—Christian
_____	_____	Senegal—Muslim	_____	_____	Zimbabwe—Syncretic Christian/Local Beliefs
_____	_____	Sierra Leone—Muslim	_____	_____	_____
_____	_____	Singapore—Buddhist	_____	_____	_____
_____	_____	Slovak Republic—R. Catholic	_____	_____	_____
_____	_____	Slovenia—R. Catholic			
_____	_____	Somalia—Muslim			
_____	_____	South Africa—Christian			
_____	_____	Spain—R. Catholic			
_____	_____	Sri Lanka—Buddhist			
_____	_____	Sudan—Muslim			
_____	_____	Suriname—Hindu			

EXPLORERS OF THE WORLD

Elem   Jr/Sr High

_____ _____ Amundsen, Roald (Norway, 1872-1928)—South Pole

_____ _____ Balboa, Vasco de (Spain, 1475-1519)— Pacific Ocean

_____ _____ Burke, Robert O'Hara (Ireland, 1820-1861)—Australia

_____ _____ Byrd, Richard (Virginia, 1888-1957)—North Pole

_____ _____ Cabot, John (Italy, 1425-c.1500)—Greenland, Labrador, Newfoundland

_____ _____ Cabral, Pedro (Portugal, c.1467-1520)—Brazil

_____ _____ Cabrillo, Rodriguez (Spain, 1542)— California

_____ _____ Cartier, Jacques (France, 1491-1557)—St. Lawrence River

_____ _____ Champlain, Samuel de (France, 1567-1635)—Quebec, Great Lakes, Canada

_____ _____ Columbus, Christopher (Italy, 1451-1506)—San Salvador, West Indies, Discovered America 1492

_____ _____ Cook, James (England, 1728-1779)—New Zealand, Australia, Antarctica, Hawaii

_____ _____ Coronado, Francisco de (Spain, 1510-1554)—Mexico, New Mexico, Texas, Oklahoma, Kansas, Grand Canyon

_____ _____ Cortes, Hernando (Spain, 1485-1547)—Mexico, Cuba, Aztecs

_____ _____ Cousteau, Jacques (France, 1910-)—Underwater Exploration

_____ _____ de Gama, Vasco (Portugal, c.1469-1525)— India, Cape of Good Hope

_____ _____ de Mendoza, Pedro de (Spain, 1487-1537)—Buenos Aires

_____ _____ de Soto, Hernando (Spain, c.1496-1542)—Florida, Mississippi, Georgia, Carolinas, Alabama, Arkansas, Louisiana

_____ _____ Dias, Batholomeu (Portugal, c.1450-1500)—Africa, Cape of Good Hope

_____ _____ Drake, Sir Francis (England, 1577-1580)— First English Circumnavigator of the Globe

_____ _____ Eriksson, Leif (Norway, 10th cent.)—Vinland, America?

_____ _____ Eric the Red (Norway, 10th cent.)—Greenland

_____ _____ Flinders, Matthew (England, 1774-1814)—Australia

_____ _____ Henry The Navigator (Portugal, 1394-1460)—Prince and Navigator: Africa, Set up Observatory, School of Scientific Navigation

_____ _____ Hillary, Edmund (New Zealand, 1919-)—Mount Everest

_____ _____ Hudson, Henry (England, c.1565-1611)—Hudson River and Bay

_____ _____ La Salle (France, 1643-1687)—Pioneer of Canada, Explored and Claimed Louisiana for France

_____ _____ Livingstone, David (England, 1813-1873)—Africa (Victoria Falls)

_____ _____ Magellan, Ferdinand (Portugal, c.1480-1521)—First to Circumnavigate the Globe, Philippines, Named Pacific Ocean

_____ _____ Marquette, Jacques (France, 1637-1675)—Upper Mississippi River to Arkansas

_____ _____ Peary, Robert (Pennsylvania, 1856-1920)—North Pole

_____ _____ Pike, Zebulon (New Jersey, 1779-1813)—Army Officer and Explorer: Mississippi River, Arkansas River, Red River, Pike's Peak, Colorado

_____ _____ Polo, Marco (Italy, 1254-1324)—China

_____ _____ Ponce de Leon (Spain, 1460-1521)—Puerto Rico, Florida, Cuba, Trinidad

_____ _____ Stanley, Henry (England, 1841-1904)—Traced Congo to the Atlantic

_____ _____ Verrazano, Giovanni da (Italy, 1485-1528)—East Coast of North America, New
York Bay, Hudson River
_____ _____ Vespucci, Amerigo (Italy, 1454-1512)—Venezuela, West Indies, Amazon, Brazil,
America Named after Him
_____ _____ _____
_____ _____ _____
_____ _____ _____
_____ _____ _____
_____ _____ _____
_____ _____ _____
_____ _____ _____
_____ _____ _____
_____ _____ _____
_____ _____ _____
_____ _____ _____

PLACES

_____ _____ Cape of Good Hope   _____ _____ _____
_____ _____ Northwest Passage   _____ _____ _____
_____ _____ Quebec   _____ _____ _____
_____ _____ West Indies   _____ _____ _____
_____ _____ _____   _____ _____ _____
_____ _____ _____   _____ _____ _____
_____ _____ _____   _____ _____ _____
_____ _____ _____   _____ _____ _____
_____ _____ _____   _____ _____ _____

TERMS

_____ _____ Circumnavigate   _____ _____ _____
_____ _____ Conquistadors   _____ _____ _____
_____ _____ Friars   _____ _____ _____
_____ _____ Line of Demarcation   _____ _____ _____
_____ _____ Maps   _____ _____ _____
_____ _____ Navigational Instruments   _____ _____ _____
_____ _____ Ships   _____ _____ _____
_____ _____ Sugar Plantations   _____ _____ _____
_____ _____ Viceroy   _____ _____ _____
_____ _____ _____   _____ _____ _____
_____ _____ _____   _____ _____ _____

U.S. HISTORY

EARLY AMERICAN SETTLEMENTS

Elem   Jr/Sr High

MAJOR EVENTS

_____ _____ 1565, St. Augustine, Florida Founded by Spaniards

_____ _____ 1584, Roanoke Island Colony

_____ _____ 1600, British and Dutch East India Companies Founded

_____ _____ 1607, Jamestown Founded

_____ _____ 1620, Plymouth Colony Founded

_____ _____ 1624, New Netherlands Founded by Dutch

_____ _____ 1629, Massachusetts Bay Colony Founded

_____ _____ 1631, First Thanksgiving Celebrated

_____ _____ 1636, Harvard College Founded

_____ _____ 1638, First Printing Press Set up in America

_____ _____ 1641, The Great Awakening

_____ _____ 1649, Toleration Act

_____ _____ 1664, New Amsterdam Renamed New York

_____ _____ 1675, Bacon's Rebellion

_____ _____ 1681, William Penn Granted Patent for Land in North America

_____ _____ 1692 - 1693, Salem Witch Trials

_____ _____ 1732, Poor Richard's Almanac Published

_____ _____ _____

_____ _____ _____

_____ _____ _____

PEOPLE

_____ _____ Bacon, Nathaniel (Virginia, 1642-1676)—Colonial Leader & Rebel

_____ _____ Bradford, William (Massachusetts, 1590?-1657)—Plymouth Colony, 1620

_____ _____ Bradstreet, Anne (England/Massachusetts, 1612-1672)—American Puritan Poet

_____ _____ Calvert, George (Lord Baltimore) (England, c.1580-1632)—Founded Baltimore,
                 Maryland-1634; Hartford, Connecticut-1636

_____ _____ Dare, Virginia (Roanoke, VA, 1587-?)—First American Born of English Descent

_____ _____ Edwards, Jonathan (Connecticut, 1703-1758)—American Theologian

_____ _____ Hooker, Thomas (England/Connecticut, c.1586-1647)—Preacher: Founded
                 Hartford, Connecticut

_____ _____ Hudson, Henry (English, 1565-1611)—Explorer

_____ _____ Hutchinson, Ann (England/Massachusetts, 1591-1643)—Religious Leader, Pioneer

_____ _____ Locke, John (England, 1632-1704)—Philosopher, Two Treatises of Government

_____ _____ Mather, Cotton (Massachusetts, 1663-1728)—American Clergyman, Author

_____ _____ Minuit, Peter (Netherlands, 1580-1638)—Established Swedish Colony on
                 Delaware Bay

_____ _____ Oglethorpe, James (England, 1696-1785)—Founded Savannah, Georgia-1732

_____ _____ Penn, William (England, 1644-1718)—Founded Pennsylvania-1681

_____ _____ Pocahontas (c.1595-1617)—American Indian Princess: Jamestown, Virginia

_____ _____ Raleigh, Sir Walter (England, 1551-1618) —English Courtier, Navigator, and Poet: Roanoke Island, Virginia

_____ _____ Rolfe, John (England, 1585-1622)—Colonist: Jamestown, Virginia

_____ _____ Smith, John (England, 1580-1631)—President of Jamestown, Virginia (1607)

_____ _____ Squanto (d. 1622)—American Indian: Aided Colonist at Plymouth Colony

_____ _____ Standish, Miles (England, 1584?-1656)—Soldier and Colonist: Mayflower, Plymouth Colony, Massachusetts

_____ _____ White, John (England, d.1593?)—Painter and Cartographer: Roanoke Colony

_____ _____ Williams, Roger (England, 1603-1683)—Clergyman: Founded Providence, Rhode Island-1636

_____ _____ Winthrop, John (England, 1588-1649)—Governor of Massachusetts Bay Colony

_____ _____ Winthrop, John (England, 1606-1676)—Governor of Connecticut and Son of John Winthrop: Paper Currency

_____ _____ _____

_____ _____ _____

_____ _____ _____

PLACES

_____ _____ Middle Colonies (NY, MD, DE, NJ, PA)

_____ _____ New England (ME, MA, CT, RI)

_____ _____ Southern Colonies (VA, NC, SC, GA)

_____ _____ _____

_____ _____ _____

TERMS

_____ _____ Apprenticeships

_____ _____ Barter

_____ _____ Blacksmith

_____ _____ Charter

_____ _____ Hard Tack

_____ _____ Horn Book

_____ _____ House of Burgess

_____ _____ Indentured Servant

_____ _____ London Company

_____ _____ Lost Colony

_____ _____ Mayflower Compact

_____ _____ Meetinghouse

_____ _____ Mercantilism

_____ _____ Navigation Act

_____ _____ Patroon System

_____ _____ Pilgrims

_____ _____ Puritans

_____ _____ Quakers

_____ _____ Separatists

_____ _____ Thanksgiving

_____ _____ Tobacco

_____ _____ Town Meetings

_____ _____ Virginia Charter

_____ _____ _____

_____ _____ _____

_____ _____ _____

DISCOVERIES/ACCOMPLISHMENTS

_____ _____ Electricity

_____ _____ Franklin Stove

_____ _____ _____

_____ _____ _____

_____ _____ _____

_____ _____ _____

_____ _____ _____

_____ _____ _____

CULTURE STUDY: COLONIAL SETTLEMENTS

_____ _____	Family Life	_____ _____ Music
_____ _____	Homes	_____ _____ Oral and Written Language
_____ _____	Food and Agriculture	_____ _____ Government, Military and
_____ _____	Clothing	Weapons of Warfare
_____ _____	Occupations	_____ _____ Economy, Technology,
_____ _____	Religion	Manufacturing, and Trade
_____ _____	Health & Medicine	_____ _____ _____
_____ _____	Recreation & Entertainment	_____ _____ _____
_____ _____	Education	_____ _____ _____
_____ _____	Arts & Crafts	_____ _____ _____

FRENCH AND INDIAN WAR (1754-1763)

Elem   Jr/Sr High

MAJOR EVENTS

_____ _____ 1754-1763, French and Indian War

_____ _____ _____

_____ _____ _____

_____ _____ _____

_____ _____ _____

_____ _____ _____

PEOPLE

_____ _____ Wolfe, James (England, 1727-1759)—Colonel, Capture of Quebec

_____ _____ _____

_____ _____ _____

_____ _____ _____

_____ _____ _____

PLACES

_____ _____ _____   _____ _____ _____

_____ _____ _____   _____ _____ _____

_____ _____ _____   _____ _____ _____

TERMS

_____ _____ French Territory   _____ _____ _____

_____ _____ British Colonies   _____ _____ _____

_____ _____ Spanish Territory   _____ _____ _____

_____ _____ Hudson Bay Company   _____ _____ _____

_____ _____ _____   _____ _____ _____

AMERICAN REVOLUTION (1775-1783)

Elem   Jr/Sr High

MAJOR EVENTS

_____ _____	1765, Stamp Act
_____ _____	1767, Townshend Acts
_____ _____	1770, Boston Massacre
_____ _____	1773, Boston Tea Party
_____ _____	1774, Intolerable Acts
_____ _____	1774, First Continental Congress
_____ _____	1775, Battle of Lexington and Concord
_____ _____	1775, Battle of Bunker Hill
_____ _____	1775, Second Continental Congress
_____ _____	1776, Common Sense Published
_____ _____	1776, Declaration of Independence Completed
_____ _____	1777, Battle of Brandywine
_____ _____	1777, Battle of Saratoga
_____ _____	1777, Articles of Confederation
_____ _____	1781, Battle of Yorktown
_____ _____	1781, Cornwallis Surrenders
_____ _____	1783, Treaty of Paris
_____ _____	1786, Shay's Rebellion
_____ _____	1787, Constitutional Convention
_____ _____	1791, Bill of Rights

_____ _____ _____

_____ _____ _____

_____ _____ _____

_____ _____ _____

_____ _____ _____

_____ _____ _____

_____ _____ _____

_____ _____ _____

PEOPLE

_____ _____	Adams, John (Massachusetts, 1767-1848)—Statesman, 2nd President (1797-1801)
_____ _____	Adams, Sam (Massachusetts, 1722-1803)—American Revolutionary: Boston Tea Party
_____ _____	Allen, Ethan (Connecticut, 1738-1789)—Green Mountain Boys: Battle o Ticonderoga-1775
_____ _____	Arnold, Benedict (Connecticut, 1741-1801)—Soldier: Assisted Ethan Allen at Battle of Ticonderoga, Traitor to America
_____ _____	Burr, Aaron (New Jersey, 1756-1836)—Corrupt Politician: Killed Alexander Hamilton in a Duel
_____ _____	Clay, Henry (Virginia, 1777-1852)—Politician
_____ _____	Dickinson, John (Maryland, 1732-1808)—Politician: Delaware

_____ _____ Franklin, Benjamin (Massachusetts, 1706-1790)—Statesman, Writer, and Scientist: Declaration of Independence, Autobiography

_____ _____ Hale, Nathan (Connecticut, 1755-1776)—Revolutionary Soldier and Spy

_____ _____ Hamilton, Alexander (West Indies, 1757-1804)—American Statesman: Federalist Papers

_____ _____ Hancock, John (Massachusetts, 1737-1793)—Statesman: First to Sign the Declaration of Independence

_____ _____ Henry, Patrick (Virginia, 1736-1799)—Lawyer and Statesman: Stamp Act

_____ _____ Howe, Sir William (England, 1729-1814)—English Soldier: Won Victory for British at Bunker Hill

_____ _____ Jay, John (New York, 1745-1829)—Jurist and Statesman

_____ _____ Jefferson, Thomas (Virginia, 1743-1826)—3rd President (1801-1809): Drafted the Declaration of Independence

_____ _____ Jones, John Paul (Scotland, 1747-1792)—American Naval Officer

_____ _____ King George III (England, 1738-1820)—King of Great Britain

_____ _____ Madison, James (Virginia, 1751-1836)—4th President (1809-1813): Constitutional Convention, Federalist Papers, Virginia Plan

_____ _____ Marshall, John (Virginia, 1755-1835)—Jurist and Soldier: American Revolution

_____ _____ Paine, Thomas (England, 1737-1809)—American Revolutionary, Philosopher, and Author: Common Sense

_____ _____ Revere, Paul (Massachusetts, 1735-1818)—Patriot, Soldier, Silversmith (also see Literature: Longfellow)

_____ _____ Ross, Betsy (Pennsylvania, 1752-1836)—First American Flag

_____ _____ Sherman, Roger (Massachusetts, 1721-1793)—Statesman and Patriot: Declaration of Independence

_____ _____ Washington, George (Virginia, 1732-1799)—Surveyor, Soldier, Farmer, Statesman, 1st President (1789-1797): Constitutional Convention

_____ _____ Witherspoon, John (Scotland, 1723-1794)—American Clergyman, President of Princeton University-1768

_____ _____ _____
_____ _____ _____
_____ _____ _____
_____ _____ _____
_____ _____ _____
_____ _____ _____
_____ _____ _____
_____ _____ _____
_____ _____ _____
_____ _____ _____
_____ _____ _____
_____ _____ _____
_____ _____ _____
_____ _____ _____
_____ _____ _____
_____ _____ _____
_____ _____ _____
_____ _____ _____
_____ _____ _____

PLACES

_____ _____ Boston   _____ _____ _____

_____ _____ Pennsylvania   _____ _____ _____

_____ _____ Philadelphia   _____ _____ _____

_____ _____ _____   _____ _____ _____

_____ _____ _____   _____ _____ _____

TERMS

_____ _____ Articles of Confederation

_____ _____ Bill of Rights

_____ _____ British East India Company

_____ _____ Declaration of Independence

_____ _____ Emancipation Proclamation

_____ _____ Federalist Papers—See Alexander Hamilton

_____ _____ Hessians

_____ _____ Intolerable Acts

_____ _____ Liberty Bell (1776)

_____ _____ Mercantilism

_____ _____ Minutemen

_____ _____ Redcoats

_____ _____ Taxation Without Representation

DISCOVERIES/ACCOMPLISHMENTS

WAR OF 1812

Elem   Jr/Sr High

MAJOR EVENTS

_____ _____ 1807, Embargo Act
_____ _____ 1814, Francis Scott Key — Star Spangled Banner (see Music, page 170)
_____ _____ 1815, Treaty of Ghent
_____ _____ _____
_____ _____ _____
_____ _____ _____
_____ _____ _____
_____ _____ _____
_____ _____ _____
_____ _____ _____

PEOPLE

_____ _____ Perry, Oliver (Rhode Island, 1785-1819)—Naval Officer
_____ _____ _____
_____ _____ _____
_____ _____ _____
_____ _____ _____
_____ _____ _____
_____ _____ _____

PLACES

_____ _____ Fort McHenry (Baltimore,   _____ _____ _____
                  Maryland)   _____ _____ _____
_____ _____ Lake Champlain   _____ _____ _____
_____ _____ New Orleans   _____ _____ _____
_____ _____ U.S.S. Constitution (Ship)   _____ _____ _____

TERMS

_____ _____ _____
_____ _____ _____
_____ _____ _____
_____ _____ _____
_____ _____ _____

FRONTIER EXPANSION AND THE LOUISIANA PURCHASE

(Also See: War of 1812, Native Americans, Mexican War)

Elem   Jr/Sr High

MAJOR EVENTS

		1791, Bill of Rights—1st Ten Amendments, Added to Constitution
____	____	1791, Bill of Rights—1st Ten Amendments, Added to Constitution

_____ _____ 1791, Bill of Rights—1st Ten Amendments, Added to Constitution
_____ _____ 1803, Louisiana Purchase from France
_____ _____ 1805, Lewis and Clark Expedition
_____ _____ 1807, Steamboat Invented
_____ _____ 1812, War of 1812 Begins
_____ _____ 1820, Missouri Compromise
_____ _____ 1821, Mexican Gains Independence from Spain
_____ _____ 1821, Horace Mann Influences Establishment of State Curriculums
_____ _____ 1823, Monroe Doctrine
_____ _____ 1825, Erie Canal Completed
_____ _____ 1836, Santa Anna Defeats Col. William Travis at the Alamo
_____ _____ 1836, Sam Houston defeats Mexican army at San Jacinto, Texas wins their independence from Mexico
_____ _____ 1845, U.S. Acquires Texas
_____ _____ 1849, California Gold Rush
_____ _____ 1862, Homestead Act
_____ _____ 1876, Custer's Last Stand
_____ _____ 1876, Battle of Little Bighorn
_____ _____ 1889, First of the Land Runs
_____ _____ Cattle Drives
_____ _____ Railroads
_____ _____ Cowboys
_____ _____ Outlaws
_____ _____ Indian Removals (see also page 91)

_____ _____ _____
_____ _____ _____
_____ _____ _____

PEOPLE

_____ _____ Adams, John Quincy (Massachusetts, 1767-1848)—6th President: 1825-1829
_____ _____ Bean, Judge Roy (Kentucky, 1825?-1903)—Frontiersman
_____ _____ Billy the Kid (New York, 1859-1881)—Bandit
_____ _____ Napoleon Bonaparte (France, 1808-1873)—Emperor, Louisiana Purchase
_____ _____ Boone, Daniel (Pennsylvania, 1735-1820)—Frontiersman
_____ _____ Bowie, Jim (Kentucky, 1790-1836)—Pioneer and Colonel: Alamo
_____ _____ Buffalo Bill Cody (Iowa, 1846-1917)—Showman, Army Scout
_____ _____ Carson, Kit (Missouri, 1809-1868)—Trapper and Guide
_____ _____ Clark, William (Virginia, 1770-1838)—Explorer: Lewis and Clark Expedition
_____ _____ Crazy Horse (South Dakota, 1842-1877)—Sioux Chief Defeated Custer at Little Big Horn

_____ _____ Crockett, Davy (Tennessee, 1786-1836)—Frontiersman: Alamo

_____ _____ Custer, George (Ohio, 1839-1876)—U.S. Soldier: Custer's Last Stand

_____ _____ Earp, Wyatt (Illinois, 1848-1929)—Gambler, Gunfighter, and Lawman

_____ _____ Fremont, John (Georgia, 1813-1890)—Explorer and Politician

_____ _____ Geronimo (Arizona, 1829-1909)—Apache Chief

_____ _____ Harrison, William Henry (Virginia, 1773-1841)—9th President (3/18/41-4/18/41)

_____ _____ Hickock, Wild Bill (Illinois, 1837-1876)—Soldier, Scout, and U.S. Marshal

_____ _____ Houston, Sam (Virginia, 1793-1863)— Cherokee Soldier and Statesman: Texas, Alamo

_____ _____ Jackson, Andrew (South Carolina, 1767-1845)—7th President (1829-1837)

_____ _____ Jones, Casey (John Luther) (Kentucky, 1864-1900)—Railroad Engineer

_____ _____ Lewis, Meriwether (Virginia, 1774-1809)—Explorer: Lewis and Clark Expedition

_____ _____ Monroe, James (Virginia, 1758-1831)—5th President (1813-1825): Monroe Doctrine

_____ _____ Oakley, Annie (Ohio, 1860-1926)—Rodeo Star and Sharpshooter

_____ _____ Sacajawea (1787?-1812?)—Native American Woman: Lewis and Clark Expedition

_____ _____ Santa Anna, Antonio Lopez de (Mexico, 1797-1876)—Mexican Dictator: Alamo

_____ _____ Sitting Bull (South Dakota,1831-1890)—Defeats Custer at Little Big Horn, Last Sioux to surrender to U.S.

_____ _____ Starr, Belle (Missouri, 1848-1889)—Outlaw

_____ _____ Tecumseh (Ohio, 1768-1813)—Shawnee Chief: Battle of Tippicanoe (1811)

_____ _____ Travis, William (South Carolina, 1809-1836)—Lawyer and Soldier: Texas

_____ _____ Tyler, John (Virginia, 1790-1862)—10th President (1841-1845)

_____ _____ Van Buren, Martin (New York, 1782-1862))—8th President (1837-1841)

_____ _____ _____

_____ _____ _____

_____ _____ _____

_____ _____ _____

_____ _____ _____

_____ _____ _____

_____ _____ _____

_____ _____ _____

_____ _____ _____

_____ _____ _____

PLACES

_____ _____ Alamo

_____ _____ California Trail

_____ _____ Chisholm Trail

_____ _____ Cumberland Road

_____ _____ Erie Canal, 1819

_____ _____ Old Spanish Trail

_____ _____ Oregon Trail

_____ _____ Santa Fe Trail

_____ _____ Wilderness Road

_____ _____ _____

_____ _____ _____

_____ _____ _____

_____ _____ _____

TERMS

_____ _____	Boomers	_____ _____ Pony Express (1860-1861)
_____ _____	Branding Irons	_____ _____ Prairie Schooners
_____ _____	Buffalo Soldiers	_____ _____ Sheriff
_____ _____	Cactus	_____ _____ Sooners
_____ _____	Canals	_____ _____ Stagecoach
_____ _____	Cattle Ranches	_____ _____ Steel Plow
_____ _____	Cattle Trails	_____ _____ Transcontinental Railroad,
_____ _____	Conestoga Wagon	1869
_____ _____	Cowboys	_____ _____ Wagon Trains
_____ _____	Curtis Act	_____ _____ Wheat
_____ _____	Erie Canal	_____ _____ Windmills
_____ _____	Gold Mines	_____ _____ Wranglers
_____ _____	Great Plains	_____ _____ _____
_____ _____	Johnny Appleseed	_____ _____ _____
_____ _____	Land Runs	_____ _____ _____
_____ _____	Locks	_____ _____ _____
_____ _____	Native American Indians	_____ _____ _____
	(see also page 91)	_____ _____ _____
_____ _____	Organic Act	_____ _____ _____
_____ _____	Paul Bunyan	_____ _____ _____
_____ _____	Pecos Bill	_____ _____ _____

DISCOVERIES/ACCOMPLISHMENTS

_____ _____ First Steam Locomotive-Tom Thumb (1804)

_____ _____ Typewriter (1829)

_____ _____ Revolver Invented (1835), see Scientist/Inventors: Samuel Colt

_____ _____ First Computer Made by Charles Babbage (1835), see Math: Computers In Math

_____ _____ Sewing Machine Invented (1846), see Scientist/Inventors: Elias Howe

_____ _____ _____

_____ _____ _____

_____ _____ _____

_____ _____ _____

CULTURE STUDY: THE WESTERN FRONTIER/PIONEERS

_____ _____	Family Life	_____ _____ Music
_____ _____	Homes	_____ _____ Oral and Written Language
_____ _____	Food and Agriculture	_____ _____ Government, Military and
_____ _____	Clothing	Weapons of Warfare
_____ _____	Occupations	_____ _____ Economy, Technology,
_____ _____	Religion	Manufacturing, and Trade
_____ _____	Health & Medicine	_____ _____ _____
_____ _____	Recreation & Entertainment	_____ _____ _____
_____ _____	Education	
_____ _____	Arts & Crafts	

MEXICAN WAR

MAJOR EVENTS

_____ _____ 1845, Annexation of Texas by U.S

_____ _____ 1846-1848, Mexican War—Conflict Between U.S. and Mexico

_____ _____ _____

_____ _____ _____

_____ _____ _____

PEOPLE

_____ _____ Fremont, John C.(Georgia, 1813-1890)—Politician, Mapmaker, Governor of
Arizona, and Explorer: Between Mississippi and West Coast

_____ _____ Gadsden, James (South Carolina, 1788-1858)—Soldier and Ambassador to Mexico

_____ _____ Polk, James (North Carolina, 1795-1849)—10th President (1845-1849)

_____ _____ Scott, Winfield (Virginia, 1786-1866)—U.S. General: Defeated Santa Anna

_____ _____ Taylor, Zachary (Virginia, 1784-1850)—General

_____ _____ _____

_____ _____ _____

_____ _____ _____

PLACES

_____ _____ Arizona

_____ _____ California

_____ _____ Mexico City

_____ _____ New Mexico

_____ _____ Rio Grande

_____ _____ _____

_____ _____ _____

_____ _____ _____

TERMS

_____ _____ Gadsden Purchase (1854)

_____ _____ Manifest Destiny

_____ _____ _____

_____ _____ _____

_____ _____ _____

_____ _____ _____

CULTURE STUDY: MEXICO

_____ _____ Family Life

_____ _____ Homes

_____ _____ Food and Agriculture

_____ _____ Clothing

_____ _____ Occupations

_____ _____ Religion

_____ _____ Health & Medicine

_____ _____ Recreation & Entertainment

_____ _____ Education

_____ _____ Arts & Crafts

_____ _____ Music

_____ _____ Oral and Written Language

_____ _____ Government, Military and
Weapons of Warfare

_____ _____ Economy, Technology,
Manufacturing, and Trade

_____ _____ _____

_____ _____ _____

GOLD RUSH (1848-1862+)

Elem   Jr/Sr High

Major Events

_____ _____ 1848, California Gold Rush Begins
_____ _____ 1896, Alaskan Gold Rush Begins

People

_____ _____ Buchanan, James (Pennsylvania, 1791-1868)—15th President (1857-1861)
_____ _____ Fillmore, Millard (New York, 1800-1874)—13th President (1850-1853)
_____ _____ Marshall, James (New Jersey, 1810-1885)—Carpenter and Gold Miner: Discovered Gold at Sutter's Mill
_____ _____ Pierce, Franklin (New Hampshire, 1804-1869)—14th President (1853-1857)
_____ _____ Taylor, Zachary (Virginia, 1784-1850)—12th President (1849-1850), General During the Mexican War

Places

_____ _____ Klondike
_____ _____ Sutter's Mill
_____ _____ Yukon

Terms

_____ _____ Forty-Niners
_____ _____ Gold Rush

THE CHECKLIST, Copyright © 2005 by Cindy Downes

NATIVE AMERICAN INDIANS

Elem   Jr/Sr High

_____ _____ How the Native Americans Came to America
_____ _____ Results of the Lewis and Clark Expedition and Frontier Expansion
_____ _____ Five Civilized Tribes
_____ _____ Other Native American Tribes
_____ _____ Forced Removal & the Trail of Tears
_____ _____ Indian Territory
_____ _____ Results of Civil War on Native Americans
_____ _____ Results of Land Runs on Native Americans (First Land Run -April 22, 1889)
_____ _____ Native Americans Today

_____ _____ _____
_____ _____ _____
_____ _____ _____
_____ _____ _____
_____ _____ _____
_____ _____ _____

PEOPLE (others included in History, Science, Music, Art)

(Biographies of Native Americans: http://www.ability.org/kids_and_teens_native_americans.htm)

_____ _____ Five Civilized Tribes (Creek, Cherokee, Choctaw, Chickasaw, Seminole)
_____ _____ Boudinet, Elias—Leader of Cherokees Who Agreed to Move West
_____ _____ Pushmataha—Leader of Choctaws
_____ _____ Ridge, John—Leader of Cherokees Who Wanted to Move West
_____ _____ Ross, John (Tennessee, 1790-1866)—Cherokee Indian Chief
_____ _____ Sequoyah (Tennessee,1770s-)—Creator of the Cherokee Alphabet
_____ _____ Watie, Stand (Georgia, 1806-1871)—Principal Chief of Confederate Cherokees
_____ _____ Mankiller, Wilma (Oklahoma,1945-)—Principal Chief of the Cherokee Nation

_____ _____ _____
_____ _____ _____
_____ _____ _____
_____ _____ _____
_____ _____ _____
_____ _____ _____
_____ _____ _____
_____ _____ _____
_____ _____ _____
_____ _____ _____
_____ _____ _____
_____ _____ _____
_____ _____ _____

PLACES

_____ _____ Surplus Lands
_____ _____ Unassigned Lands
_____ _____ _____
_____ _____ _____

_____ _____ _____
_____ _____ _____
_____ _____ _____
_____ _____ _____

TERMS

_____ _____ American Bison (Buffalo)
_____ _____ Arrowheads
_____ _____ Moccasins
_____ _____ Pottery

_____ _____ Reservations
_____ _____ _____
_____ _____ _____
_____ _____ _____

DISCOVERIES/ACCOMPLISHMENTS

_____ _____ Cherokee Alphabet
_____ _____ _____
_____ _____ _____
_____ _____ _____

_____ _____ _____
_____ _____ _____
_____ _____ _____
_____ _____ _____

CULTURE OF NATIVE AMERICAN INDIANS (TRIBE: _____)

_____ _____ Family Life
_____ _____ Homes
_____ _____ Food and Agriculture
_____ _____ Clothing
_____ _____ Occupations
_____ _____ Religion
_____ _____ Health & Medicine
_____ _____ Recreation & Entertainment
_____ _____ Education
_____ _____ Arts & Crafts

_____ _____ Music
_____ _____ Oral and Written Language
_____ _____ Government, Military and
             Weapons of Warfare
_____ _____ Economy, Technology,
             Manufacturing, and Trade
_____ _____ _____
_____ _____ _____

THE CIVIL WAR (1861-65) AND RECONSTRUCTION

Elem   Jr/Sr High

MAJOR EVENTS

_____ _____ 1820, Missouri Compromise

_____ _____ 1831, Liberator Published

_____ _____ 1846, Mexican-American War Begins, See Mexican-American War

_____ _____ 1849, Harriet Tubman Escapes

_____ _____ 1850, Compromise of 1850

_____ _____ 1850, Fugitive Slave Act

_____ _____ 1852, Uncle Tom's Cabin is written by Harriet Beecher Stowe, See Literature: American Authors

_____ _____ 1854, Kansas-Nebraska Act

_____ _____ 1857, Dred Scott Decision

_____ _____ 1858, Lincoln-Douglas Debates

_____ _____ 1859, John Brown's Raid on Harper's Ferry

_____ _____ 1860, Lincoln Elected President and Succession of First Southern States

_____ _____ 1861, Confederated States Formed and Jefferson Davis is Named as President

_____ _____ 1861, Battle of Bull Run

_____ _____ 1861, South Fires on Fort Sumter

_____ _____ 1861, First Battle of Bull Run

_____ _____ 1862, Battle of Shiloh

_____ _____ 1862, Second Battle of Bull Run

_____ _____ 1862, Battle of Antietam

_____ _____ 1862, Battle of Fredericksburg

_____ _____ 1863, Emancipation Proclamation

_____ _____ 1863, Battle of Chancellorsville

_____ _____ 1863, Battle of Gettysburg

_____ _____ 1863, Fall of Vicksburg

_____ _____ 1863, Gettysburg Address

_____ _____ 1864, Sherman Sets Fire to Atlanta

_____ _____ 1865, Surrender of General Lee at Appomattox Courthouse

_____ _____ 1865, Assassination of Lincoln

_____ _____ 1865, Andrew Johnson Succeeds Lincoln as President

_____ _____ 1865, 13th Amendment Abolishes Slavery

_____ _____ 1865-1877, Reconstruction

_____ _____ 1866, Civil Rights Act

_____ _____ 1868, 14th Amendment Made all Former Slaves U.S. Citizens

_____ _____ 1868, President Johnson Impeached

_____ _____ 1869, Ulysses S. Grant becomes President

_____ _____ 1870, 15th Amendment Gives African-American Men the Vote

_____ _____ 1870, All Confederate States Readmitted to the Union

_____ _____ 1877, Rutherford B. Hayes becomes President

_____ _____ _____

_____ _____ _____

_____ _____ _____
_____ _____ _____
_____ _____ _____
_____ _____ _____
_____ _____ _____

PEOPLE

_____ _____ Astor, John Jacob(Germany, 1763-1848)—Fur Trader and Financier

_____ _____ Barton, Clara (Massachusetts, 1821-1912)—Nurse of Civil War: Founder of American Red Cross

_____ _____ Booth, John Wilkes (Maryland, 1839-1865)—Assassin of President Lincoln

_____ _____ Brown, John (Connecticut, 1800-1859)—White Abolitionist: Harper's Ferry

_____ _____ Calhoun, John C. (South Carolina, 1782-1850)—Statesman

_____ _____ Clay, Henry (Virginia, 1777-1852)—Senator: Compromise of 1850

_____ _____ Davis, Jefferson (Kentucky, 1808-1889)—President of Confederate States

_____ _____ Douglas, Stephen A. (Vermont, 1813-1861)—Political Leader: Compromise of 1850

_____ _____ Douglass, Frederick (Maryland, 1817-1895)—Escaped Slave, Abolitionist

_____ _____ Garrison, William L. (Massachusetts, 1805-1879)—Abolitionist and Publisher

_____ _____ Grant, Ulysses S. (Ohio, 18922-1885)—General, 18th President (1869-1877)

_____ _____ Hayes, Rutherford B. (Ohio, 1822-1893)—19th President (1877-1881)

_____ _____ Jackson, Stonewall (West Virginia, 1824-1863)—Confederate General

_____ _____ Johnson, Andrew (New Carolina, 1808-1875)—17th President (1865-1869)

_____ _____ Lee, Robert E. (Virginia, 1807-1870)—Confederate General

_____ _____ Lincoln, Abraham (Kentucky, 1809-1865)—16th President (1861-1865)

_____ _____ Mann, Horace (Massachusetts, 1796-1859)—Lawyer and Statesman: Called "Father of American Public Education"

_____ _____ McClellan, George B. (Pennsylvania, 1826-1885)—Union General

_____ _____ Scott, Dred (Virginia, ?1795-1858)—Slave: Dred Scott Decision

_____ _____ Seward, William H. (New York, 1801-1872)—Statesman

_____ _____ Sherman, William T. (Ohio, 1820-1891)—Union General

_____ _____ Smith, Joseph (Vermont, 1805-1844)—Mormon Leader

_____ _____ Stowe, Harriet Beecher (Connecticut, 1811-1896)—Abolitionist: Wrote Uncle Tom's Cabin, 1852

_____ _____ Truth, Sojourner (New York, 1777-1883)—Freed Slave: Spoke Against Slavery

_____ _____ Tubman, Harriet (Maryland, 1821-1913)—Escaped Slave: Underground Railroad

_____ _____ Turner, Nat (Virginia, c.1800-1831)—Slave Leader, Led an Unsuccessful Revolt

_____ _____ Webster, Daniel (New Hampshire, 1782-1852)—Orator, Lawyer, and Statesman: Compromise of 1850

_____ _____ _____
_____ _____ _____
_____ _____ _____
_____ _____ _____
_____ _____ _____
_____ _____ _____
_____ _____ _____
_____ _____ _____

PLACES

_____ _____ Erie Canal (1819)
_____ _____ Harper's Ferry (1859)
_____ _____ Mason-Dixon Line
_____ _____ Valley Forge

TERMS

_____ _____ Abolition
_____ _____ Border States
_____ _____ Carpetbaggers
_____ _____ Compromise
_____ _____ Confederacy
_____ _____ Cotton Gin
_____ _____ Debate
_____ _____ Emancipation
_____ _____ Free States
_____ _____ Fugitive Slave Law
_____ _____ Gag Rule
_____ _____ Impeachment
_____ _____ Jim Crow Laws
_____ _____ Ku Klux Klan
_____ _____ Minstrels
_____ _____ Plantations
_____ _____ Republican Party
_____ _____ Scalawags
_____ _____ Secede
_____ _____ Slave States
_____ _____ Slavery
_____ _____ Succession
_____ _____ Thirteenth Amendment

_____ _____ Underground Railroad
_____ _____ Union

AFRICAN AMERICAN HISTORY

Elem   Jr/Sr High

_____ _____ Life in Africa (homes, clothing, religion, work, economy, education, customs, folklore, government)
_____ _____ How African Americans came to America
_____ _____ Life in America (slavery, homes, clothing, food, religion, work, education, customs, folklore)
_____ _____ Results of Civil War on African Americans
_____ _____ Segregation in America
_____ _____ Results of Civil Rights Movement
_____ _____ _____
_____ _____ _____
_____ _____ _____

PEOPLE (Others included in History, Science, Music, Art)

_____ _____ Attucks, Crispus (c.1723 -1770)—Leader of an American Patriot Revolt Against British Troops.
_____ _____ Bethune, Mary McLeod (South Carolina, 1875-1955)—College President and Adviser to Franklin D. Roosevelt
_____ _____ Cole, Nat King (Alabama,1917-1965)—American Singer and Pianist
_____ _____ Marshall, Thurgood (Maryland, 1908-1993)—Supreme Court Justice, 1967
_____ _____ Parks, Rosa (Alabama, 1913-)—Civil Rights Pioneer
_____ _____ Powell, Colin (New York, 1937-)—Secretary of State
_____ _____ Rice, Dr. Condoleezza (Alabama, 1954-)—Secretary of State, 2004. First African American Woman to Have This Post.
_____ _____ Robinson, Jackie (Georgia, 1919-1972)—Baseball Player: Began the Acceptance of Black Athletics
_____ _____ Wheatley, Phillis (West Africa, c.1754 - 1784)—Poet
_____ _____ _____
_____ _____ _____
_____ _____ _____
_____ _____ _____

PLACES

____ ___ _____   ____ ___ _____
____ ___ _____   ____ ___ _____

TERMS

_____ _____ Emancipation Proclamation   _____ _____ _____
_____ _____ NAACP   _____ _____ _____
_____ _____ Civil Rights   _____ _____ _____

SPANISH-AMERICAN WAR (1898)

Elem   Jr/Sr High

MAJOR EVENTS

_____ _____ 1898, Spanish-American War

_____ _____ 1898, Charge of San Juan Hill

_____ _____ 1898, U.S. Gains Control of Philippines, Puerto Rico, and Guam

_____ _____ _____

_____ _____ _____

_____ _____ _____

PEOPLE

_____ _____ Dewey, Commodore George—Destroyed Spanish Fleet in Philippines

_____ _____ Hurst, William Randolf—American Newspaper Publisher

_____ _____ Pulitzer, Joseph (Hungary, 1847-1911)—American Newspaper Publisher

_____ _____ Roosevelt, Theodore (New York, 1858-1919)—U.S. Navy Commander: San Juan
               Hill, Cuba (also see Industrial Revolution)

_____ _____ _____

_____ _____ _____

PLACES

_____ _____ Cuba

_____ _____ Guam

_____ _____ Philippines

_____ _____ Puerto Rico

_____ _____ _____

_____ _____ _____

TERMS

_____ _____ U. S. Battleship-Maine

_____ _____ Nobel Peace Prize

_____ _____ _____

_____ _____ _____

CULTURE STUDY: SPAIN

_____ _____ Family Life   _____ _____ Music

_____ _____ Homes   _____ _____ Oral and Written Language

_____ _____ Food and Agriculture   _____ _____ Government, Military and

_____ _____ Clothing   Weapons of Warfare

_____ _____ Occupations   _____ _____ Economy, Technology,

_____ _____ Religion   Manufacturing, and Trade

_____ _____ Health & Medicine

_____ _____ Recreation & Entertainment _____ _____ _____

_____ _____ Education   _____ _____ _____

_____ _____ Arts & Crafts

INDUSTRIAL REVOLUTION & IMMIGRATION —1850 -1928

Elem   Jr/Sr High

MAJOR EVENTS

_____ _____ Late 1800's, Socialism and Marxism
_____ _____ 1859, Darwin Publishes Origin of the Species
_____ _____ 1867, Alaska Bought from Russian
_____ _____ 1869, Transcontinental Railroad
_____ _____ 1870, John D. Rockefeller Founds Standard Oil Company
_____ _____ 1871, Great Fire of Chicago
_____ _____ 1876, Alexander Graham Bell Invents Telephone
_____ _____ 1879, Thomas Edison Invents Electric Light Bulb
_____ _____ 1881, Assassination of Garfield
_____ _____ 1881, American Red Cross Founded
_____ _____ 1886, American Federation of Labor Founded
_____ _____ 1890, Sherman Antitrust Act
_____ _____ 1898, Spanish-American War Begins, See Spanish-American War
_____ _____ Early 1900's, Labor Unions
_____ _____ 1901, Assassination of McKinley
_____ _____ 1901, Theodore Roosevelt Becomes President
_____ _____ 1902, Sherman-Antitrust Act
_____ _____ 1903, Establishment of Commerce and Labor Department
_____ _____ 1909, Henry Ford /Assembly Line Production of Motor Car
_____ _____ 1913, 16th Amendment Authorizes Income Tax
_____ _____ 1914-1918, World War I Begins. See World War I

_____ _____ _____
_____ _____ _____
_____ _____ _____
_____ _____ _____
_____ _____ _____
_____ _____ _____
_____ _____ _____

PEOPLE

_____ _____ Addams, Jane (Illinois, 1860-1935)—Feminist and Social Reformer: Hull House, Immigrants
_____ _____ Arthur, Chester A. (Vermont, 1830-1886)—21st President (1881-1885)
_____ _____ Barton, Clara (Massachusetts, 1821-1912)—Founded American Red Cross
_____ _____ Bell, Alexander Graham (Scotland/Massachusetts, 1847-1922)—American Inventor: Telephone
_____ _____ Bessemer, Henry (England, 1813-1898)—Engineer and Inventor: Steel
_____ _____ Bryan, William Jennings (Illinois, 1860-1925)—Political Leader and Lawyer: Scopes Trial, Evolution in Schools
_____ _____ Carnegie, Andrew (Scotland/Pennsylvania, 1835-1919)—Industrialist and Humanitarian: Steel

_____ _____ Chaplin, Charlie (England, 1889-1977)—Silent Movie Star

_____ _____ Cleveland, Grover (New Jersey, 1837-1908)—22nd & 24th President (1885-1889 and 1893-1897)

_____ _____ Darrow, Clarence (Ohio, 1857-1938)—Defense Lawyer: Scopes Trial, Evolution in Schools

_____ _____ Darwin, Charles (England, 1809-1882)—Evolutionist: Origin of Species-1859

_____ _____ Dewey, John (Vermont, 1859-1952)—Teacher and Education Reformer

_____ _____ Garfield, James (Ohio, 1831-1881)—20th President (March 1881- September 1881)

_____ _____ Harrison, Benjamin (Ohio, 1833-1901)—23rd President (1889-1893)

_____ _____ Hearst, William Randolph (California, 1863-1951)—Newspaper Publisher: "Yellow Journalism"

_____ _____ Holmes, Oliver Wendall, Jr. (Massachusetts, 1841-1935)—Jurist and Chief Justice: U.S. Supreme Court, Freedom of Speech

_____ _____ McKinley, William (Ohio, 1843-1901)—25th President (1897-1901)

_____ _____ Pillsbury, Charles (New Hampshire, 1842-1899)—Industrialist: Flour

_____ _____ Rockefeller, John D. (New York, 1839-1937)—Industrialist: Oil

_____ _____ Roosevelt, Theodore (New York, 1858-1919)—Volunteer Cavalry: Rough Riders, 26th President (1901-1909), Panama Canal-1903, Square Deal

_____ _____ Sanger, Margaret (New York, 1879-1966)—Feminist: Birth Control

_____ _____ Taft, William H.(Ohio, 1857-1930)—27th President (1909-1913)

_____ _____ Vanderbilt, Cornelius (New York, 1794-1877)—Industrialist: Railroads

_____ _____ Washington, Booker T. (Virginia, 1856-1915)—Alabama Slave and Educator: Tuskegee Institute, Up From Slavery (also see page 96)

_____ _____ _____
_____ _____ _____
_____ _____ _____
_____ _____ _____
_____ _____ _____
_____ _____ _____
_____ _____ _____
_____ _____ _____
_____ _____ _____
_____ _____ _____

PLACES

_____ _____ Ellis Island (1890)
_____ _____ Guam
_____ _____ Panama Canal
_____ _____ Yellowstone Park

_____ _____ _____
_____ _____ _____
_____ _____ _____
_____ _____ _____
_____ _____ _____
_____ _____ _____
_____ _____ _____

TERMS

_____ _____	Arbitration	_____ _____ Robber Barons
_____ _____	Airplanes	_____ _____ Steel
_____ _____	Citizen	_____ _____ Strike
_____ _____	Closed Shop	_____ _____ Strikebreaker
_____ _____	Collective Bargaining	_____ _____ Theory of Evolution
_____ _____	Grievance	_____ _____ Walkout
_____ _____	Immigrants	_____ _____ Yellow Journalism
_____ _____	Labor Unions	_____ _____ _____
_____ _____	Lockout	_____ _____ _____
_____ _____	Mediate	_____ _____ _____
_____ _____	Monopolies	_____ _____ _____
_____ _____	Negotiate	_____ _____ _____
_____ _____	Oil	_____ _____ _____
_____ _____	Peanuts	_____ _____ _____
_____ _____	Pickets	_____ _____ _____
_____ _____	Progressive Education	_____ _____ _____

DISCOVERIES/ACCOMPLISHMENTS

_____ _____ Steel Production Begins, Henry Bessemer (1855)

_____ _____ Color Photography (1861)

_____ _____ Telegraph (1866)

_____ _____ Pasteurization, See Scientist/Inventors: Louis Pasteur (1867)

_____ _____ Transcontinental Railroad (1869)

_____ _____ Stock Ticker (1870)

_____ _____ Electric Typewriter, See Scientist/Inventors: Thomas Edison (1872)

_____ _____ Telephone (1876)

_____ _____ Phonograph (1877)

_____ _____ Electric Light, See Scientist/Inventors: Thomas Edison (1879)

_____ _____ Statue of Liberty (1886)

_____ _____ Grammaphone Record (1888)

_____ _____ Photographic Film, See Scientist/Inventors: George Eastman (1889)

_____ _____ X-Ray, See Scientist/Inventors: Wilhem Röntgen (1895)

_____ _____ First Model T Ford Made, See Scientist/Inventors: Henry Ford (1908)

_____ _____ _____

_____ _____ _____

_____ _____ _____

_____ _____ _____

_____ _____ _____

_____ _____ _____

_____ _____ _____

_____ _____ _____

WORLD WAR I —1914-1918

Elem   Jr/Sr High

MAJOR EVENTS

_____ _____ 1914, Archduke Franz Ferdinand of Austria-Hungary Assassinated
_____ _____ 1914, Panama Canal Opened
_____ _____ 1914, World War I Begins in Europe
_____ _____ 1914, Charlie Chaplin Films Are Produced
_____ _____ 1915, Germans Sink the Lusitania
_____ _____ 1917, United States Enters War I
_____ _____ 1917, Balfour Declaration
_____ _____ 1918, Armistice and World War I Ends
_____ _____ 1919, Treaty of Versailles
_____ _____ 1920, Palestine Established as Jewish State
_____ _____ 1920, Radio Broadcasting Begins
_____ _____ 1922, USSR is formed—See World History
_____ _____ 1926, Hirohito Become Emperor of Japan
_____ _____ 1927, Talking Pictures Begin

_____ _____ _____
_____ _____ _____
_____ _____ _____
_____ _____ _____
_____ _____ _____
_____ _____ _____
_____ _____ _____
_____ _____ _____

PEOPLE

_____ _____ Churchill, Winston (England, 1874-1965)—Soldier, Writer, War Strategist
_____ _____ Clemenceau, Georges Benjamin (France, 1841-1929)—Premier of France during World War I
_____ _____ Lawrence, T. E. (Wales, 1888-1935)—Soldier and Author: Lawrence of Arabia, Army Intelligence, Revolt in the Desert
_____ _____ Lloyd-George, David (England, 1863-1945)—Prime Minister of Britain: 1916-1922
_____ _____ Lodge, Henry Cabot (Massachusetts, 1850-1924)—Politician and Author: League of Nations
_____ _____ Nicolas II (Russia, 1868-1918)—Russian Czar: Joined Allies in WWI
_____ _____ Pershing, John J. (Missouri, 1860-1948)—Army Commander
_____ _____ Thorpe, Jim (Oklahoma, 1886-1953)—Athlete (also see page 91)
_____ _____ Wilhelm II, Kaiser (Germany, 1859-1941)—German Emperor (1888-1918)
_____ _____ Wilson, Woodrow (Virginia, 1856-1924)—28th President (1913-1921): Prohibition, Women's Suffrage, Clayton Antitrust Act, Child Labor Law, League of Nations

_____ _____ _____
_____ _____ _____
_____ _____ _____
_____ _____ _____
_____ _____ _____
_____ _____ _____
_____ _____ _____
_____ _____ _____
_____ _____ _____
_____ _____ _____
_____ _____ _____
_____ _____ _____

PLACES

_____ _____ _____   _____ _____ _____
_____ _____ _____   _____ _____ _____
_____ _____ _____   _____ _____ _____
_____ _____ _____   _____ _____ _____
_____ _____ _____   _____ _____ _____
_____ _____ _____   _____ _____ _____

TERMS

_____ _____ Allies   _____ _____ _____
_____ _____ Central Powers   _____ _____ _____
_____ _____ Propaganda   _____ _____ _____
_____ _____ Trench Warfare   _____ _____ _____
_____ _____ U-Boats   _____ _____ _____
_____ _____ Western Front   _____ _____ _____
_____ _____ _____   _____ _____ _____
_____ _____ _____   _____ _____ _____
_____ _____ _____   _____ _____ _____
_____ _____ _____   _____ _____ _____

1920'S

MAJOR EVENTS

_____	_____	1919, 18th Amendment Began Prohibition
_____	_____	1920, 19th Amendment Gave Women the Right to Vote
_____	_____	1920, League of Nations Established
_____	_____	1920, American Civil Liberties Union Formed
_____	_____	1925, The Scopes Monkey Trial
_____	_____	1927, Lindbergh's Solo Flight
_____	_____	1927, Talking Motion Pictures
_____	_____	1929, Rocket Engines

PEOPLE

Anthony, Susan B. (Massachusetts, 1820-1906)—Women's Rights and Suffrage

Coolidge, Calvin (Vermont, 1872-1933)—30th President (1923-1929)

Harding, Warren G. (Ohio, 1865-1923)—29th President (1921-1923): Opposed League of Nations

Hoover, J. Edgar (Washington, DC, 1895-1972)—Lawyer: FBI, Dept of Justice

Lenin, Vladimir (Russia, 1870-1924)—Marxist Communist Leader and Revolutionary: Bolshevik Revolution

Stalin, Joseph (Russia, 1879-1953)—Dictator

PLACES

TERMS

Equal Rights

Isolationism

Roaring Twenties

Suffrage

DISCOVERIES/ACCOMPLISHMENTS

_____	_____	_____	_____	_____	_____
_____	_____	_____	_____	_____	_____
_____	_____	_____	_____	_____	_____
_____	_____	_____	_____	_____	_____
_____	_____	_____	_____	_____	_____
_____	_____	_____	_____	_____	_____
_____	_____	_____	_____	_____	_____

LIFE IN AMERICAN DURING ROARING 20'S

_____ _____ Family Life

_____ _____ Homes

_____ _____ Food and Agriculture

_____ _____ Clothing

_____ _____ Occupations

_____ _____ Religion

_____ _____ Health & Medicine

_____ _____ Recreation & Entertainment

_____ _____ Education

_____ _____ Arts & Crafts

_____ _____ Music

_____ _____ Economy, Technology, Manufacturing, and Trade

_____ _____ _____

_____ _____ _____

THE GREAT DEPRESSION

Elem   Jr/Sr High

MAJOR EVENTS

_____ _____ 1929, Stock Market Crashes (October 29, 1929)
_____ _____ 1929, The Great Depression Begins
_____ _____ 1932, Franklin Roosevelt Elected President
_____ _____ 1933, Adolf Hitler Becomes German Chancellor
_____ _____ 1933, 20th Amendment Changed the Term of the President and Vice President
_____ _____ 1933, 21st Amendment Repealed Prohibition
_____ _____ 1935, Social Security Act
_____ _____ 1939, The New Deal
_____ _____ 1947, Taft-Hartley Act
_____ _____ 1946, Welfare Legislation
_____ _____ Devaluation of the Dollar
_____ _____ _____
_____ _____ _____
_____ _____ _____
_____ _____ _____
_____ _____ _____

PEOPLE

_____ _____ Earhart, Amelia (1898-1937)—Aviator
_____ _____ Taft, Robert A (Ohio, 1889-1953)—Senator: Taft-Hartley Act (1947)
_____ _____ Roosevelt, Franklin D. (New York, 1882-1945)—32nd President (1933-1945):
                       New Deal (1939)
_____ _____ Roosevelt, Eleanor (New York, 1884-1962)—Author, Diplomat, and Humanitarian:
                       Delegate to the United Nations
_____ _____ _____
_____ _____ _____
_____ _____ _____
_____ _____ _____
_____ _____ _____
_____ _____ _____

PLACES

_____ _____ Empire State Building
_____ _____ New York Stock Exchange
_____ _____ _____
_____ _____ _____
_____ _____ _____
_____ _____ _____
_____ _____ _____
_____ _____ _____

TERMS

_____ _____	Banking	
_____ _____	Federal Reserve	
_____ _____	Inflation	
_____ _____	Investments	
_____ _____	Loans	
_____ _____	Surplus	
_____ _____	Stocks	

DISCOVERIES/ACCOMPLISHMENTS

_____ _____ Nylon (1937)

LIFE IN AMERICA DURING THE GREAT DEPRESSION

_____ _____ Homes, Food, Clothing, Family Life

_____ _____ Economy, Technology, Manufacturing, and Trade

_____ _____ Religion

_____ _____ Health & Medicine

_____ _____ Recreation, Arts, Crafts, Music, Entertainment

_____ _____ Education

WORLD WAR II (1939-45)

Elem   Jr/Sr High

MAJOR EVENTS

_____ _____ 1933, Hitler Forms Third Reich (1933)

_____ _____ Persecution of the Jews

_____ _____ Concentration Camps

_____ _____ 1939, Great Purge in Soviet Union and World War II Begins (1939)

_____ _____ 1940, Battle of Britain

_____ _____ 1941, Japanese Attack Pearl Harbor, U.S. Enters War II

_____ _____ 1942, Pledge of Allegiance Becomes Official U.S. Pledge

_____ _____ 1942, Americans Defeat Japan at Midway

_____ _____ 1943, Surrender of Germans at Stalingrad

_____ _____ 1944, D-Day Landing at Normandy (June 6, 1944)

_____ _____ 1945, Battle of the Bulge (Dec.1944-Jan. 1945)

_____ _____ 1945, U.S. Drops Atomic Bomb on Nagasaki and Hiroshima

_____ _____ 1945, End of World War II and United Nations Established

PEOPLE

_____ _____ Chamberlain, Neville (England, 1869-1940)—Prime Minister of Britain: Partition of Czechoslovakia

_____ _____ Churchill, Sir Winston (England, 1874-1965)—Prime Minister of Britain and Author

_____ _____ de Gaulle, Charles (France, 1890-1970)—French General and Statesman

_____ _____ Eisenhower, Dwight D.(Texas, 1890-1969)—34th President (1953-1961), General: Allied Invasion of France, D-Day; Korean War, School Integration, Cuba

_____ _____ Hitler, Adolf (Germany, 1889-1945)—German Nazi and Fuhrer of the 3rd Reich: Jewish Extermination

_____ _____ Lindbergh, Charles A. (Michigan, 1902-1974)—Aviator: First Nonstop
           TransAtlantic Flight

_____ _____ MacArthur, Douglas (Arkansas, 1880-1964)—General

_____ _____ Nimitz, Chester W. (Texas, 1885-1966)—Naval Officer

_____ _____ Oppenheimer, Robert (New York, 1904-1967)—U.S. Physicist: Manhattan Project,
           Atomic Bomb

_____ _____ Patton, George S. (California, 1885-1945)—Army Officer: Mexico, Europe,
           Mobile Tank Warfare

_____ _____ Stalin, Joseph (Russia, 1879-1953)—Revolutionary and Dictator

_____ _____ Tojo, Hideki (Japan, 1884-1948)—Dictator: New World Order

_____ _____ Truman, Harry S. (Missouri, 1884-1972)—Vice President, 33rd President (1945-
           1949): Marshall Plan, Atomic Bombing of Hiroshima and Nagasaki, Truman
           Doctrine, NATO, CIA, Berlin Airlift, Korean War

_____ _____ Tse-tung, Mao (China, 1893-1976)—President of People's Republic of China

_____ _____ _____

_____ _____ _____

_____ _____ _____

_____ _____ _____

_____ _____ _____

_____ _____ _____

_____ _____ _____

_____ _____ _____

_____ _____ _____

_____ _____ _____

_____ _____ _____

_____ _____ _____

_____ _____ _____

PLACES

_____ _____ East Berlin   _____ _____ _____

_____ _____ Guadalcanal   _____ _____ _____

_____ _____ Hiroshima   _____ _____ _____

_____ _____ Iwo Jima   _____ _____ _____

_____ _____ Nagasaki   _____ _____ _____

_____ _____ Nuremberg   _____ _____ _____

_____ _____ Okinawa   _____ _____ _____

_____ _____ West Berlin   _____ _____ _____

_____ _____ _____   _____ _____ _____

_____ _____ _____   _____ _____ _____

_____ _____ _____   _____ _____ _____

_____ _____ _____

TERMS

_____ _____	Axis Powers	
_____ _____	Berlin Wall	
_____ _____	Bismarck	
_____ _____	"Blitz"	
_____ _____	Concentration Camps	
_____ _____	Dictator	
_____ _____	Holocaust	
_____ _____	Infantry	
_____ _____	Kamikaze	
_____ _____	Nazi Party	
_____ _____	Nuclear Bomb	
_____ _____	Persecution	
_____ _____	_____	
_____ _____	_____	

CULTURE STUDY: GERMANY

_____ _____ Family Life

_____ _____ Homes

_____ _____ Food and Agriculture

_____ _____ Clothing

_____ _____ Occupations

_____ _____ Religion

_____ _____ Health & Medicine

_____ _____ Recreation & Entertainment

_____ _____ Education

_____ _____ Arts & Crafts

_____ _____ Music

_____ _____ Oral and Written Language

_____ _____ Government, Military and Weapons of Warfare

_____ _____ Economy, Technology, Manufacturing, and Trade

_____ _____ _____

_____ _____ _____

COLD WAR (1945-1989) AND MODERN AMERICA

Elem   Jr/Sr High

MAJOR EVENTS

_____ _____ 1945, United Nations Established

_____ _____ 1946, Iron Curtain

_____ _____ 1947, Truman Doctrine

_____ _____ 1948, Organization of American States (OAS) Formed

_____ _____ 1949, North Atlantic Treaty Organization (NATO) Formed

_____ _____ 1950-1953, Korean War

_____ _____ 1951, 22nd Amendment Limited the President to Serving Only Two Terms

_____ _____ 1954, Desegregation of Schools Begins

_____ _____ 1955, Bus Boycott in Montgomery Led by Dr. Martin Luther King, Jr.

_____ _____ 1957, Civil Rights Violence at Little Rock, Arkansas

_____ _____ 1957-1975, Vietnam War

_____ _____ 1961, Bay of Pigs Invasion

_____ _____ 1961, First American in Space, Alan B. Shepard, New Hampshire, 1923-1998

_____ _____ 1961, U.S. Enters Vietnam War

_____ _____ 1961, 23rd Amendment Gave Residents of District of Columbia the Right to Vote For President and Vice President

_____ _____ 1962, Cuban Missile Crisis—Soviet Installation of Missile Bases

_____ _____ 1963, President Kennedy Assassinated

_____ _____ 1964, 24th Amendment Prohibited Tax Payment as a Requirement to Vote in the Federal Elections

_____ _____ 1964, Civil Rights Bill

_____ _____ 1965, Medicare Established

_____ _____ 1966, First Space Docking

_____ _____ 1966, National Organization for Women (NOW) Founded

_____ _____ 1967, 25th Amendment Provides for the Filling of Vacancies in the Office of President and Vice President

_____ _____ 1968, Dr. Martin Luther King, Jr. Assassinated

_____ _____ 1969, Neil Armstrong's Moon Landing—1st Man on the Moon

_____ _____ 1970, Environmental Protection Agency (EPA) Founded

_____ _____ 1971, 26th Amendment Lowers the Voting Age to 18

_____ _____ 1972, Watergate, Nixon

_____ _____ 1973, Roe vs. Wade Legalizes Abortion

_____ _____ 1974, First "Test-Tube Babies"

_____ _____ 1974, Strategic Arms Limitation Treaty (SALT) Signed

_____ _____ 1975, First Docking Between U.S. and Russian Spacecraft

_____ _____ 1977, Department of Energy Created

_____ _____ 1978, Camp David Treaty Between Egypt and Israel

_____ _____ 1979, Iran Takes U.S. Hostages, U.S. and China Establish Diplomatic Relations

_____ _____ 1981, First space Shuttle Launched in U.S.

_____ _____ 1981, AIDS Epidemic is Officially Recognized

_____ _____ 1983, U.S. Proposes "Star Wars" Missile Program

_____	._____	1986, U.S. Bombs Libya
_____	_____	1986, Challenger Spacecraft Explodes
_____	_____	1986, Iran-Contra Affair
_____	_____	1989, Invasion of Panama by U.S.
_____	_____	1990, Launch of Hubble Spacecraft
_____	_____	1990-91, Persian Gulf War
_____	_____	1992, 27th Amendment Affected Pay Raises for Members of Congress
_____	_____	1993, North American Free Trade Agreement (NAFTA) Ends Trade Barriers Between U.S., Canada, and Mexico
_____	_____	2001, 911 - Terrorist Attack World Trade Center
_____	_____	2001, U.S. War in Afghanistan
_____	_____	2002, Department of Homeland Security Formed
_____	_____	2003, Operation Iraqi Freedom
_____	_____	2004, Tsunami Kills over 100,000 People in Indonesia

_____ _____ _____

_____ _____ _____

_____ _____ _____

_____ _____ _____

_____ _____ _____

PEOPLE

_____	_____	Begin, Menachem (Russia, 1913-1992)—Israeli Prime Minister: Camp David, Peace Treaty with Sadat 1979, Zionist,
_____	_____	Bush, George (Massachusetts, 1924-)—41st President (1989-1993): Operation Desert Storm in Persian Gulf War
_____	_____	Bush, George W. (Connecticut, 1946 -)—43rd President (2001-Present); Created Department of Homeland Security, War in Afghanistan and Iraq
_____	_____	Carter, James (Georgia, 1924-)—39th President (1977-1981): Panama Treaty
_____	_____	Clinton, William (Arkansas, 1946-)—42nd President (1992-2000)
_____	_____	Ford, Gerald R. (Nebraska, 1913-)—38th President (1973-1977)
_____	_____	Gorbachev, Mikhail (Russia, 1931-)—Leader Soviet Union
_____	_____	Hussein, Saddam (Iraq, 1937-)—Iraqi Leader
_____	_____	Johnson, Lyndon B. (Texas, 1908-1973)—36th President (1963-1969): Voting Rights Act, Vietnam War
_____	_____	Kennedy, John F. (Massachusetts, 1917-1963)—35th President (1961-1963): Federal Desegregation of Schools, Civil Rights Reform, Nuclear Test Ban Treaty
_____	_____	King, Martin Luther, Jr. (Georgia, 1929-1968)—Clergyman, Civil Rights Leader
_____	_____	Kissinger, Henry A. (Germany, 1923-)—U.S. Secretary of State: Emigrated to U.S. Because of Jewish Persecution, Vietnam War Negotiations
_____	_____	Nixon, Richard M. (California, 1913-)—37th President (1969-1974): End of Vietnam War, Wage and Price Controls, China Relations, Watergate
_____	_____	O'Connor, Sandra Day (Texas, 1930-)—1st Female Supreme Court Justice (1981)
_____	_____	Reagan, Ronald W. (Illinois, 1911-2004)—40th President (1981-1989), Actor: Reduction of Government Spending and Inflation, Anti-Communist, Strategic Defense Initiative, Iran-Contra Scandal
_____	_____	Sadat, Anwar (Egypt, 1918-1981)—Egyptian President: Camp David Accords

_____ _____ Schwarzkopf, H. Norman (New Jersey, 1934-)—U.S. General: Operation Desert Storm

_____ _____ Wallace, George C. (Alabama, 1919-)—Governor of Alabama: Segregation

_____ _____ _____

_____ _____ _____

_____ _____ _____

_____ _____ _____

_____ _____ _____

_____ _____ _____

PLACES

_____ _____ Afghanistan

_____ _____ Baghdad

_____ _____ Iraq (also see page 53)

_____ _____ Persian Gulf

_____ _____ Selma, Alabama

_____ _____ _____

_____ _____ _____

_____ _____ _____

TERMS

_____ _____ Astronauts

_____ _____ Computers

_____ _____ Detente

_____ _____ Glasnost

_____ _____ Perestroika

_____ _____ Sputnik

_____ _____ Television

_____ _____ Terrorists

_____ _____ _____

_____ _____ _____

_____ _____ _____

_____ _____ _____

LIFE IN AMERICA DURING THE 1940'S

_____ _____ Homes, Food, Clothing, Family Life

_____ _____ Economy, Technology, Manufacturing, and Trade

_____ _____ Religion

_____ _____ Health & Medicine

_____ _____ Recreation, Arts, Crafts, Music, Entertainment

_____ _____ Education

LIFE IN AMERICA DURING THE 1950'S

_____ _____ Homes, Food, Clothing, Family Life

_____ _____ Economy, Technology, Manufacturing, and Trade

_____ _____ Religion

_____ _____ Health & Medicine

_____ _____ Recreation, Arts, Crafts, Music, Entertainment

_____ _____ Education

LIFE IN AMERICA DURING THE 1960's

_____ _____	Homes, Food, Clothing, Family Life	_____ _____ Health & Medicine
_____ _____	Economy, Technology, Manufacturing, and Trade	_____ _____ Recreation, Arts, Crafts, Music, Entertainment
_____ _____	Religion	_____ _____ Education

LIFE IN AMERICA DURING THE 1970's

_____ _____	Homes, Food, Clothing, Family Life	_____ _____ Health & Medicine
_____ _____	Economy, Technology, Manufacturing, and Trade	_____ _____ Recreation, Arts, Crafts, Music, Entertainment
_____ _____	Religion	_____ _____ Education

LIFE IN AMERICA DURING THE 1980's

_____ _____	Homes, Food, Clothing, Family Life	_____ _____ Health & Medicine
_____ _____	Economy, Technology, Manufacturing, and Trade	_____ _____ Recreation, Arts, Crafts, Music, Entertainment
_____ _____	Religion	_____ _____ Education

LANDMARKS & SYMBOLS OF THE UNITED STATES

Elem   Jr/Sr High

_____ _____	Alamo	_____ _____ Mt. Rushmore
_____ _____	Bald Eagle	_____ _____ Pentagon
_____ _____	Bill of Rights	_____ _____ Statue of Liberty
_____ _____	California Redwoods	_____ _____ Uncle Sam
_____ _____	Capitol	_____ _____ Vietnam War Veteran
_____ _____	Constitution	Memorial
_____ _____	Declaration of Independence	_____ _____ Washington Monument
		_____ _____ White House
_____ _____	Golden Gate Bridge	_____ _____ Yellowstone National Park
_____ _____	Grand Canyon	_____ _____ _____
_____ _____	Empire State Building	_____ _____ _____
_____ _____	Flag	_____ _____ _____
_____ _____	Jefferson Memorial	_____ _____ _____
_____ _____	Liberty Bell	_____ _____ _____
_____ _____	Lincoln Memorial	

U.S. STATES AND CAPITALS

* Indicates First 13 States

Elem	Jr/Sr High	STATE	ABBREVIATION	CAPITAL	STATE ENTERED UNION
_____	_____	Alabama	AL	Montgomery	1819
_____	_____	Alaska	AK	Juneau	1959
_____	_____	Arizona	AZ	Phoenix	1912
_____	_____	Arkansas	AR	Little Rock	1836
_____	_____	California	CA	Sacramento	1850
_____	_____	Colorado	CO	Denver	1876
_____	_____	Connecticut*	CT	Hartford	1788
_____	_____	Delaware*	DE	Dover	1787
_____	_____	Florida	FL	Tallahassee	1845
_____	_____	Georgia*	GA	Atlanta	1788
_____	_____	Hawaii	HI	Honolulu	1959
_____	_____	Idaho	ID	Boise	1890
_____	_____	Illinois	IL	Springfield	1818
_____	_____	Indiana	IN	Indianapolis	1816
_____	_____	Iowa	IA	Des Moines	1846
_____	_____	Kansas	KS	Topeka	1861
_____	_____	Kentucky	KY	Frankfort	1792
_____	_____	Louisiana	LA	Baton Rouge	1812
_____	_____	Maine	ME	Augusta	1820
_____	_____	Maryland*	MD	Baltimore	1788
_____	_____	Massachusetts*	MA	Boston	1788
_____	_____	Michigan	MI	Lansing	1837
_____	_____	Minnesota	MN	St. Paul	1858
_____	_____	Mississippi	MS	Jackson	1817
_____	_____	Missouri	MO	Jefferson City	1821
_____	_____	Montana	MT	Helena	1889
_____	_____	Nebraska	NE	Lincoln	1867
_____	_____	Nevada	NV	Carson City	1864
_____	_____	New Hampshire*	NH	Concord	1788
_____	_____	New Jersey*	NJ	Trenton	1787
_____	_____	New Mexico	NM	Sante Fe	1912
_____	_____	New York*	NY	Albany	1788
_____	_____	North Carolina*	NC	Raleigh	1789
_____	_____	North Dakota	ND	Bismarck	1889
_____	_____	Ohio	OH	Columbus	1803
_____	_____	Oklahoma	OK	Oklahoma City	1907
_____	_____	Oregon	OR	Salem	1859
_____	_____	Pennsylvania*	PA	Harrisburg	1787
_____	_____	Rhode Island*	RI	Providence	1790
_____	_____	South Carolina*	SC	Columbia	1788

		STATE	ABBREVIATION	CAPITAL	STATE ENTERED UNION
_____	_____	South Dakota	SD	Pierre	1889
_____	_____	Tennessee	TN	Nashville	1796
_____	_____	Texas	TX	Austin	1845
_____	_____	Utah	UT	Salt Lake City	1896
_____	_____	Vermont	VT	Montpelier	1791
_____	_____	Virginia*	VA	Richmond	1788
_____	_____	Washington	WA	Olympia	1889
_____	_____	West Virginia	WV	Charleston	1863
_____	_____	Wisconsin	WI	Madison	1848
_____	_____	Wyoming	WY	Cheyenne	1890

STATE HISTORY - _____

Elem	Jr/Sr High	
_____	_____	History of State (Major Events)
_____	_____	Map Study of State
_____	_____	State Flag, State Seal, Nickname
_____	_____	State Symbols (Flower, Bird, Tree, Mammal, etc.)
_____	_____	State Song
_____	_____	Major People
_____	_____	Major Places
_____	_____	Government
_____	_____	Wildlife (plants & animals)
_____	_____	Natural Resources
_____	_____	Agriculture
_____	_____	Manufacturing & Industry
_____	_____	Geography
_____	_____	Weather

_____ _____ _____
_____ _____ _____
_____ _____ _____
_____ _____ _____
_____ _____ _____
_____ _____ _____
_____ _____ _____
_____ _____ _____
_____ _____ _____
_____ _____ _____
_____ _____ _____
_____ _____ _____
_____ _____ _____
_____ _____ _____

GOVERNMENT

_____ _____ International Relationships
_____ _____ Godly Submission to Authority (1 Pet. 2:13-14, Rom. 13:1-7)
_____ _____ U.S. State and Local Government
_____ _____ U.S. Voting and the Election Process
_____ _____ U.S. Constitution
_____ _____ U.S. Bill of Rights
_____ _____ U.S. Government Agencies
_____ _____ U.S. Pledge of Allegiance
_____ _____ U.S. National Symbols
_____ _____ U.S. National Holidays
_____ _____ Presidents of the United States

_____ _____
_____ _____
_____ _____
_____ _____

FORMS OF GOVERNMENT

_____ _____ Democracy   _____ _____ Parliamentary
_____ _____ Dictatorship   _____ _____ Republic
_____ _____ Federation   _____ _____ Theocracy
_____ _____ Imperialism   _____ _____ Totalitarianism
_____ _____ Monarchy   _____ _____ _____

U.S. FEDERAL GOVERNMENT EXECUTIVE BRANCH

_____ _____ Executive Office of the   _____ _____ Department of Health and
President   Human Services
_____ _____ Department of Agriculture   _____ _____ Department of Labor
_____ _____ Department of Commerce   _____ _____ Department of State
_____ _____ Department of Defense   _____ _____ Department of
_____ _____ Department of Education   Transportation
_____ _____ Department of Energy   _____ _____ Department of Treasury
_____ _____ Department of the Interior   _____ _____ Department of Homeland
_____ _____ Department of Justice   Security

U.S. FEDERAL GOVERNMENT LEGISLATIVE BRANCH

_____ _____ Senate
_____ _____ House of Representatives

U.S. FEDERAL GOVERNMENT JUDICIAL BRANCH

_____ _____ Supreme Court   _____ _____ Other Federal Courts
_____ _____ Federal Court of Appeals

ECONOMICS

Elem	Jr/Sr High	
_____	_____	History of Money and Banking
_____	_____	History of Economics
_____	_____	Definition of Economics
_____	_____	Major Fields—Microeconomics, Macroeconomics
_____	_____	U.S. and World Economies (International Trade, Exports, Imports)
_____	_____	_____
_____	_____	_____
_____	_____	_____

PEOPLE IN ECONOMICS

_____	_____	Engels, Friedrich (Germany, 1820-1895)—Revolutionary Political Economist and Co-founder (with Karl Marx) of Communism: Communist Manifesto
_____	_____	Keynes, John Maynard (England, 1883-1946)—Economist: Planned Economy, Influenced the "New Deal"
_____	_____	Malthus, Thomas Robert (England, 1766-1834)—Economist: Classical
_____	_____	Marshall, Alfred —Principles of Economics (1890)
_____	_____	Mill, John Stuart (England, 1806-1873)—Social Reformer: Classical Economics, Principles of Political Economy
_____	_____	Ricardo, David (England, 1772-1823)—Political Economist: Classical Economics
_____	_____	Smith, Adam (England, 1723-1890)—Economist: Classical Economics, Wealth of Nations
_____	_____	_____
_____	_____	_____
_____	_____	_____
_____	_____	_____

ECONOMIC TERMS

Elem	Jr/Sr High		Elem	Jr/Sr High	
_____	_____	Bureaucracy	_____	_____	Marxism
_____	_____	Business Cycle	_____	_____	Mercantilism
_____	_____	Capitalism	_____	_____	Money Supply
_____	_____	Communism	_____	_____	Neoclassicist
_____	_____	Communist Manifesto	_____	_____	Physiocracy
_____	_____	Consumption	_____	_____	Production
_____	_____	Depression	_____	_____	Rationing
_____	_____	Deregulation	_____	_____	Recession
_____	_____	Diminishing Returns	_____	_____	Socialist
_____	_____	Food Supply	_____	_____	Supply and Demand
_____	_____	Free Enterprise	_____	_____	Unemployment
_____	_____	Gold, Silver	_____	_____	Welfare State
_____	_____	Gross National Product	_____	_____	Wages
_____	_____	Inflation	_____	_____	_____
_____	_____	Laissez-Faire Economics	_____	_____	_____

WISDOM, PART 2—ACQUIRE KNOWLEDGE ABOUT GOD'S CREATION

READING

Elem   Jr/Sr High

READING SKILLS

Elem	Jr/Sr High	
_____	_____	Sings the Alphabet Song
_____	_____	Reads Uppercase of the Alphabet
_____	_____	Reads Lowercase of the Alphabet
_____	_____	Rhymes Words
_____	_____	Knows Consonant Sounds
_____	_____	Knows Short Vowel Sounds
_____	_____	Knows Long Vowel Sounds
_____	_____	Knows How to Blend Letters Such as "s" and "h" to make "sh"
_____	_____	Reads Words with Blends
_____	_____	Reads Words with Digraphs
_____	_____	Reads Words with Diphthongs
_____	_____	Reads Dolch Sight Words
_____	_____	Reads Picture Books with Comprehension
_____	_____	Reads "Step-Up" Books with Comprehension
_____	_____	Reads Chapter Books with Comprehension
_____	_____	Reads Juvenile/Youth Literature with Comprehension
_____	_____	Reads Adult Literature with Comprehension
_____	_____	Reads the Bible Daily (Rom. 12:2)
_____	_____	Reads Books that Edify (Phil 4:8)
_____	_____	Reads for Enjoyment (Prov. 17:22)
_____	_____	Reads to Learn (1 Cor. 10:10-11)
_____	_____	Reads and Understands Maps, Charts, Graphs (also see Math & Geography)

LITERATURE

Study authors in light of their relationship with God and how their relationship affected their work. Check library for additional books by same authors. Books marked with an * are ones I've personally read and recommend. Many of these can be used as read-alouds for all ages. Dates and birthplace are added if known.

See <u>Recommended Preschool Literature</u> on the Oklahoma Homeschool website for a list of more books for preschoolers & beginning readers. (http://www.oklahomahomeschool.com/PreKLit.html).

Elem   Jr/Sr High

AMERICAN AUTHORS

_____ _____ Alcott, Louisa May (Pennsylvania, 1832-1888)— *Little Women**, *Little Men**, *Eight Cousins**, *The Inheritance**

_____ _____ Aldrich, Bess Streeter (Iowa, 1881-1954)— *A Lantern in Her Hand**, *Miss Bishop*

_____ _____ Alger, Horatio (Massachusetts, 1934-1899)—*The Young Adventurer**, *Ragged Dick*

_____ _____ Anderson, C. W.—*Billy and Blaze**

_____ _____ Audubon, John James (Haiti/Pennsylvania, 1785-1851)—National Audubon Society, *The Birds of America*

_____ _____ Armour, Richard (California, ?) —Satire: *It All Started With Columbus**, *Twisted Tales of Shakespeare** (Fun after you've read the real Shakespeare!)

_____ _____ Atwater, Richard—*Mr. Popper's Penguins**

_____ _____ Babbitt, Natalie (Ohio, 1932-) —*Tuck Everlasting**

_____ _____ Bagnold, Enid (1889-1991)—*National Velvet**

_____ _____ Barron, Stephanie (?)—Mysteries: *Jane and the Unpleasantness at Scargrave Manor**, a Jane Austen mystery series

_____ _____ Baum, L. Frank (New York, 1856-1919)—*The Wizard of Oz*, *Tik-Tok of Oz*

_____ _____ Benet, Stephen Vincent (Pennsylvania, 1898-1943)—Poet and Short Story Writer: "John Brown's Body"

_____ _____ Bradford, William (England/Massachusetts, 1590-1657)—Mayflower, Plymouth Colony, Separatist, *History of Plimouth Plantation**

_____ _____ Brooks, Walter (Connecticut?, 1886-1958)—*Freddy the Detective**

_____ _____ Bryant, William Cullen (Massachusetts, 1794-1878)—Poet and Journalist: New York Evening Post, *Thanatopsis*

_____ _____ Burgess, Thornton (Massachusetts, 1874-1965)—*Old Mother West Wind*, *The Adventures of Jimmy Skunk**

_____ _____ Burnett, Frances Hodgson (England/Tennessee, *1849-1924)—Little Lord Fauntleroy**, *The Secret Garden**, *The Lost Prince*, *A Little Princess**, *The Shuttle*, *T. Temberom**

_____ _____ Byars, Betsy (North Carolina, 1928-)—*The Midnight Fox*, *Seven Treasure Hunts**

_____ _____ Campbell, Julie & others—*Trixie Belden** series

_____ _____ Cather, Willa (Virginia, 1876-1947)—Novelist and Poet: *O Pioneers!*, *Death Comes for the Archbishop*

_____ _____ Chandler, Gertrude (Connecticut,1890-1979)—*Boxcar Children** series

_____ _____ Cleary, Beverly (Oregon, 1916-)—*Henry Huggins** series

_____ _____ Clemens, Samuel L. (see Mark Twain)

_____ _____ Cohn, Amy—*From Sea to Shining Sea, A Treasury of American Folklore**

_____ _____ Cooper, James Fenimore (New Jersey, 1789-1851)—*The Deerslayer, The Last of the Mohicans*

_____ _____ Crane, Stephen (New Jersey, 1871-1900)—War Correspondent: *Red Badge of Courage, Maggie, A Girl of the Streets*

_____ _____ Curtis, Christopher (Michigan)—*Bud, Not Buddy**

_____ _____ Dalgliesh, Alice (1892-1979)—*The Courage of Sarah Noble**

_____ _____ Dick, Lois Hadley—*Devil on the Deck**

_____ _____ Dickinson, Emily (Massachusetts, 1830-1886)—Poet

_____ _____ du Bois, William Pene—(New York, 1884-1958) *Twenty-One Balloons**

_____ _____ Edmonds, Walter—*The Matchlock Gun**

_____ _____ Edwards, Jonathan (Connecticut, 1703-1758)—Theologian and Philosopher: *The Great Awakening, Sinners in the Hands of an Angry God**

_____ _____ Emerson, Ralph Waldo (Massachusetts, 1803-1882)—Transcendentalist, Poet: "Nature,"

_____ _____ Estes, Eleanor—*Ginger Pye**

_____ _____ Farley, Walter (New York, 1915-1989)—*Black Stallion** series.

_____ _____ Felleman, Hazel—*Best Loved Poems of the American People**

_____ _____ Field, Rachel (New York, 1894–1942)—*Hitty, Her First Hundred Years**

_____ _____ Forbes, Esther (Massachusetts, 1891-1967)—*Johnny Tremaine*

_____ _____ Franklin, Benjamin (Massachusetts, 1706-1790)—*Autobiography**

_____ _____ Fritz, Jean (China/New York, 1915-)—Daughter of a missionary, *Shh! We're Writing the Constitution**

_____ _____ Gardiner, John—*Stonefox**

_____ _____ Gray, Elizabeth (Pennsylvania, 1902-1999)—*Adam of the Road*

_____ _____ Harris, Joel Chandler (Georgia, 1848-1908)—Humorist: *Uncle Remus, Tar Baby*

_____ _____ Hawthorne, Nathaniel (Massachusetts, 1804-1864)—*The House of Seven Gables, The Scarlet Letter, Twice-Told Tales*

_____ _____ Hemingway, Ernest (Illinois, 1899-1961)—*The Sun Also Rises, For Whom the Bell Tolls, The Old Man and The Sea, A Farewell To Arms*

_____ _____ Henry, Marguerite (Wisconsin, 1902-1997)—*Misty of Chincoteague**

_____ _____ Irving, Washington (New York, 1783-1859)—Biographer and Historian: *Legend of Sleepy Hollow, Rip Van Winkle*

_____ _____ Jackson, Dave—Trailblazer Series: John Newton, Martin Luther, John Wesley, Harriet Tubman, D.L. Moody, etc.

_____ _____ James, Will—*Smoky, the Cow Horse*

_____ _____ Johnson, Lois Walfrid—Adventures of the Northwoods* series

_____ _____ Kjelgaard, Jim (New York, 1910-1959)—*Big Red* and others

_____ _____ Lawhead, Stephen—Similar to Tolkien, *In the Halls of the Dragon King** series, *Byzantium** Some of his adult fiction is not suitable for children.

_____ _____ L'Engle, Madeleine (New York, 1918)—*A Wrinkle in Time*

_____ _____ Lenski, Lois (Ohio, 1893-1974)—*Strawberry Girl*

_____ _____ Leppard, Lois Gladys—*Mandie** series

_____ _____ Lewis, Sinclair (Minnesota, 1885-1951)—*Main Street, Elmer Gantry, Babbitt*

_____ _____ London, Jack (California, 1876 - 1916)— *White Fang, The Call of the Wild, Sea Wolf*

_____ _____ Longfellow, Henry Wadsworth (Maine, 1807-1882)—Poet: "The Village Blacksmith," "The Courtship of Miles Standish," "Paul Revere's Ride"

_____ _____ Lovelace, Maud Hart (Minnesota, 1892-1980)—*Betsy-Tacy** series

_____ _____ Lucas, Leanne—*Addie McCormick** series

_____ _____ MacLachlan, Patricia (Wyoming, 1938-)—*Sarah, Plain and Tall*

_____ _____ Marshall, Catherine (Tennessee, 1914-1983)—*Christy**, *Julie**

_____ _____ Marshall, Peter (Scotland, 1902-1949)—*The Light and the Glory**

_____ _____ Mather, Cotton (Massachusetts, 1663-1728)—Writer and Minister: Salem
Witchcraft Trials Historian, *The Wonders of the Invisible World*, Botany

_____ _____ Mather, Increase (Massachusetts, 1639-1723)—Theologian: *A Brief History of the
War with the Indians*

_____ _____ Melville, Herman (New York, 1819-1891)—*Moby Dick, Billy Budd*

_____ _____ Morey, Walter—*Gentle Ben**

_____ _____ Morris, Gilbert—Christian Historical Fiction*, Children's Fiction*, many titles

_____ _____ Mowat, Farley—*Owls in the Family**

_____ _____ North, Sterling (Wisconsin)—*Rascal*

_____ _____ O'Brien, Jack—*Silver Chief, Dog of the North*

_____ _____ O'Hara, Mary (New Jersey, 1885-1980)—*My Friend Flicka**

_____ _____ O'Neill, Eugene (New York, 1888-1953)—Playwright: *Long Day's Journey Into
Night, The Iceman Cometh*

_____ _____ Oke, Jeanette—Christian Historical Fiction about the West & *Spunky's
Diary**, *Trouble in a Fur Coat**

_____ _____ Osborne, Mary—*Magic Treehouse** series

_____ _____ Paine, Thomas (England/Pennsylvania, 1737-1809)—"Common Sense"

_____ _____ Parrish, Peggy—*Amelia Bedelia* series*.

_____ _____ Peretti, Frank (Washington, 1951-)—*This Present Darkness**, *The Prophet**,
*Piercing The Darkness**

_____ _____ Phillips, Michael—Historical Fiction: *Jamie Macloed**, *Stonewyck Trilogy**,
*Secrets of Heathersleigh Hall**, *The Russians**

_____ _____ Poe, Edgar Allen (Massachusetts, 1809-1849)—Novelist and Poet: *The Pit and the
Pendulum, The Tell-Tale Heart, Murders in the Rue Morgue, The Raven*

_____ _____ Porter, Eleanor H. (New Hampshire, 1868-1920)—*Pollyanna**

_____ _____ Porter, Gene Stratton—*Freckles, A Girl of the Limberlost*

_____ _____ Price, Eugenia—Historical fiction about the South: *The Lighthouse**

_____ _____ Pyle, Howard (New York, Delaware, 1853-1911)—*Otto of the Silver Hand**

_____ _____ Rawlings, Marjorie Kinnan (Wash. D.C., 1896-1953)—*The Yearling*

_____ _____ Roberts, Willo Davis—Children's Mystery: *Megan's Island**

_____ _____ Sandburg, Carl (Illinois, 1878-)—Biographer and Poet: *Abraham Lincoln: The
Prairie Years, Abraham Lincoln: The War Years*

_____ _____ Sewell, Anna (England, 1820-1878)—*Black Beauty**

_____ _____ Smith, Betty (New York immigrant, 1904-1972) —*A Tree Grows in Brooklyn**

_____ _____ Sobol, Donald—*Encyclopedia Brown** series.

_____ _____ Speare, Elizabeth George—Historical Fiction: *The Bronze Bow, Calico Captive**,
*The Sign of the Beaver, The Witch From Blackbird Pond**

_____ _____ Spinelli, Jerry—*Maniac Magee**

_____ _____ Stahl, Hilda—*Sadie* Series*

_____ _____ Stanley, Diane—*Bard of Avon: The Story of William Shakespeare**

_____ _____ Stowe, Harriet Beecher (Connecticut, 1811-1896)—*Uncle Tom's Cabin, The Minister's Wooing, Dred: A Tale of the Great Dismal Swamp*

_____ _____ Taylor, Theodore—Children's Historical Fiction: *The Cay**

_____ _____ Terhune, Albert—*Lad, A Dog**, and others

_____ _____ Thoreau, Henry David (Massachusetts, 1817-1862)—Poet and Essayist: *Civil Disobedience, Walden, Life in the Woods*

_____ _____ Traylor, Ellen Gunderson—Historical Fiction about Bible Characters: *Moses**, *Joshua**, *Abraham**, etc

_____ _____ Twain, Mark (Missouri, 1835-1910)—*The Prince and the Pauper**, *A Connecticut Yankee in King Arthur's Court, Huckleberry Finn**, *Tom Sawyer**

_____ _____ Wallace, Lew (Indiana, 1827-1905)—*Ben Hur*

_____ _____ Warner, Gertrude—*Boxcar Children** series

_____ _____ Webster, Jean (New York, 1876-1916)—*Daddy Long Legs**

_____ _____ West, Jerry—*Happy Hollisters** series

_____ _____ Wharton, Edith (New York, 1861-1937)—*The Age of Innocence, Ethan Frome*

_____ _____ White, John—*The Archives of Anthropos Series**- similar to C.S.Lewis

_____ _____ Whitman, Walt (New York, 1819-1892)—Poet: *Leaves of Grass*

_____ _____ Whittier, John Greenleaf (Massachusetts, 1807-1892)—Quaker Poet and Abolitionist: *In War Time, At Sundown, Legend of New England*

_____ _____ Wiggins, Kate Douglas (Pennsylvania, 1856-1923)—*Rebecca of Sunnybrook Farm**, *Mother Carey's Chickens, The Birds' Christmas Carol*

_____ _____ Wilder, Laura Ingalls (Wisconsin, 1867-1957)—*Little House in the Big Woods**, *By the Shores of Silver Lake**, *Those Happy Golden Years**

_____ _____ Wilder, Thornton (Wisconsin, 1897-1975)—Writer and Playwright: *The Bridge of San Luis Rey, Our Town, The Matchmaker, The Ides of March*

_____ _____ _____

_____ _____ _____

_____ _____ _____

_____ _____ _____

_____ _____ _____

_____ _____ _____

_____ _____ _____

_____ _____ _____

_____ _____ _____

_____ _____ _____

_____ _____ _____

_____ _____ _____

_____ _____ _____

_____ _____ _____

_____ _____ _____

_____ _____ _____

_____ _____ _____

_____ _____ _____

_____ _____ _____

_____ _____ _____

Authors From Around The World

_____ _____ Chaucer, Geoffrey (England, c.1343-1400)—Poet: "Canterbury Tales" Look for a copy edited by Geraldine McCaughrean or Barbara Cohen.

_____ _____ Chekhov, Anton Pavlovich (Ukraine, 1860-1904)—Playwright and Short Stories: *Uncle Vanya*

_____ _____ Coleridge, Samuel (England, 1772-1834)—Poet: "The Rime of the Ancient Mariner," "Kubla Khan"

_____ _____ Collins, Wilkie (England, 1824-1889)—*The Woman in White*, The Moonstone**

_____ _____ Collodi (See Carlo Lorenzini)

_____ _____ Confucius (Shantung, 551-479BC)—Chinese Philosopher

_____ _____ Conrad, Joseph (England, 1857-1924)—*Lord Jim, The Secret Agent*

_____ _____ Dante, Alighieri (Italy, 1265-1321)—Poet: "The Divine Comedy"

_____ _____ Defoe, Daniel (England, 1660-1731)—*Robinson Crusoe** (read the original version for a Christian emphasis), *Moll Flanders*

_____ _____ Dejong, Meindert (Netherlands,1906-)—*Along Came a Dog*, The House of Sixty Fathers*, Shadrach*, Good Luck Duck**

_____ _____ Descartes, René (France, 1596-1650)—Philosopher: *Principles of Philosophy*

_____ _____ Dickens, Charles (England, 1812-1870)—*Oliver Twist*, The Old Curiosity Shop, Pickwick Papers, A Christmas Carol*, David Copperfield*, A Tale of Two Cities*, Great Expectations, Nicolas Nickleby*

_____ _____ Donne, John (England, 1572-1631)—Poet: "Songs and Sonnets"

_____ _____ Dostoevski, Fyodor (Russia, 1821-1881)—*The Brother's Karamozov, Crime and Punishment, The Idiot*

_____ _____ Doyle, Sir Arthur Conan (Scotland, 1859-1930)—*The Adventures of Sherlock Holmes*, A Study in Scarlet*, The White Company*, The War in South Africa*

_____ _____ Dumas, Alexandre (France,1802-1870)—Novelist and Playwright: *The Three Musketeers, The Count of Monte Cristo, Henry III, The Black Tulip*

_____ _____ Eliot, George (England,1819-1880)—Pen Name of Homeschooled Author Marian Evans: *Adam Bede, The Mill on the Floss, Silas Marner*, Middlemarch*

_____ _____ Eliot, T. S. (Missouri/England, 1888-1965)—Playwright: *Four Quartets, Murder in the Cathedral, The Waste Land*

_____ _____ Frank, Anne (Germany, 1929-1945)—*The Dairy of Anne Frank**

_____ _____ Gibbon, Edward (England, 1737-1794)—Historian: *The History of the Decline and Fall of the Roman Empire*

_____ _____ Goldsmith, Oliver (Ireland, 1728-1774)—Playwright and Novelist: *The Vicar of Wakefield, She Stoops to Conquer*

_____ _____ Grahame, Kenneth (Scotland, 1856-1932)—*The Reluctant Dragon*, The Wind and the Willows**

_____ _____ Hardy, Thomas (England, 1840-1928)—Atheist: *The Mayor of Casterbridge*

_____ _____ Henty, G. A. (England, 1832-1902)—*Cat of Bubastes, In Freedom's Cause*

_____ _____ Homer (Greece, b.1200 BC?)—Poet: "Iliad," "Odyssey". Look for an edited version by Geraldine McCaughrean for an easy-to-read introduction.

_____ _____ Hugo, Victor (France, 1802-1885)—*The Hunchback of Notre Dame, Les Misérables*

_____ _____ Jacques, Brian (England)—*Redwall** series

_____ _____ Keats, John (England, 1795-1821)—Poet: "Letters," "The Eve of St. Agnes,"

_____ _____ Kempis, Thomas à. (German, c.1380-1471)—Monk: *Imitation of Christ*

_____ _____ Kipling, Rudyard (India, 1865-1936)—*Gunga Din, Jungle Book*, Just So Stories, Puck of Pook's Hill*

_____ _____ Knight, Eric (England, 1897-1943)—*Lassie Come Home**

_____ _____ Lamb, Charles (England, 1775–1834) and Mary —*Tales from Shakespeare**

_____ _____ Lear, Edward (England, 1812-1888)—Artist and Writer: *A Book of Nonsense, Sketches of Rome*

_____ _____ Lewis, C.S. (England, 1898-1963)—Christian Apologist and Novelist: *The Screwtape Letters*, The Chronicles of Narnia**

_____ _____ Locke, John (England, 1632-1704)—Diest Philosopher: Essay Concerning Human Understanding

_____ _____ Lofting, Hugh (England & U.S., 1886–1947)—*Dr. Doolittle** series

_____ _____ Lorenzini, Carlo (Collodi)(Italy, 1826-1890)—*Pinocchio**

_____ _____ MacDonald, George (Scotland, 1824-1905)—Novelist and Preacher: *A Fisherman's Lady*, The Marquis Secret*, The Shepherd of the Castle*, The Baronet's Song*, At the Back of the North Wind**

_____ _____ Marlowe, Christopher (England, 1564-1593)—Atheist Playwright: *Dr. Faustus, The Jew of Malta*

_____ _____ Maupassant, Guy de (France, 1850-1893)—*The Necklace*

_____ _____ Milne, A. A. (England, 1882-1956)—*Winnie-the-Pooh*, The Red House Mystery, Now We Are Six, When We Were Very Young*

_____ _____ Milton, John (England, 1608-1674)—Poet: "Paradise Lost," "Paradise Regained"

_____ _____ Molière (France, 1622-1673)—Playwright: *The School for Wives, The Misanthropist*

_____ _____ Montgomery, Lucy Maud (Canada, 1874-1942)—*Anne of Green Gables*, Anne of Avonlea**, and *Emily* Series

_____ _____ Orczy, Baroness (Hungary, 1865-1947)—Novelist and Playwright: *The Scarlet Pimpernel*

_____ _____ Orwell, George (India, 1903-1950)—*Animal Farm*, Nineteen Eighty-Four*

_____ _____ Ovid (Italy, 43 BC-AD 17)—Poet: "Metamorphoses"

_____ _____ Plato (Greece, 427-347 BC)—Philosopher and Founder of the 'Academy', *Apology, Republic, Symposium*

_____ _____ Pliny the Elder (Gaul, 23-79 AD)—*Historia Naturalis* (Natural History)

_____ _____ Potter, Beatrix (England, 1866-1943)—Writer and Illustrator: *The Tale of Peter Rabbit*, Jeremiah Puddleduck, The Tale of Tom Kitten, Benjamin Bunny*

_____ _____ Raleigh, Sir Walter (England, 1552-1618)—Courtier, Writer, and Navigator: *History of the World*

_____ _____ Raschid, Haround Al (Persia)—*Tales of Arabian Nights*

_____ _____ Scott, Sir Walter (Scotland, 1771-1832)—Novelist and Poet: *Ivanhoe*, The Lady of the Lake, The Talisman, Woodstock, Waverley*

_____ _____ Shakespeare (England, 1564-1616)—Elizabethan Drama: *Antony and Cleopatra, Romeo and Juliet, Julius Caesar, A Midsummer's Night Dream, The Tempest* (*A Midsummer's Night Dream for Kids* by Lois Burdett is a good place to start.)

_____ _____ Sharp, Margery (England, 1905-1991)—*The Rescuers**

_____ _____ Shaw, Bernard (Ireland, 1856-1950)—Socialist Playwright: *The Devil's Disciple, Major Barbara, Adrocles and the Lion, Pygmalion (My Fair Lady)*

_____ _____ Shelley, Mary (England, 1797-1851)—*Frankenstein*

_____ _____ Socrates (Greece, 469-399 BC)—Philosopher: Socratic Method

_____ _____ Sophocles (Greece, 496-406 BC)—Tragic Playwright: *Odepus Rex, Antigone*

_____ _____ Spyri, Johanna (Switzerland, 1827–1901)—*Heidi**

_____ _____ Stevenson, Robert Louis (Scotland, 1850-1894)—*Treasure Island**, *Kidnapped, The Strange Case of Dr. Jekyll and Mr. Hyde, The Master of Ballantrae, Weir of Hermiston*

_____ _____ Swift, Jonathan (Ireland, 1667-1745)—Novelist and Clergyman: *Gulliver's Travels**, *A Tale of a Tub*

_____ _____ Tacitus (Rome, c.55-120)—Roman Historian: *Histories*

_____ _____ Tennyson, Alfred (England, 1809-1892)—Poet: "Idylls of the King"

_____ _____ Thucydides (Greece, c.460-c.400BC)—*Greek Historian, Peloponnesian War*

_____ _____ Tolkien, J. R. R. (Africa/England, 1892-1973)—Philologist and Writer: *The Hobbit**, *The Lord of the Rings, Silmarillion*

_____ _____ Tolstoy, Count Leo (Russia, 1828-1910)— *Anna Karenina, War and Peace*

_____ _____ Verne, Jules (France, 1828-1905)—*20,000 Leagues Under The Sea**, *Journey to the Center of the Earth**, *The Mysterious Island**, *Around the World in 80 Days**

_____ _____ Virgil (70-19 BC)—Latin Poet: "Aeneid." Read *The Aeneid for Boys and Girls* by Alfred Church as an easy-to-read version. ISBN 0027184005.

_____ _____ Voltaire (France, 1694-1778)—*Oedipe, Candide, Dictionnaire Philosophique*

_____ _____ Wells, H.G. (England, 1866-1946)—Novelist and Historian: *The Time Machine, The War of the Worlds, The Outline of History*

_____ _____ Wilde, Oscar (Ireland, 1854-1900)—*The Importance of Being Earnest**

_____ _____ Wordsworth, William (England, 1770-1850)—Poet: "The Prelude"

_____ _____ Wyss, Johann (Switzerland, 1781–1830)—*Swiss Family Robinson**

COMMUNICATION (ORAL, SPEECH)

Elem	Jr/Sr High	
_____	_____	Able to Speak Grammatically Correct at All Times
_____	_____	Able to Give an Oral Presentation
_____	_____	Able to Participate in a Dramatic Production (Play, Puppets, Television, Etc.)
_____	_____	Able to Read or Tell a Story to Others
_____	_____	Speaks a Foreign Language (If Needed)
_____	_____	Has Developed Memorization Skills
_____	_____	_____
_____	_____	_____

COMMUNICATION (WRITTEN, GRAMMAR)

Elem   Jr/Sr High

BASIC WRITING SKILLS—PART I

Elem	Jr/Sr High	
_____	_____	Knows and Is Able to Write the Alphabet
_____	_____	Knows and Is Able to Write Numbers in the Correct Order
_____	_____	Knows and Is Able to Write Name, Address, Telephone Number
_____	_____	Writes in Manuscript
_____	_____	Writes in Cursive
_____	_____	Is Able to Copy Selections of Writing
_____	_____	Is Able to Take Dictation
_____	_____	Writes Neatly and Legibly
_____	_____	Knows the History of Bookmaking (Papyrus, Rosetta Stone, Printing Press)
_____	_____	_____
_____	_____	_____

IS FAMILIAR WITH WRITTEN CODES:

Elem	Jr/Sr High		Elem	Jr/Sr High	
_____	_____	Hieroglyphics (see page 30)	_____	_____	Semaphore
_____	_____	Morse Code	_____	_____	_____
_____	_____	Braille	_____	_____	_____
_____	_____	Sign Language	_____	_____	_____

CAPITALIZATION

Elem	Jr/Sr High		Elem	Jr/Sr High	
_____	_____	First Word of Sentence	_____	_____	Outlines
_____	_____	Proper Nouns	_____	_____	Quotations
_____	_____	Proper Adjectives	_____	_____	_____
_____	_____	Letter Parts	_____	_____	_____

ABBREVIATIONS

Elem	Jr/Sr High		Elem	Jr/Sr High	
_____	_____	Days of Week	_____	_____	States
_____	_____	Months	_____	_____	Cities
_____	_____	Titles	_____	_____	_____
_____	_____	Streets	_____	_____	_____

PUNCTUATION

____ ____	Apostrophe	____ ____ Parenthesis
____ ____	Colon	____ ____ Period
____ ____	Comma	____ ____ Question Mark
____ ____	Contractions	____ ____ Quotation Marks
____ ____	Exclamation Point	____ ____ Semicolon
____ ____	Hyphens	____ ____ _____
____ ____	Paragraph Indentation	____ ____ _____

SENTENCE CONSTRUCTION

____ ____	Subject	____ ____ Exclamatory
____ ____	Predicate	____ ____ Imperative
____ ____	Simple	____ ____ Interrogative
____ ____	Compound	____ ____ _____
____ ____	Complex Sentences	____ ____ _____
____ ____	Declarative	

ANTONYMS, HOMONYMS, PREFIXES, ETC.

____ ____	Antonyms	____ ____ Prefixes
____ ____	Base words	____ ____ Suffixes
____ ____	Compound Words	____ ____ Synonyms
____ ____	Contractions	____ ____ _____
____ ____	Homonyms	____ ____ _____

BASIC WRITING SKILLS—PART II

____ ____ Consistently Uses Correct Subject and Verb Agreement

____ ____ Consistently Uses Correct Pronoun Forms

____ ____ Is Able to Proofread and Make Corrections

____ ____ Has a Good Vocabulary

____ ____ Is Able to Form Plurals and Add Word Endings

____ ____ Is Able to Form Possessives

____ ____ Correctly Spells Words Used in Daily Writing on a Consistent Basis

____ ____ Uses a Dictionary, as Needed (also see Research Skills page 129)

____ ____ Understands and Uses Analogies

____ ____ Is Able to Paraphrase and Summarize

____ ____ Is Able to Play Word Games Such as Scrabble and Boggle

____ ____ Is Able to Distinguish Between Fact, Fiction, Opinion, Inference

____ ____ Keeps a Journal

____ ____ Knowledgeable in Formal Grammar (Parts of Speech, Diagramming, etc.)

____ ____ Is Able to Take Notes Quickly and Accurately

____ ____ _____

____ ____ _____

____ ____ _____

WRITING/LITERATURE TERMS

_____ _____	Alliteration	_____ _____ Personification
_____ _____	Allusion	_____ _____ Plot
_____ _____	Cacophony	_____ _____ Point of View
_____ _____	Character	_____ _____ Prose
_____ _____	Cliche	_____ _____ Setting
_____ _____	Climax	_____ _____ Simile
_____ _____	Composition	_____ _____ Subject
_____ _____	Dialogue	_____ _____ Symbolism
_____ _____	Figure of Speech	_____ _____ Theme
_____ _____	Hyperbole	_____ _____ Tone
_____ _____	Imagery	_____ _____ Topic
_____ _____	Metaphor	_____ _____ _____
_____ _____	Meter	_____ _____ _____
_____ _____	Onomatopoeia	_____ _____ _____
_____ _____	Parable	_____ _____ _____

WRITING SKILLS—COMPUTER

_____ _____ Uses Word Processing Software

_____ _____ Uses Page Layout Software

_____ _____ Uses Database Software

_____ _____ Types at 40 Words Per Minute, Minimum

_____ _____ _____

_____ _____ _____

RESEARCH SKILLS

Elem	Jr/Sr High	
_____	_____	Is Able to Arrange Words in Alphabetical Order
_____	_____	Is Familiar with the Reference Section of the Library
_____	_____	Is Able to Use Encyclopedias
_____	_____	Is Able to Use a Thesaurus
_____	_____	Is Able to Use an Atlas
_____	_____	Is Able to Use an Almanac
_____	_____	Is Able to Use a Dictionary (Guide Words, Accents, Pronunciation Guide)
_____	_____	Is Able to Use the Periodical Index
_____	_____	Is Able to Access the Local Library Using a Modem
_____	_____	Is Able to Use the Internet
_____	_____	Bible Research Skills (see page 17)
_____	_____	_____
_____	_____	_____
_____	_____	_____
_____	_____	_____
_____	_____	_____

WRITING PROJECT IDEAS

_____	_____	Advertisement
_____	_____	Anecdote
_____	_____	Announcement
_____	_____	Autobiography
_____	_____	Bibliography (Author, Book Title, Publisher, Publication Date)
_____	_____	Biography
_____	_____	Book Review
_____	_____	Brochure
_____	_____	Captions to Photos
_____	_____	Cartoon
_____	_____	Catalog
_____	_____	Charts and Graphs
_____	_____	Consumer Guide
_____	_____	Contract
_____	_____	Dedication
_____	_____	Definitions
_____	_____	Dialogs
_____	_____	Diary
_____	_____	Dictionaries
_____	_____	Directions
_____	_____	Directories (Address Book, Databases)
_____	_____	Editorial (Letter to Editor)
_____	_____	Entertainment Guide
_____	_____	Envelope
_____	_____	Essays (Persuade, Inform, Entertain)
_____	_____	Eulogy
_____	_____	Explanation
_____	_____	Fable
_____	_____	Fact Sheet
_____	_____	Family Tree
_____	_____	Fax
_____	_____	Fiction
_____	_____	Flyer
_____	_____	Greeting Cards
_____	_____	Handbook
_____	_____	Historical Fiction
_____	_____	Instructions
_____	_____	Interview
_____	_____	Invitations
_____	_____	Itineraries
_____	_____	Labels
_____	_____	Lists
_____	_____	Letter: Personal (Heading, Greeting, Body, Closing, Signature, Envelope)
_____	_____	Letter: Business (Heading, Greeting, Body, Closing, Signature, Envelope)
_____	_____	Magazine

_____ _____		Memo
_____ _____		Menu, Recipes
_____ _____		Minutes of a Meeting
_____ _____		Movie/TV/Video Review
_____ _____		Mystery
_____ _____		News Article/Newspaper
_____ _____		Newsletter
_____ _____		Order Form
_____ _____		Play
_____ _____		Postcard
_____ _____		Questionnaire/Survey
_____ _____		Quiz
_____ _____		Reports (Topic Sentence, Details, Organization, Closing Statement)
_____ _____		Research Paper (Note Taking, Outline, First Draft, Editing, Rewriting, Bibliography)
_____ _____		Resume
_____ _____		Riddles
_____ _____		Rules
_____ _____		Schedules
_____ _____		Signs, Posters
_____ _____		Song
_____ _____		Speech
_____ _____		Story (Character, Plot, Theme, Setting, Point of View, Conflict)
_____ _____		Summaries
_____ _____		Table of Contents
_____ _____		Telegram
_____ _____		Telephone Message
_____ _____		Thank You Note
_____ _____		Tongue Twisters
_____ _____		Travel Guide

_____ _____ _____

_____ _____ _____

_____ _____ _____

_____ _____ _____

_____ _____ _____

_____ _____ _____

_____ _____ _____

_____ _____ _____

Poetry:

_____ _____ Sonnet		_____ _____ Ode	
_____ _____ Ballad		_____ _____ Stanza	
_____ _____ Haiku		_____ _____ Couplet	
_____ _____ Epic		_____ _____ Blank Verse	
_____ _____ Limerick		_____ _____ _____	
_____ _____ Cinquain			

MATH

_____ _____ God's Purpose for Math
_____ _____ Practical Uses of Math
_____ _____ Careers in Math

BASIC MATH SKILLS—PART I

_____ _____ Is Able to Use Manipulatives
_____ _____ Is Able to Count to 100+
_____ _____ Is Able to Recognize and Complete Patterns
_____ _____ Is Able to Recognize and Predict Number Sequences
_____ _____ Knows Ordinals (First, Second, Third, etc.)
_____ _____ Knows Place Values (Ones, Tens, Hundreds, etc.)
_____ _____ Reads and Writes Word Names for Numbers
_____ _____ Identifies, Counts, and Calculates Money
_____ _____ Is Able to Read and Write Roman Numerals
_____ _____ Is Able to Tell Time (Watch)-also see Earth's Motion, page 151
_____ _____ Is Familiar With Math Games: Dominos, Yahtzee, Battleship, Math Mouse, Playing
      Store
      Is Able to Use a Compass and Straightedge to Create Geometric Shapes

_____ _____ _____
_____ _____ _____
_____ _____ _____
_____ _____ _____
_____ _____ _____
_____ _____ _____
_____ _____ _____
_____ _____ _____

COUNTING

_____ _____ 2's   _____ _____ 6's
_____ _____ 3's   _____ _____ 7's
_____ _____ 5's   _____ _____ 8's
_____ _____ 10's   _____ _____ 9's
_____ _____ 12's   _____ _____ 11's
_____ _____ 100's   _____ _____ 12's
_____ _____ 4's

SORTING—SAME & DIFFERENT

_____ _____ Sizes   _____ _____ Amounts
_____ _____ Colors   _____ _____ _____
_____ _____ Shapes   _____ _____ _____

RECOGNIZING SHAPES

_____ _____	Square	_____ _____ Cone
_____ _____	Circle	_____ _____ Pyramid
_____ _____	Triangle	_____ _____ Cylinder
_____ _____	Rectangle	_____ _____ Rectangular Solid
_____ _____	Polygon	_____ _____ _____
_____ _____	Sphere	_____ _____ _____

100 BASIC FACTS (DRILL WORK)

_____ _____	Addition	_____ _____ Multiplication
_____ _____	Subtraction	_____ _____ Division

LINEAR MEASUREMENTS

_____ _____	Inch	_____ _____ Metric Linear
_____ _____	Foot	Measurements
_____ _____	Yard	_____ _____ _____
_____ _____	Mile	_____ _____ _____

WEIGHT MEASUREMENTS

_____ _____	Ounce	_____ _____ Metric Weight
_____ _____	Pounds	Measurements
_____ _____	Tons	_____ _____ _____

VOLUME MEASUREMENTS

_____ _____	Teaspoon	_____ _____ Gallon
_____ _____	Tablespoon	_____ _____ Metric Volume
_____ _____	Cup	Measurements
_____ _____	Pint	_____ _____ _____
_____ _____	Quart	_____ _____ _____

BASIC MATH SKILLS—PART II

_____ _____ Area of Circles
_____ _____ Area of Rectangles
_____ _____ Area of Triangles
_____ _____ Averaging
_____ _____ Circumference of Circles
_____ _____ Decimals
_____ _____ Estimation
_____ _____ Exponents
_____ _____ Fractions
_____ _____ Fractions (Adding, Subtracting, Multiplying and Dividing)
_____ _____ Fractions, Converting to Decimals and Vice Versa
_____ _____ Fractions, Simplifying
_____ _____ Greater Than, Less Than, Equal To
_____ _____ Greatest Common Factor, Least Common Multiple
_____ _____ Isolation of X and Equations (Simple Algebra)
_____ _____ Logic Problems
_____ _____ Mean, Median, Mode, and Range of a Set of Numbers
_____ _____ Metrics
_____ _____ Negative Numbers
_____ _____ Percentages
_____ _____ Perimeter
_____ _____ Prime Numbers, Composite, Odd, Even
_____ _____ Rate, Time, and Distance Problems
_____ _____ Ratios and Proportions
_____ _____ Rounding Numbers
_____ _____ Square Roots
_____ _____ Temperature—Degrees Fahrenheit (also see page 146, 160, 165)
_____ _____ Temperature—Degrees Celsius (also see page 146, 160, 165)
_____ _____ Volume
_____ _____ Word Problems
_____ _____ _____
_____ _____ _____
_____ _____ _____
_____ _____ _____

GRAPHS, CHARTS, AND TABLES

_____ _____ Bar Graphs   _____ _____ Charts
_____ _____ Line Graphs   _____ _____ Tables
_____ _____ Picture Graphs   _____ _____ _____
_____ _____ Circle or Pie Graphs   _____ _____ _____

GEOMETRIC TERMS

_____	_____	Point	_____	_____	_____
_____	_____	Line	_____	_____	_____
_____	_____	Line Segment	_____	_____	_____
_____	_____	Ray	_____	_____	_____
_____	_____	Parallel Lines	_____	_____	_____
_____	_____	Perpendicular Lines	_____	_____	_____
_____	_____	Angles	_____	_____	_____

FAMOUS MATHEMATICIANS

Elem   Jr/Sr High

_____ _____ Archimedes (Greece, c.287-212 BC)—Mathematician and Engineer: Discovered the Lever and the Principle of Buoyancy

_____ _____ Babbage, Charles (England, 1792-1871)—Mathematician and Inventor: Developed One of the First Early Computers Called the "Difference Machine."

_____ _____ Boole, George S. (England, 1815-1864)—Developed a Method for Representing Logic with Mathematical Formulas, Boolean Algebra Named After Him

_____ _____ Descartes, René (France, 1596-1650)—Mathematician and Philosopher: Principles of Philosophy ("I think, therefore I am."), Diest, Geometry, Optics

_____ _____ Euclid (Greece, c.330-c.260 BC)—Geometry, Elements

_____ _____ Gates, William Henry (Washington, 1955-)—Computer Scientist: Developed Microsoft Disk Operating System

_____ _____ Hopper, Grace Murray (1906-1834)—Computer Programmer: Invented COBOL Programming Language

_____ _____ Jobs, Steven Paul (California, 1955-)—Computer Scientist: Co-Founder of Apple Computer Company, Graphical User Interface, High-Resolution Graphics, Digital Sound Processing

_____ _____ Lamb, Sir Horace (England, 1849-1934)—Mathematician and Geophysicist: Airflow Over Airplane Surfaces

_____ _____ Napier, John (England, 1550-1617)—Invented Logarithm as a Mathematical Device to Aid in Calculation

_____ _____ Oughtred, William (England, 1575-1660)—Invented the Earliest Form of the Slide Rule

_____ _____ Pacioli, Luca (Italy, c.1445-?)—Wrote the First Algebra Book

_____ _____ Pascal, Blaise (France, 1623-1662)—Founded the Modern Theory of Probabilities

_____ _____ Pythagoras (Greece, c.540-510 BC)—Geometry, Pythagorean Theorem for Right Triangles, Music Intervals

_____ _____ Wozniak, Stephen (California, 1951-)—Computer Scientist: Co-Founded Apple Computer Company (See Steven Jobs)

_____ _____ _____

_____ _____ _____

_____ _____ _____

_____ _____ _____

_____ _____ _____

MATH HISTORY/READING (LIST TITLE & AUTHOR)

Elem   Jr/Sr High

_____ _____ _____
_____ _____ _____
_____ _____ _____
_____ _____ _____
_____ _____ _____
_____ _____ _____
_____ _____ _____
_____ _____ _____
_____ _____ _____
_____ _____ _____
_____ _____ _____
_____ _____ _____
_____ _____ _____
_____ _____ _____
_____ _____ _____
_____ _____ _____

COMPUTERS IN MATH

_____ _____ History of the Computer
_____ _____ Calculator Use
_____ _____ Computers—Programming
_____ _____ Spreadsheet Software to Create Charts and Graphs
_____ _____ Positive and Negative Uses of Computers
_____ _____ _____
_____ _____ _____

ADVANCED MATH

_____ _____ Algebra I
_____ _____ Geometry
_____ _____ Logic (Word) Problems
_____ _____ _____
_____ _____ _____

COLLEGE PREP MATH SKILLS

_____ _____ Advanced Geometry
_____ _____ Calculus
_____ _____ Algebra II
_____ _____ Trigonometry
_____ _____ Statistics
_____ _____ _____
_____ _____ _____

BIBLICAL FINANCES & CONSUMER MATH (also see Economics)

DIVISION OF INCOME:

_____ _____ **Tithe**-Malachi 3:8

_____ _____ **Government**-Matthew 22:21

_____ _____ **Family Needs**-1 Tim. 5:8

_____ _____ **Debts**-Psalms 37:21

_____ _____ **Surplus** - Savings (Deut.28:4) and Gifts (2 Cor. 8:14]

_____ _____ Budgeting

_____ _____ Borrowing vs. Lending

_____ _____ Checking/Savings Account

_____ _____ History of Money and the Banking System

_____ _____ Home Ownership—Mortgage Interest and Taxes

_____ _____ Insurance

_____ _____ Interest Rates

_____ _____ Investments

_____ _____ Markdowns

_____ _____ Sales Tax

_____ _____ Savings Account

_____ _____ Taxes and Tax Preparation

_____ _____ _____

_____ _____ _____

_____ _____ _____

BUSINESS MATH

_____ _____ Accounting

_____ _____ Advertising

_____ _____ Bookkeeping

_____ _____ Commissions

_____ _____ Depreciation

_____ _____ Discounts

_____ _____ Marketing

_____ _____ Profit and Loss

_____ _____ _____

_____ _____ _____

_____ _____ _____

_____ _____ _____

_____ _____ _____

SCIENCE (GEN. 1:28)

GOD'S CREATION

_____ _____ Creationism vs. Evolutionary Theory (Jer. 10:12), See page 24
_____ _____ Practical Uses for Science
_____ _____ Scientific Method

_____ _____ _____
_____ _____ _____
_____ _____ _____
_____ _____ _____
_____ _____ _____
_____ _____ _____

TERMS

_____ _____ Science
_____ _____ Applied Science
_____ _____ Technology

_____ _____ _____
_____ _____ _____
_____ _____ _____
_____ _____ _____
_____ _____ _____
_____ _____ _____

SCIENTISTS & INVENTORS

Study each scientist or inventor in light of their religion and it's influence on their work.

_____ _____ Ampère, André-Marie (France, 1775-1836)—Mathematician and Physicist: Ampere=Unit of Current, Electronics, Physics, Mathematics

_____ _____ Appleton, Sir Edward Victor (England, 1892-1965)—Physicist: Ionosphere Layer of Atmosphere

_____ _____ Archimedes (Greece, c.287-212 BC)—Mathematician, Archimedes Screw, Formula for Areas and Volumes of Spheres, Cylinders, etc.

_____ _____ Aristotle (Greece, 384-322 BC)—Philosopher and Scientist: Classification of Animals, Logic, Metaphysics, Spontaneous Generation

_____ _____ Avery, Oswald Theodore (Canada/New York, 1877-1955)—Bacteriologist: DNA and Heredity

_____ _____ Bacon, Roger (England, c.1214-1294)—Philosopher and Scientist: Magnifying Glass, Gunpowder

_____ _____ Barnard, Christiaan (South Africa, 1922-)—Surgeon: First Successful Human Heart Transplant

_____ _____ Bayer, Johann (German, 1572-1625)—Astronomer: Star Atlas

_____ _____ Beaumont, William (Connecticut, 1785-1853)—Physician: Contributed to the Modern Studies on Digestion

_____ _____ Bell, Alexander Graham (Scotland/Massachusetts, 1847-1922)—Physicist: Telephones, Electronics

_____ _____ Benz, Karl (Germany, 1844-1929)—Internal Combustion Engines

_____ _____ Bernoulli, Daniel (Switzerland, 1700-1782)—Bernoulli's Principle, Physics, Trigonometry

_____ _____ Blackwell, Elizabeth (New York, 1821-1910)—First Woman Physician in U.S.

_____ _____ Bohr, Niels (Denmark,1885-1962)—Bohr Model, Atomic Structure, Radiation

_____ _____ Boyle, Robert (Ireland, 1627-1691)—Christian Physicist: Vacuum Pump, Boyle's Law, founder of Modern Chemistry

_____ _____ Brahe, Tycho (Sweden, 1546-1601)—Astronomer: Astronomical Tables

_____ _____ Bunsen, Robert (German, 1811-99)—Chemist and Physicist: Spectroscope, Bunsen Burner, Galvanic Battery

_____ _____ Burbank, Luther (Massachusetts/California, 1849-1926)—Botanist: Potato

_____ _____ Carver, George Washington (Missouri/Alabama, 1864-1943)—Scientist and Teacher: Botany, Peanuts, Sweet Potatoes, Soybeans, Tuskegee Institute, Chemistry

_____ _____ Cavendish, Henry (England, 1731-1810)—Chemist and Physicist: Discovered Hydrogen, Determined the Mass of the Earth

_____ _____ Celsius, Anders (Sweden, 1701-1744)—Developed the Celsium Scale for Measuring Temperature

_____ _____ Charles, Jacques (France, 1746-1823)—Physicist: Charles' Law, Pressure, Hydrogen Balloon, Physics

_____ _____ Colt, Samuel (Connecticut, 1836-1962)—Inventor: Handgun, Chemistry

_____ _____ Copernicus, Nicolas (Poland, 1473-1543)—Astronomer: Heliocentric Theory, On The Revolution of the Heavenly Bodies

_____ _____ Coriolis, Gustave-Gaspard (France, 1792-1843)—Physicist: Coriolis Effect, First to Coin the Term "Kinetic Energy"

_____ _____ Coulomb, Charles (France, 1736-1806)—Laws of Magnetic and Electrical Attraction and Repulsion, Coulomb=Unit of Electrical Quantity, Friction, Physics, Electronics

_____ _____ Cousteau, Jacques (France, 1910-)—Naval Officer and Underwater Explorer

_____ _____ Crick, Francis Harry (England, 1916-)—Molecular Biologist: Discovered the Structure of DNA (along with James Watson, Maurice Wilkins, and Rosalind Franklin)

_____ _____ Curie, Marie (Poland/France, 1867-1934)—Radium, Chemistry, Geology, Magnetism, Radioactivity, Physics

_____ _____ Dalton, John (England, 1766-1844)—Quaker Chemist: Atomic Theory, Dalton's Law, Color Blindness

_____ _____ Darwin, Charles (England, 1809-1882)—Evolutionary Theory

_____ _____ Descartes, René du Perron (France, 1596-1650)—Philosopher, Scientist, and Mathematician: Rainbow Formation

_____ _____ Doppler, Christian Johann (Austria, 1803-1853)—Doppler Effect

_____ _____ Eastman, George (New York, 1854-1932)—Inventor: Photography, Box Camera

_____ _____ Edison, Thomas Alva (Ohio, 1847-1931)—Inventor: Electricity, Phonographs, Battery, Light Bulb, Mimeograph Machine, Motion Picture Equipment, Physics, Electronics

_____ _____ Einstein, Albert (Germany/New Jersey, 1879-1955)—Physicist: Theory of Relativity, Manhattan Project, Mathematics

_____ _____ Ehrlich, Paul (Germany, 1854-1915)—Physician: Bacteriologist, and Chemist, First to Use Chemotherapy

_____ _____ Espy, James Pollard (Pennsylvania, 1785-1860)—Meteorologist: First Annual Weather Reports (1843), Pioneer in Weather Forecasting

_____ _____ Ewing, William Maurice (Texas, 1913-1974)—Oceanographer: Ocean Mapping

_____ _____ Fahrenheit, Gabriel (Poland, 1686-1736)—Physicist: Fahrenheit Scale of Measuring Temperature, Alcohol Thermometer, Mercury Thermometer

_____ _____ Faraday, Michael (England, 1791-1867)—Physicist: Magnetic "Lines of Force," Developed First Electric Generator, Laws of Electrolysis, Chemistry

_____ _____ Fermi, Enrico (Italy, 1901-1954)—Physicist: Investigated the Neutron Bombardment of Uranium Which Led to the Development of the Atomic Bomb

_____ _____ Fleming, Sir Alexander (Scotland, 1881-1955)—Physicist and Bacteriologist: Penicillin, Invented First Vacuum Tube, Biology

_____ _____ Ford, Henry (Michigan, 1863-1947)—Industrialist: Gasoline Engine, Automobile, Assembly Line Production, Physics, Electronics

_____ _____ Foucault, Jean Bernard (France, 1819-1868)—Physicist: Measuring Velocity of Light Using Mirrors, Invented Foucault Pendulum

_____ _____ Franklin, Benjamin (Massachusetts, 1706-1790)—Statesman, Writer, Scientist, and Deist: Electricity, Physics, Lightning Rod

_____ _____ Galileo, Galilei (Italy, 1564-1642)—Astronomer: Telescope, Acceleration, Motion, Gravity, Jupiter moons, Physics, Mathematics

_____ _____ Galton, Sir Francis (England, 1822-1911)—Anthropologist and Explorer: Introduced Modern Symbols for Mapping the Weather

_____ _____ Gilbert, William (England, 1544-1603)—Physician and Physicist: Discovered Terrestrial Magnetism, Earth Science, Geology, Physics

_____ _____ Goddard, Robert (Massachusetts, 1882-1945)—Physicist: Rockets

_____ _____ Grosseteste, Robert (England,1168-1253)—Father of Scientific Method

_____ _____ Gutenberg, Johann (German, 1398-1468)—Printer: Printing Press, Movable Type, Gutenberg Bible

_____ _____ Hale, George Ellery (Illinois, 1868-1938)—Astrophysicist: Hale Telescope

_____ _____ Halley, Edmond (England, 1650-1742)—Astronomer: Halley's Comet

_____ _____ Hansen, Armauer Gerhard (Norway, 1841-1912)—Bacteriologist: Discovered Bacterium Responsible for Leprosy

_____ _____ Hippocrates (Greece, 460?-377? BC)—Physician: School of Medicine, Biology, Anatomy, Father of Medicine, Hippocratic Oath

_____ _____ Herschel, Sir William (England, 1738-1822)—Astronomer: Reflecting Telescope, Celestial Photography, Photo Active Chemicals, Wave Theory of Light

_____ _____ Hooke, Robert (England, 1635-1703)—Chemist and Physicist: Compound Microscope, Hooke's Law, Balance Spring for Watches, Physics

_____ _____ Hounsfield, Sir Godfrey (England, 1919-)—Physicist: Developed CAT (X-Ray Computer-Assisted Tomography)

_____ _____ Howard, Luke (England, 1772-1864)—Amateur Meteorologist: First to Publish a Classification System for Clouds

_____ _____ Howe, Elias (Massachusetts, 1819-1867)—Inventor: Sewing Machine

_____ _____ Hubble, Edwin Powell (Missouri, 1889-1953)—Astronomer: Expanding Universe, Hubble Constant, Hubble Space Telescope Named after Him

_____ _____ Huygens, Christiaan (Netherlands, 1629-1695)—Astronomer: Wave Theory of Light, Pendulum Clock, Physics, Saturn, Polarization

_____ _____ Jenner, Edward (England, 1749-1823)—Physician: Immunology, Vaccine for Smallpox, Life Science, Chemistry

_____ _____ Joule, James (England, 1818-1889)—First Law of Thermodynamics

_____ _____ Kelvin, Lord (Ireland, 1824-1907)—Mathematician, Physicist, and Chemist: Absolute Scale of Temperature: Kelvin Scale, Weather, Thermodynamics, Electricity, Magnetism, Hydrodynamics

_____ _____ Kepler, Johannes (Germany, 1571-1630)—Astronomer: Laws of Planetary Motion

_____ _____ Land, Edwin Herbert (Connecticut, 1909-1991)—Physicist: Photography, Polarizing Filter

_____ _____ Lavoisier, Antoine (France, 1743-1794)—Chemist: Oxygen, Foundations of Modern Chemistry

_____ _____ Leakey, Dr. Louis (Kenya, 1903-1972)—Archaeologist: Anthropologist

_____ _____ Leeuwenhoek, Anton van (Holland, 1632-1723)—Microscopist: Circulation of Blood, Discovered Numerous Organisms

_____ _____ Linnaeus, Carolus (Sweden, 1707-1778)—Botanist: Plant Classification System, Botany

_____ _____ Lister, Joseph (Scotland, 1827-1912)—Surgeon: Antiseptics, Medicine, Biology

_____ _____ Lyell, Sir Charles (Scotland, 1797-1875)—Geological Time, Uniformitarianism

_____ _____ Mach, Ernst (Austria, 1838-1916)—Airflow and the Speed of Sound, Mach Speed was Named After Him

_____ _____ Malpighi, Marcello (Italy, 1628-1684)—Botanist: Plant Anatomy

_____ _____ Marconi, Guglielmo (Italy, 1874-1937)—Physicist and Inventor: Radio Signals, Electronics, Physics

_____ _____ Maxwell, James Clerk (Scotland, 1831-1879)—Founder of Modern Physics

_____ _____ McCormick, Cyrus (Virginia, 1809-1884)—Industrialist and Inventor: Mechanical Reaper

_____ _____ Mendel, Gregor Johann (Austria, 1822-1884)—Botanist: Genetics, Hybrids

_____ _____ Mendeleyv, Dmitri (Russia, 1834-1907)—Chemist: Periodic Classification of Chemical Elements, Chemistry

_____ _____ Michelson, Albert (Illinois, 1852-1931)—Physicist: Speed of Light

_____ _____ Milne, John (England, 1850-1913)—Seismologist and Geologist: Invented Seismograph for Measuring Earthquake Waves

_____ _____ Mohs, Friedrich (Germany, 1773-1839)—Mineralogist: Developed Mohs' Scale for Hardness (Minerals), Geology

_____ _____ Morse, Samuel (Massachusetts, 1791-1872)—Artist and Inventor: Telegraph, Morse Code, Electronics, Physics, Communication, "What hath God wrought?"

_____ _____ Napier, John (Scotland, 1550-1617)—Mathematician: Logarithm Tables

_____ _____ Needham, John (England, 1713-1781)—Naturalist: Spontaneous Generation

_____ _____ Newton, Sir Isaac (England, 1642-1727)—Physicist and Mathematician: White Light, Constructed First Reflecting Telescope, Laws of Motion, Theory of Universal Gravitation, Invented Calculus, Author of Principia

_____ _____ Nobel, Alfred (Sweden, 1833-1896)—Chemist, Industrialist, Inventor: Dynamite, Instituted the Nobel Peace Prize

_____ _____ Ohm, Georg (Germany,1787-1854)—Physicist: Ohm's Law, Electricity

_____ _____ Oppenheimer, Robert (New York, 1904-1967)—Nuclear Physicist: First Atomic Bomb

_____ _____ Pascal, Blaise (France, 1623-1662)—Physicist and Theologian: Pascal's Law, Mathematics, Pressure, Adding Machine, Barometer, Hydraulic Press, Syringe, Physics

_____ _____ Pasteur, Louis (France, 1822-1895)—Microbiologist: Bacteria, Pasteurization, Rabies, Chemistry, Micro-organisms

_____ _____ Pavlov, Ivan (Russia, 1849-1936)—Physiologist: Circulation, Digestion, Pavlov Conditioning, Psychology (also see Psychology)

_____ _____ Piccard, August (Sweden, 1884-1962)—Physicist: First Human to Enter the Stratosphere, Developed the Bathyscaphe

_____ _____ Planck, Max (Germany, 1858-1947)—Physicist, Originator of Quantum Theory.

_____ _____ Ptolemy (Egypt, c.90-168)—Astronomer and Geographer: Geographia

_____ _____ Reed, Walter (Virginia, 1851-1902)—Military Surgeon: Bacteria, Typhoid Fever, Mosquito, Virus, Biology, Cuba

_____ _____ Richter, Charles Francis (Ohio, 1900-1985)—Seismologist: Developed Richter Scale for Measuring Intensity or Magnitude of Earthquakes

_____ _____ Roentgen, Wilhelm Conrad (Germany, 1845-1923)—Physicist: Discovered X-Rays

_____ _____ Salk, Jonas E.(New York, 1914-)—Physician: Polio Vaccine (1954), Medicine, Bacteria, Biology

_____ _____ Sørensen, Søren Peter Lauritz (Denmark, 1868-1939)—Chemist: Developed Standard pH Scale to Measure Acidity

_____ _____ Thales (Turkey, 624BC-547BC)—Greek Philosopher, Astronomer, and Mathematician

_____ _____ Torricelli, Evangelista (Italy, 1608-1647)—Physicist: Mercury Barometer, Weather, Meteorology, Called the "Father of Hydrodynamics."

_____ _____ Van Allen, James Alfred (Iowa, 1914-)—Physicist: Discovered Radiation Belts Circling the Earth (Van Allen Belts)

_____ _____ Vesalius, Andreas (Belgium,1514-64)— Anatomist, First Book of Human Anatomy

_____ _____ Volta, Alessandro (Italy, 1745-1827)—Physicist: Electroscope, Condenser, "Volt"=Unit of Electromotive Force, Static Electricity, Methane Gas, Electronics

_____ _____ von Braun, Wernher (Germany/Alabama, 1912-1977)—Rocket Engineer: Explorer I, Saturn Rocket

_____ _____ Watt, James (Scotland, 1736-1819)—Inventor and Engineer: Steam Engine, "Watt"=Unit of Electricity, Physics, Electronics, "horsepower"

_____ _____ Wegener, Alfred (Germany, 1880-1930)—Geologist and Meteorologist: Continental Drift, Plate Tectonics

_____ _____ Werner, Abraham Gottlob (Germany, 1750-1817)—M=Mineralogist and Geologist: Developed First Systematic Classification of Minerals

———— ———— Whitney, Eli (Massachusetts, 1765-1825)—Inventor: Cotton Gin, Process of Mass
Production
———— ———— Wright Brothers, Orville (Ohio, 1871-1948) and Wilbur (Indiana, 1867-1912)—
Aviation Pioneers: First to Fly Powered Aircraft
———— ———— ——————————————————————————————————————
———— ———— ——————————————————————————————————————
———— ———— ——————————————————————————————————————
———— ———— ——————————————————————————————————————
———— ———— ——————————————————————————————————————
———— ———— ——————————————————————————————————————
———— ———— ——————————————————————————————————————
———— ———— ——————————————————————————————————————
———— ———— ——————————————————————————————————————
———— ———— ——————————————————————————————————————

EARTH SCIENCES

GEOLOGY

(Also see Dinosaurs & The Bible, Archaeology & The Bible, and Scientist & Inventors)

Elem   Jr/Sr High

_____ _____ God's Purpose for the Earth
_____ _____ Ecology, Conservation, and Stewardship
_____ _____ Careers in Geology
_____ _____ Creationism vs. Evolutionary Theory (See Creation pg. 24, Archaeology, pg. 22)
_____ _____ _____
_____ _____ _____
_____ _____ _____
_____ _____ _____
_____ _____ _____

EARTH'S COMPOSITION AND LANDFORMS

_____ _____ Composition of the Earth (Crust, Mantle, Outer Core, Inner Core)
_____ _____ Soil Types (Clay, Silt, Sand, Loam)
_____ _____ Landforms (Mountains, Hills, Valleys, Plains, Plateaus, Caves)
_____ _____ Geological Time Scale
_____ _____ _____
_____ _____ _____
_____ _____ _____
_____ _____ _____
_____ _____ _____

ROCKS & MINERALS

_____ _____ Chemical Properties (Burning, Acid Reaction)
_____ _____ Coal
_____ _____ Common Uses of Rocks (i.e. Roads, Dental Powders, Steel, Glass, Cement, Monuments, Table Tops, Roofing, Building Stones, Railroad Beds)
_____ _____ Common Uses of Minerals (i.e. Sandpaper, Aluminum Products, Cement, Chalk, China, Electrical Wire, Gems, Insecticides, Batteries, Thermometers, Paints, Lead Pencils, Wallboard, Salt, Coins, Jewelry, Fillings, Tin Products)
_____ _____ Composition
_____ _____ Crystals
_____ _____ Double Refraction
_____ _____ Fluorescence
_____ _____ Identification (Hardness, Mohs' Scale of Hardness, Color, Streak, Cleavage, Fracture, Crystal Shape, Luster, Specific Gravity, Striations)
_____ _____ Magma
_____ _____ Magnetism
_____ _____ Oil and Natural Gas

_____ _____ Radioactivity
_____ _____ Sedimentary, Metamorphic, Igneous
_____ _____ _____
_____ _____ _____
_____ _____ _____
_____ _____ _____
_____ _____ _____
_____ _____ _____
_____ _____ _____

THE EARTH'S MOVEMENTS

_____ _____ Movement of Earth's Crust (Plate Tectonics)
_____ _____ Erosion and Weathering
_____ _____ Earthquakes (Richter Scale, Mercalli Scale, Seismologist)
_____ _____ Volcanoes (Active, Intermittent, Dormant, Extinct)
_____ _____ Tsunamis
_____ _____ _____
_____ _____ _____
_____ _____ _____
_____ _____ _____

PEOPLE (see Scientists & Inventors, page 138)

_____ _____ _____
_____ _____ _____
_____ _____ _____
_____ _____ _____
_____ _____ _____
_____ _____ _____
_____ _____ _____
_____ _____ _____
_____ _____ _____
_____ _____ _____

TERMS

_____ _____	Catastrophism		_____ _____	Silt
_____ _____	Cavern		_____ _____	Soil
_____ _____	Column		_____ _____	Stalagmite
_____ _____	Crust		_____ _____	Stalactite
_____ _____	Dikes		_____ _____	Unconformity
_____ _____	Erosion		_____ _____	Uniformitarianism
_____ _____	Groundwater		_____ _____	Weathering
_____ _____	Humus		_____ _____	_____
_____ _____	Intrusion		_____ _____	_____
_____ _____	Magma		_____ _____	_____
_____ _____	Sediments		_____ _____	_____
_____ _____	Sills			

METEOROLOGY
(Weather & Climate)

Elem   Jr/Sr High

_____ _____ Air Pollution and Stewardship

_____ _____ Careers in Meteorology

_____ _____ _____

WEATHER

_____ _____ Effects of Weather on Man

_____ _____ Effects of Weather on Plants and Animals

_____ _____ Storms (Blizzards, Cyclone, Hurricanes, Rainstorms, Snowstorms, Thunderstorm, Tornadoes, Typhoon)

_____ _____ Weather Forecasts (Short Range, Long Range)

_____ _____ Weather Fronts (Warm, Cold, Stationary, Occluded)

_____ _____ Weather Safety

_____ _____ Weather Map

_____ _____ _____

_____ _____ _____

_____ _____ _____

_____ _____ _____

_____ _____ _____

_____ _____ _____

CLIMATE

_____ _____ Barometers—Atmospheric Pressure

_____ _____ Causes of Wind (Convection Eell, Coriolis Effect)

_____ _____ Cloud Formations (Altostratus, Altocumulus, Cirrocumulus, Cirrostratus, Cirrus, Cumulonimbus, Cumulus, Nimbostratus, Stratus, Stratocumulus,)

_____ _____ Composition of the Atmosphere

_____ _____ Conduction, Convection

_____ _____ Evaporation, Humidity, Condensation, Ground Fog, Dew Point

_____ _____ Major Wind Systems (Anticyclones, Chinook, Cyclone, Doldrums, Easterly Trades, Horse Latitude, Jet Streams, Land breezes, Monsoons, Prevailing Winds, Sea Breezes)

_____ _____ Precipitation (Dew, Drizzle, Fog, Freezing Rain, Hail, Rain, Sleet, Snow)

_____ _____ Rainbow

_____ _____ Structure of Atmosphere (Exosphere, Mesosphere, Stratosphere, Thermosphere, Troposphere)

_____ _____ Temperature (also see page 134, 160, 165)

_____ _____ Weather Balloons

_____ _____ _____

_____ _____ _____

_____ _____ _____

PEOPLE (see Scientists & Inventors, page 138)

_____ _____ _____
_____ _____ _____
_____ _____ _____
_____ _____ _____
_____ _____ _____
_____ _____ _____
_____ _____ _____
_____ _____ _____

TERMS

_____ _____	Air Mass	_____ _____ Polar
_____ _____	Air Pressure	_____ _____ Precipitation
_____ _____	Arid	_____ _____ Rain Gauge
_____ _____	Atmosphere	_____ _____ Rotation
_____ _____	Ball Lightning	_____ _____ Seasons
_____ _____	Barometer	_____ _____ Sleet
_____ _____	Beaufort Wind Scale	_____ _____ Solar Radiation
_____ _____	Breeze	_____ _____ Storm Surge
_____ _____	Climate	_____ _____ Temperature
_____ _____	Cloud	_____ _____ Thunderstorm
_____ _____	Condensation	_____ _____ Tornado
_____ _____	Dew Point	_____ _____ Tornado Watch
_____ _____	Doppler Radar	_____ _____ Tropical
_____ _____	Evaporation	_____ _____ Water Cycle
_____ _____	Eye of Storm	_____ _____ Weather Station
_____ _____	Fog	_____ _____ Weather Tracking
_____ _____	Forecast	_____ _____ Weather Vane
_____ _____	Front	_____ _____ Wind
_____ _____	Frost	_____ _____ Wind Chill
_____ _____	Greenhouse Warming	_____ _____ Wind Direction
_____ _____	Halo	_____ _____ Wind Speed
_____ _____	Hail	_____ _____ Windmill
_____ _____	Humidity	
_____ _____	Hurricane	
_____ _____	Ice Age	
_____ _____	Isobars	
_____ _____	Jet Stream	
_____ _____	Lightning	
_____ _____	Mediterranean	
_____ _____	Monsoon	
_____ _____	Occluded	
_____ _____	Ozone	

OCEANOGRAPHY & MARINE BIOLOGY

Elem   Jr/Sr High

_____ _____ Glaciers
_____ _____ Water Travel and Transportation
_____ _____ Water Pollution and Stewardship
_____ _____ Careers in Oceanography
_____ _____ Water Safety

_____ _____ _____
_____ _____ _____

MAIN BODIES OF WATER ON EARTH

_____ _____ Location of World's Main Bodies of Water (Arctic Ocean, Atlantic Ocean, Indian
                   Ocean, Pacific Ocean, and Mediterranean Sea)
_____ _____ Lakes & Ponds
_____ _____ Rivers & Streams (Source, Banks, Mouth, Courses)
_____ _____ Animal Life in Fresh Water
_____ _____ Plant Life in Fresh Water
_____ _____ Animal Life in Brackish Water
_____ _____ Plant Life in Brackish Water

_____ _____ _____
_____ _____ _____

OCEAN LIFE AND COMPOSITION

_____ _____ Composition of Water
_____ _____ Currents, Waves
_____ _____ Hydrosphere
_____ _____ Natural Resources in Oceans (Availability and Use of)
_____ _____ Ocean Floor (Continental Shelf, Abyssal Plains, Mountain Ridges, Ridges)
_____ _____ Animal Life in Salt Water
_____ _____ Plant Life in Salt Water
_____ _____ Temperature
_____ _____ Zones (Photic, Bathyl, Midnight)

_____ _____ _____
_____ _____ _____
_____ _____ _____

EFFECT OF OCEANS ON HUMAN AND ANIMAL LIFE

_____ _____ Effect of Ocean on Climate and Shoreline
_____ _____ Tides (Low or Ebb Tide, High or Flood Tide, High Spring Tide, Neap Tide)

_____ _____ _____
_____ _____ _____
_____ _____ _____

OCEAN EXPLORATION

_____ _____ Sound Waves-Echo Sounder

_____ _____ _____

_____ _____ _____

_____ _____ _____

_____ _____ _____

_____ _____ _____

PEOPLE (see Scientists & Inventors, page 138)

_____ _____ _____

_____ _____ _____

_____ _____ _____

_____ _____ _____

_____ _____ _____

_____ _____ _____

TERMS

_____ _____ Abyss	_____ _____ Plankton
_____ _____ Anemone	_____ _____ Pond
_____ _____ Archipelago	_____ _____ Port
_____ _____ Battleship	_____ _____ River
_____ _____ Bay	_____ _____ Reef
_____ _____ Beach	_____ _____ Sand Dunes
_____ _____ Blubber	_____ _____ Shore
_____ _____ Bow	_____ _____ Sonar
_____ _____ Canal	_____ _____ Starboard
_____ _____ Clipper Ship	_____ _____ Stern
_____ _____ Continental Shelf	_____ _____ Stream
_____ _____ Continental Slope	_____ _____ Submarine
_____ _____ Crest	_____ _____ Tentacles
_____ _____ Crustacean	_____ _____ Tide Pool
_____ _____ Current	_____ _____ Tsunami
_____ _____ Fjord	_____ _____ Univalve
_____ _____ Gulf	_____ _____ Water Cycle
_____ _____ Gulf Stream	_____ _____ _____
_____ _____ Ichthyologist	_____ _____ _____
_____ _____ Kelp	_____ _____ _____
_____ _____ Lake	_____ _____ _____
_____ _____ Lichen	_____ _____ _____
_____ _____ Lighthouse	_____ _____ _____
_____ _____ Mollusk	_____ _____ _____
_____ _____ Ocean	_____ _____ _____
_____ _____ Ocean Liner	_____ _____ _____
_____ _____ Oceanographer	_____ _____ _____
_____ _____ Offshore Drilling	_____ _____ _____
_____ _____ Paddle Boat	_____ _____ _____

ASTRONOMY

Elem	Jr/Sr High	
_____	_____	God's Purpose for the Heavenly Bodies
_____	_____	Uses for Astronomy (Navigation, Space Travel)
_____	_____	Careers in Astronomy
_____	_____	_____
_____	_____	_____

ASTRONOMICAL TOOLS

_____	_____	Camera
_____	_____	Hale Telescope
_____	_____	Hubble Space Telescope
_____	_____	Spectroscope
_____	_____	Telescope (Refracting, Reflecting, Radio)
_____	_____	_____
_____	_____	_____
_____	_____	_____

UNIVERSE AND SOLAR SYSTEM

_____	_____	Asteroids
_____	_____	Circumpolar Constellations (Big and Little Dipper)
_____	_____	Comets
_____	_____	Constellations
_____	_____	Distance of Stars (Parallax, Actual Brightness)
_____	_____	Galaxy
_____	_____	Light Year
_____	_____	Meteors and Meteor Showers
_____	_____	Milky Way
_____	_____	Moon (See Earth's Motion)
_____	_____	Nebulae
_____	_____	Stars (Size, Magnitude, Temperature, Composition, Colors)
_____	_____	Structure of Sun (Chromosphere, Core, Corona, Photosphere, Prominences, Solar Flares, Sunspots)
_____	_____	Sun (Composition, Solar Eclipse, Size)
_____	_____	_____
_____	_____	_____

PLANETS

_____	_____	Inner Planets, Outer Planets
_____	_____	Mercury, Venus, Earth, Mars, Jupiter, Saturn, Uranus, Neptune, Pluto (**M**ost **V**ultures **E**at **M**arshmallows and **J**apanese **S**ubs, **U**sually **N**ot **P**izza)
_____	_____	Motion

_____ _____ Planet Study—Compare to Earth: Composition, Rings, Distance from Sun, Moons, Diameter, Length of Year, Length of Day, Gravity, Atmosphere, Temperature, Weight of Objects

_____ _____ Revolution

_____ _____ Rotation, Period of Rotation

_____ _____ _____

_____ _____ _____

_____ _____ _____

_____ _____ _____

EARTH'S MOTION

_____ _____ Atomic Time

_____ _____ Calendars (Julian Calendar, Gregorian Calendar)

_____ _____ Daylight Savings Time

_____ _____ Eclipses (Umbra, Penumbra)

_____ _____ Greenwich Mean Time (Universal Time)

_____ _____ International Date Line

_____ _____ Lunar Eclipses

_____ _____ Military Time (24-Hour)

_____ _____ Moon Phases, Lunar Eclipse

_____ _____ Tides and Moon (Neap, Spring Tides), also see Oceanography, page148

_____ _____ Night and Day

_____ _____ Prime Meridian (also see Geography)

_____ _____ Rotation, Axis, Tilt

_____ _____ Seasonal Time (Summer Solstice, Winter Solstice, Fall Equinox, Spring Equinox)

_____ _____ Solar Eclipse

_____ _____ _____

_____ _____ _____

TIME (also see Math, page 132)

_____ _____ Seconds   _____ _____ Days

_____ _____ Minutes   _____ _____ Months

_____ _____ Hours   _____ _____ Years

_____ _____ U.S. Time Zones

_____ _____ Standard Time

_____ _____ Daylight Savings Time

_____ _____ _____

_____ _____ _____

AVIATION & SPACE TRAVEL

_____	_____	Jet Engines, Rockets
_____	_____	Space Exploration
_____	_____	Space Shuttle
_____	_____	Space Stations
_____	_____	Space Vehicles
_____	_____	Unmanned Spacecraft

_____ _____ _____

_____ _____ _____

_____ _____ _____

_____ _____ _____

_____ _____ _____

PEOPLE (ASTRONAUTS*), see Scientists & Inventors, page 138

_____ _____ Aldrin, Edwin (New Jersey, 1930-)—Astronaut: 1966 Gemini 12 Mission, Moon Landing (1969)

_____ _____ Armstrong, Neil (Ohio, 1930-)—Astronaut: Apollo 11, First Man on Moon (1969)

_____ _____ Carpenter, Scott (Colorado, 1925-)—Astronaut: Mercury, 1959

_____ _____ Gagarin, Yuri A. (U.S.S.R., 1934-1968)—Astronaut: First Human in Space

_____ _____ Glenn, John (Ohio, 1921-)—Senator and Astronaut: First U.S. Astronaut to Orbit the Earth

_____ _____ Shepard, Alan B. (New Hampshire, 1923-)—Astronaut: First American in Space

_____ _____ _____

_____ _____ _____

_____ _____ _____

_____ _____ _____

_____ _____ _____

_____ _____ _____

_____ _____ _____

_____ _____ _____

*Astronaut Biographies: http://www.jsc.nasa.gov/Bios/astrobio_former.html\

TERMS

LIFE SCIENCES

BIOLOGY & HUMAN ANATOMY

Elem   Jr/Sr High

_____ _____ Careers in Biology
_____ _____ Biology Lab
_____ _____ Creation vs. Evolutionary Theory (also see page 24)
_____ _____ Heredity and Genetics
_____ _____ Nutrition and Metabolism
_____ _____ Disease and Immunity

CLASSIFICATION SYSTEM (ORGANISMS AND MICROORGANISMS)

_____ _____ Kingdom, Phylum, Subphylum, Class, Order, Family, Genus, Species
_____ _____ Vertebrates, Invertebrates (also see page 148 & 155)
_____ _____ _____
_____ _____ _____

KINGDOMS

_____ _____ Animalia—Animals (also see page 148 & 155)
_____ _____ Fungi
_____ _____ Monera—Algae
_____ _____ Plantae—Flowering Plants, Ferns
_____ _____ Protista—Protozoa, Algae

HUMAN ANATOMY

_____ _____ God's Purpose for Man
_____ _____ _____
_____ _____ _____
_____ _____ _____
_____ _____ _____
_____ _____ _____

FIVE SENSES

_____ _____ Touch   _____ _____ Hearing
_____ _____ Taste   _____ _____ Sight
_____ _____ Smell

BODY SYSTEMS

_____ _____ Circulatory   _____ _____ Muscular
_____ _____ Digestive   _____ _____ Nervous
_____ _____ Endocrine   _____ _____ Reproductive
_____ _____ Excretory   _____ _____ Respiratory
_____ _____ Integumentary (Skin, Hair,   _____ _____ Skeletal
                 Nails)

PEOPLE (see Scientists & Inventors, page 138)

_____ _____ _____
_____ _____ _____
_____ _____ _____
_____ _____ _____
_____ _____ _____
_____ _____ _____
_____ _____ _____
_____ _____ _____
_____ _____ _____
_____ _____ _____
_____ _____ _____

TERMS

_____ _____ Arteries

_____ _____ Autonomic Nervous System

_____ _____ Axial Skeleton

_____ _____ Axons

_____ _____ Basal Metabolic Rate

_____ _____ Capillaries

_____ _____ Carnivore

_____ _____ Cells

_____ _____ Consumers

_____ _____ Decomposers

_____ _____ Dendrites

_____ _____ Digestion

_____ _____ DNA

_____ _____ Eukaryotic Cell

_____ _____ Exoskeleton

_____ _____ Gland

_____ _____ Herbivore

_____ _____ Hormone

_____ _____ Living Organism

_____ _____ Motor Nervous System

_____ _____ Omnivore

_____ _____ Organs

_____ _____ Pathogen

_____ _____ Prokaryotic Cell

_____ _____ Producers

_____ _____ Receptors

_____ _____ Sensory Nervous System

_____ _____ Skeleton

_____ _____ Symbiosis

_____ _____ Synapse

_____ _____ Tissues

_____ _____ Vaccine

_____ _____ Vegetative Reproduction

_____ _____ Veins

_____ _____ Vitamin

_____ _____ _____

_____ _____ _____

_____ _____ _____

_____ _____ _____

_____ _____ _____

_____ _____ _____

_____ _____ _____

_____ _____ _____

_____ _____ _____

_____ _____ _____

_____ _____ _____

_____ _____ _____

ZOOLOGY
Also see Oceanography & Marine Biology, page 148

Elem   Jr/Sr High

_____ _____ God's Purpose for Animals
_____ _____ Careers in Zoology
_____ _____ Animal Identification
_____ _____ Conservation and Stewardship
_____ _____ Animal Dissection (Lab—Needed For College)
_____ _____ Microscopic Life
_____ _____ Food chains (Producers, Consumers, Decomposers)
_____ _____ Life Cycles (Animal Reproduction)
_____ _____ Animal Habitats
_____ _____ _____
_____ _____ _____
_____ _____ _____

ANIMAL STUDY & ANATOMY (INVERTEBRATES)

_____ _____ Arachnids   _____ _____ Mollusks
_____ _____ Crustaceans   _____ _____ One-Celled
_____ _____ Enchinoderms   _____ _____ Sponges, Worms
_____ _____ Insects

ANIMAL STUDY & ANATOMY (VERTEBRATES)

_____ _____ Amphibians   _____ _____ Mammals
_____ _____ Birds   _____ _____ Reptiles
_____ _____ Fish

ANIMAL HABITS AND INSTINCTS

_____ _____ Adaptation, Camouflage, and Extinction
_____ _____ Diurnal and Nocturnal
_____ _____ Migration and Hibernation
_____ _____ _____
_____ _____ _____
_____ _____ _____
_____ _____ _____

PEOPLE (see Scientists & Inventors, page 138)

_____ _____ _____
_____ _____ _____
_____ _____ _____
_____ _____ _____
_____ _____ _____
_____ _____ _____
_____ _____ _____
_____ _____ _____

_____ _____ _____   _____ _____ _____
_____ _____ _____   _____ _____ _____
_____ _____ _____   _____ _____ _____
_____ _____ _____   _____ _____ _____
_____ _____ _____   _____ _____ _____
_____ _____ _____   _____ _____ _____
_____ _____ _____   _____ _____ _____
_____ _____ _____   _____ _____ _____
_____ _____ _____   _____ _____ _____

_____ _____ **MICROBIOLOGY**

_____ _____ **ENTOMOLOGY (INSECTS)**

_____ _____ **ORNITHOLOGY (BIRDS)**

_____ _____ **HERPETOLOGY (REPTILES)**

DINOSAURS AND THE BIBLE*

Unit study and book recommendations on the Oklahoma Homeschool website:
http://www.oklahomahomeschool.com/dinosaurUnit.html.

_____ _____ Dinosaurs in the Bible
_____ _____ How Fossils are Formed
_____ _____ Restoring Dinosaur Fossils
_____ _____ Dinosaurs Types and Names
_____ _____ Dinosaur Proposed Timeline (Mesozoic Era: Triassic, Jurassic, Cretaceous)
_____ _____ Dinosaurs Life: Homes, Food, Protection
_____ _____ Dinosaur Excavation
_____ _____ Dinosaur Extinction and The Great Flood
_____ _____ Dinosaur Relatives of Today

*See also Archaeology and the Bible, page 22; Creation, page 24

BOTANY

Elem   Jr/Sr High

_____   _____   God's Purpose for Plants
_____   _____   Plant Identification and Classification
_____   _____   Practical Uses of Plants
_____   _____   Interdependency of Plants and Humans (Water Cycle, Carbon and Oxygen Cycle, Nitrogen Cycle)
_____   _____   Plant Dissection (Lab—Needed For College)
_____   _____   Unusual Plants
_____   _____   Endangered Plants
_____   _____   Gardening (Lab)
_____   _____   Careers in Botany

_____   _____   _____
_____   _____   _____
_____   _____   _____
_____   _____   _____
_____   _____   _____
_____   _____   _____

PLANT HABITATS AND BIOMES

_____   _____   Coniferous Forests   _____   _____   Scrublands
_____   _____   Deciduous Forests   _____   _____   Tropical Rain Forests
_____   _____   Deserts   _____   _____   Tundra
_____   _____   Grasslands   _____   _____   _____

PLANT ANATOMY

_____   _____   Flowers   _____   _____   Root
_____   _____   Fruit   _____   _____   Stem
_____   _____   Leaves   _____   _____   Seed

PARTS OF FLOWER

_____   _____   Ovary   _____   _____   Sepal
_____   _____   Petal   _____   _____   Stamen
_____   _____   Pistil   _____   _____   Stigma
_____   _____   Pollen Tube

PEOPLE (See Scientists & Inventors, page 138)

_____   _____   _____
_____   _____   _____
_____   _____   _____
_____   _____   _____
_____   _____   _____

LIFE CYCLE OF PLANTS & REPRODUCTION

_____ _____ What Plants Need to Grow

_____ _____ Photosynthesis

_____ _____ Respiration

_____ _____ Transpiration

_____ _____ _____

_____ _____ _____

_____ _____ _____

TERMS

_____ _____ Angiosperms   _____ _____ Pome

_____ _____ Anther   _____ _____ Radicle

_____ _____ Biennial   _____ _____ Receptacle

_____ _____ Bud   _____ _____ Rhizomes

_____ _____ Cellulose   _____ _____ Root

_____ _____ Chlorophyll   _____ _____ Root Cap

_____ _____ Chloroplast   _____ _____ Root Hair

_____ _____ Compound Leaf   _____ _____ Runners

_____ _____ Cone   _____ _____ Seed

_____ _____ Conifers   _____ _____ Sepals

_____ _____ Cotyledon   _____ _____ Spore

_____ _____ Cuttings   _____ _____ Stamen

_____ _____ Deciduous   _____ _____ Stem

_____ _____ Dicotyledon (dicot)   _____ _____ Stigma

_____ _____ Filament   _____ _____ Style

_____ _____ Flower   _____ _____ Tap Root

_____ _____ Fruit   _____ _____ Tendril

_____ _____ Gymnosperms   _____ _____ Tropism

_____ _____ Leaf   _____ _____ Tubers

_____ _____ Legume   _____ _____ Xylem

_____ _____ Monocotyledon (monocot)   _____ _____ _____

_____ _____ Node   _____ _____ _____

_____ _____ Ovaries   _____ _____ _____

_____ _____ Ovule   _____ _____ _____

_____ _____ Perennial   _____ _____ _____

_____ _____ Phloem   _____ _____ _____

_____ _____ Photosynthesis   _____ _____ _____

_____ _____ Pistil   _____ _____ _____

_____ _____ Pollen   _____ _____ _____

_____ _____ Pollination   _____ _____ _____

PHYSICAL SCIENCES

PHYSICS

Elem   Jr/Sr High

_____ _____ Physics Defined

_____ _____ Branches of Physics (Classical: Newtonian Mechanics, Thermodynamics,
Statistical Mechanics, Acoustics, Optics, Electricity, and Magnetism; Modern
Physics: Relativistic Mechanics, Atomic, Nuclear and Particle Physics, and
Quantum Physics.)

_____ _____ Careers in Physics

_____ _____ _____

_____ _____ _____

MASS AND GRAVITATION

_____ _____ Mass

_____ _____ Matter

_____ _____ Gravitation

_____ _____ _____

_____ _____ _____

MOTION

_____ _____ Acceleration

_____ _____ Angular Momentum

_____ _____ Centripetal and Centrifugal Forces

_____ _____ Force

_____ _____ Inertia

_____ _____ Momentum

_____ _____ Speed = Distance x Time

_____ _____ Torque

_____ _____ Velocity

_____ _____ _____

_____ _____ _____

BASIC LAWS OF MOTION (SIR ISAAC NEWTON)

_____ _____ Law 1 (Law of Inertia): An object at rest tends to stay at rest and an object in
motion tends to stay in motion.

_____ _____ Law 2 (Law of Constant Acceleration): The more force on an object, the more it
accelerates. The more massive it is, the more it resists acceleration.
(Force=Mass x Acceleration)

_____ _____ Law 3 (Law of Conservation of Momentum): When one object exerts a force on a
second object, the second object exerts an equal but opposite force on the first
(Action = Reaction).

WORK AND ENERGY

_____ _____ Atomic Energy
_____ _____ Conservation of Energy
_____ _____ Friction
_____ _____ Kinetic and Potential Energy
_____ _____ Measuring Energy (Joules, Calories, British Thermal Units-BTU's)
_____ _____ Measuring Force (Newtons)
_____ _____ Nuclear Energy (Radioactivity, Fission, Fusion)
_____ _____ Power = Work Divided by Time
_____ _____ Static Energy
_____ _____ Uses of Energy
_____ _____ Work = Force x Distance Object Moves in Direction of Force

_____ _____ _____
_____ _____ _____
_____ _____ _____
_____ _____ _____

SIMPLE MACHINES

_____ _____ Complex Machines
_____ _____ Force
_____ _____ Fulcrum
_____ _____ Gear
_____ _____ Inclined Plane

_____ _____ Lever (1st, 2nd, 3rd Class)
_____ _____ Pulley
_____ _____ Screw
_____ _____ Wheel & Axle
_____ _____ Wedge

SOURCES OF ENERGY

_____ _____ Coal
_____ _____ Crude Oil
_____ _____ Electricity
_____ _____ Hydro Energy

_____ _____ Natural Gas
_____ _____ Nuclear Energy
_____ _____ _____
_____ _____ _____

HEAT AND TEMPERATURE (see page 134, 146, 165)

_____ _____ Absolute Zero
_____ _____ Celsius Scale
_____ _____ Fahrenheit Scale
_____ _____ Thermodynamics

_____ _____ _____
_____ _____ _____
_____ _____ _____

LIGHT

_____ _____ Electromagnetic Waves
_____ _____ Fiber Optics
_____ _____ Light Sources
_____ _____ Light Characteristics
_____ _____ Rainbow
_____ _____ Reflection
_____ _____ Refraction
_____ _____ Spectrum
_____ _____ Speed of Light
_____ _____ _____
_____ _____ _____

SOUND

_____ _____ Doppler Effect
_____ _____ Echoes and Reverberation
_____ _____ Frequency, Pitch
_____ _____ How Sound Travels
_____ _____ Measuring Sound (Intensity, Sound Level, Decibels)
_____ _____ Sound Effects
_____ _____ Speed of Sound
_____ _____ Ultrasound
_____ _____ Waves
_____ _____ _____
_____ _____ _____
_____ _____ _____

LAB WORK (Needed For College)

_____ _____ Model Building
_____ _____ Scientific Method
_____ _____ _____
_____ _____ _____
_____ _____ _____

USES OF PHYSICS

_____ _____ Navigation
_____ _____ Transportation (Air, Land, Sea)
_____ _____ Warfare
_____ _____ Construction
_____ _____ _____
_____ _____ _____
_____ _____ _____

PEOPLE (see Scientists & Inventors, page 138)

_____ _____ _____
_____ _____ _____
_____ _____ _____
_____ _____ _____
_____ _____ _____
_____ _____ _____
_____ _____ _____
_____ _____ _____
_____ _____ _____

TERMS

_____ _____ _____   _____ _____ _____
_____ _____ _____   _____ _____ _____
_____ _____ _____   _____ _____ _____
_____ _____ _____   _____ _____ _____
_____ _____ _____   _____ _____ _____
_____ _____ _____   _____ _____ _____
_____ _____ _____   _____ _____ _____
_____ _____ _____   _____ _____ _____
_____ _____ _____   _____ _____ _____
_____ _____ _____   _____ _____ _____

ELECTRICITY AND ELECTRONICS

Elem   Jr/Sr High

ELECTRICITY AND MAGNETISM

_____ _____ Battery
_____ _____ Charge (Positive, Negative)
_____ _____ Compass
_____ _____ Conductors of Electricity
_____ _____ Electric Current (Alternating Current-AC, Direct Current-DC)
_____ _____ Electromagnetism
_____ _____ Electrons, Neutrons, Protons, Ions
_____ _____ Generating Electricity (Galvanometer, Michael Faraday)
_____ _____ Ground (Electrical)
_____ _____ Insulators
_____ _____ Magnetism, Magnetic Lines of Force, Earth's Magnetic Pole
_____ _____ Measuring Electricity (Amperes, Volts, Ohms, Watts)
_____ _____ Ohm's Law (Force = Current x Resistance)
_____ _____ Polarization
_____ _____ Resistance
_____ _____ Volts
_____ _____ Watts

_____ _____ _____
_____ _____ _____
_____ _____ _____

CIRCUITS

_____ _____ Closed   _____ _____ Parallel
_____ _____ Open   _____ _____ Series

ELECTRONIC COMPONENTS

_____ _____ Capacitor   _____ _____ Silicon Chip
_____ _____ Circuit Board   _____ _____ Switch
_____ _____ Connectors   _____ _____ Transformer
_____ _____ Diode   _____ _____ _____
_____ _____ LED   _____ _____ _____
_____ _____ Photoelectric Cell   _____ _____ _____

USES OF ELECTRONICS

_____ _____ Appliances (Household)   _____ _____ _____
_____ _____ Computer Equipment   _____ _____ _____
_____ _____ Entertainment Equipment   _____ _____ _____
_____ _____ Tools   _____ _____ _____

CHEMISTRY

Elem   Jr/Sr High

_____ _____ Practical Uses of Chemistry (Archaeology, Warfare, Nutrition, Energy, Astronomy, Consumer Goods, Forensic Science, Art, Medicine)

_____ _____ Environment (Air Pollution and Hazardous Wastes)

_____ _____ Careers in Chemistry

_____ _____ _____

_____ _____ _____

_____ _____ _____

_____ _____ _____

_____ _____ _____

_____ _____ _____

_____ _____ _____

_____ _____ _____

MATTER

_____ _____ Catalyst—Affects Speed of Chemical Reaction

_____ _____ Changes in States (Physical, Chemical, and Nuclear Changes)

_____ _____ Chemical Change—Forms New Substance

_____ _____ Chemical Properties—Describes its Ability to Form New Substances

_____ _____ Mass, Weight, and Volume

_____ _____ Matter—Anything That Has Mass and Occupies Space

_____ _____ Matter—Made up of Elements, Compounds, and Mixtures

_____ _____ Metals and Nonmetals

_____ _____ Physical Properties—Describes Matter As It Is (Density, Specific Gravity, Hardness, Odor, Color)

_____ _____ Physical Change—Modification of Properties, No Change in Substance

_____ _____ States of Matter (Solids, Liquids, and Gases)

_____ _____ _____

_____ _____ _____

_____ _____ _____

_____ _____ _____

_____ _____ _____

ATOMS AND MOLECULES

_____ _____ Atom—Smallest Particle of Element

_____ _____ Atomic Structure (Electrons, Protons, Neutrons)

_____ _____ Atomic Number

_____ _____ Atomic Weight

_____ _____ Bohr Model

_____ _____ Elements

_____ _____ Isotopes

_____ _____ Periodic Table

_____ _____ Radicals
_____ _____ _____
_____ _____ _____
_____ _____ _____
_____ _____ _____
_____ _____ _____
_____ _____ _____

HEAT AND TEMPERATURE (see page 134, 146, 160)

_____ _____ Evaporation
_____ _____ Freezing Point, Boiling Point, Melting Point
_____ _____ Heat Flow (Radiation, Conduction, Convection)
_____ _____ Thermodynamics and Heat Energy
_____ _____ Three Laws of Thermodynamics (1) Energy cannot be created or destroyed.
　　　　　　　　(2) Heat will always flow from an area of higher temperature to an area of
　　　　　　　　lower temperature. (3) It is impossible to reach the state of absolute zero.
_____ _____ Measuring Heat (Joules, Calories, British Thermal Units-BTU's)
_____ _____ Measuring Temperature (Fahrenheit, Celsius, Converting Fahrenheit to Celsius and
　　　　　　　　vice versa, Kelvin)
_____ _____ _____
_____ _____ _____
_____ _____ _____
_____ _____ _____

ORGANIC CHEMISTRY

_____ _____ Acids
_____ _____ Alcohols
_____ _____ Esters
_____ _____ Ethers
_____ _____ Hydrocarbons
_____ _____ Ketones
_____ _____ Liquid Crystals
_____ _____ Oxidation and Reduction

_____ _____ Plastics and Synthetics
_____ _____ _____
_____ _____ _____
_____ _____ _____
_____ _____ _____
_____ _____ _____
_____ _____ _____
_____ _____ _____

PEOPLE (see Scientists & Inventors, page 138)

_____ _____ _____
_____ _____ _____
_____ _____ _____
_____ _____ _____
_____ _____ _____
_____ _____ _____
_____ _____ _____
_____ _____ _____

_____ _____	Acid	_____ _____ Molecules
_____ _____	Alkali	_____ _____ Molecular Weight
_____ _____	Bases	_____ _____ Neutralize
_____ _____	Bonding (Hydrogen, Covalent, Ionic)	_____ _____ Oxidation and Reduction
_____ _____	Cations, Anions, Molecular Orbitals	_____ _____ pH
_____ _____	Chromatography	_____ _____ Precipitate
_____ _____	Colloids	_____ _____ Reactions
_____ _____	Compounds	_____ _____ Reaction Rates
_____ _____	Decompose	_____ _____ Salts
_____ _____	Dehydrating	_____ _____ Saturated
_____ _____	Dilution	_____ _____ Solute
_____ _____	Distillation	_____ _____ Solution
_____ _____	Equilibrium	_____ _____ Solvent
_____ _____	Extraction	_____ _____ Solubility
_____ _____	Filtration	_____ _____ Substance
_____ _____	Formula	_____ _____ Valence
_____ _____	Inert	_____ _____ Volatile
_____ _____	Ions	_____ _____ _____
_____ _____	Isotopes	_____ _____ _____
_____ _____	Magnetic Separation	_____ _____ _____
_____ _____	Mixture	_____ _____ _____
_____ _____	Mole	_____ _____ _____

ART & ART HISTORY/APPRECIATION

Elem   Jr/Sr High

_____ _____ God's Purpose for Art (Ex. 35:30-35, 1 Chron. 23:5)
_____ _____ Practical Uses of Art
_____ _____ Careers in Art

Art Technique and Principles

_____ _____ Knows the Primary Colors
_____ _____ Understands the Color Wheel
_____ _____ Basic Drawing Skills —Colored Pencils
_____ _____ Basic Drawing Skills —Pencil
_____ _____ Basic Drawing Skills —Chalk
_____ _____ Basic Drawing Skills —Cartooning
_____ _____ Basic Drawing Skills —Pen & Ink
_____ _____ Basic Painting Skills—Tempera Paints
_____ _____ Basic Painting Skills—Watercolors
_____ _____ Basic Painting Skills—Oils
_____ _____ Basic Painting Skills—Acrylic

_____ _____ _____
_____ _____ _____

Other Art Mediums

_____ _____ Calligraphy
_____ _____ Ceramics and Pottery
_____ _____ Clay
_____ _____ Costuming for Drama
_____ _____ Crayon
_____ _____ Crewel
_____ _____ Crochet
_____ _____ Cut Paper & Origami
_____ _____ Embroidery
_____ _____ Jewelry and Metalwork
_____ _____ Knitting
_____ _____ Leather Crafting

_____ _____ Makeup for Drama
_____ _____ Musical Instruments (Creating)
_____ _____ Photography
_____ _____ Quilt Making
_____ _____ Sculpting
_____ _____ Staging for Drama
_____ _____ Tatting
_____ _____ Wood Carving
_____ _____ Weaving
_____ _____ _____
_____ _____ _____

Computer Graphics

_____ _____ Animation Software
_____ _____ Draw/Paint Software
_____ _____ Presentation Software
_____ _____ 3-D Software
_____ _____ Video Editing Software

_____ _____ _____
_____ _____ _____

FAMOUS WORKS OF ARCHITECTURE

_____ _____	Arc de Triomphe	_____ _____ World Trade Center
_____ _____	Empire State Building	_____ _____ _____
_____ _____	Leaning Tower of Pisa	_____ _____ _____
_____ _____	Pantheon	_____ _____ _____
_____ _____	St. Louis Gateway Arch	_____ _____ _____
_____ _____	Taj Mahal	_____ _____ _____

NOTE: USE CAUTION IN SELECTING ART WORKS FOR YOUR CHILDREN TO VIEW.

AMERICAN ARTISTS

_____ _____ Audubon, John James (Haiti/Pennsylvania, 1785-1851)—Ornithologist and Bird Artist: *Birds of America*, National Audubon Society

_____ _____ Butcher, Sam (Michigan, 1939-)—Illustrator, Precious Moments Figures

_____ _____ Calder, Alexander (Pennsylvania, 1898-1976)—Mobiles

_____ _____ Cassatt, Mary (Pennsylvania, 1845-1926)—Impressionism: *The Cup of Tea*

_____ _____ Homer, Winslow (Massachusetts, 1836-1910)—Painter: *Prisoners at the Front*

_____ _____ Kinkade, Thomas (California, 1958-)—Christian called the "Painter of Lights"

_____ _____ Lawrence, Jacob (New Jersey, 1917-2000)—Abstracts: Historical Works

_____ _____ O'Keeffe, Georgia (Wisconsin, 1887-1986)—Modern Art: Flowers

_____ _____ Remington, Frederic (New York, 1861-1909)—Painter, Sculptor, and Illustrator: *American West, Bronco Buster, Calvary Charge on the South Plain*

_____ _____ Ringgold, Faith (New York, 1930-)—Painted Story Quilts

_____ _____ Rockwell, Norman (New York, 1894-1978)—Illustrator: Small Town America, *The Four Freedoms*

_____ _____ Stuart, Gilbert (Rhode Island, 1755-1828)—Portrait Painter: *Washington, Jefferson*

_____ _____ Trumball, John (Connecticut, 1756-1843)—Historical Painter: *The Declaration of Independence*

_____ _____ Warhol, Andy (Pennsylvania, 1928-1987)—Pop Art Movement

_____ _____ West, Benjamin (Pennsylvania/England, 1738-1820)—Painter: Portraits, Founded Royal Academy, *The Death of Wolfe*

_____ _____ Whistler, James McNeill (Massachusetts, 1834-1903)—Painter: Etchings, *Evening Scenes, Whistler's Mother*

_____ _____ Wright, Frank Lloyd (Wisconsin, 1869-1959)—Architect: Imperial Hotel

_____ _____ Wyeth, Andrew (Pennsylvania, 1917-)—Painter of Landscapes: *Christina's World*

_____ _____ _____

_____ _____ _____

_____ _____ _____

_____ _____ _____

_____ _____ _____

ARTISTS OF THE WORLD

_____ _____ Botticelli, Sandro (Italy, 1444-1510)—Painter: Frescoes, *Birth of Venus*

_____ _____ Cezanne, Paul (France, 1839-1906)—Post-Impressionistic: *Peaches & Pears*

_____ _____ Chagall, Marc (Russia, 1887-1985)— *Eu e a vila (Enchanted Village)*

_____ _____ Dali, Salvador (Spain, 1904-1989)—Surrealist: *The Rose, The Melting Watch*

_____ _____ da Vinci, Leonardo (Italy, 1452-1519)—Painter, Architect, Inventor, and Sculptor: *Mona Lisa, The Last Supper*

_____ _____ Degas, Edgar (France, 1834-1917)—Artist: *Dancer Lacing Her Shoe*

_____ _____ Dürer, Albrecht (Germany, 1471-1528)—Painter, Engraver: *Adam and Eve*

_____ _____ El Greco (Greece, 1541-1614)—Renaissance Art, *Assumption of the Virgin*

_____ _____ Gainsborough, Thomas (England, 1727-1788)—Landscapes, Portraits: *The Blue Boy*

_____ _____ Gauguin, Paul (France, 1848-1903)—Painter: *Breton Girls Dancing, Pont-Aven*

_____ _____ Giotto di Bondone (Italy, 1266-1337)—Painter, Architect, Frescoes, Florentine School of Painting

_____ _____ Goya (Spain, 1746-1828)—Frescoes, Portraits, *The Sleep of Reason Produces Monsters*

_____ _____ Kahlo, Frida (Mexico, 1907-1954)—Communist Militant, Surrealism: *Still Life With Parrot* (Recommended. Use caution viewing his website.)

_____ _____ Klee, Paul (Switzerland, 1879-1940)—Modernistic Painter: *Dream City*

_____ _____ Hokusai, Katsushika (Japan, 1760-1849)—Painter, Engraver: *Boy On Mt. Fuji*

_____ _____ Holbein, Hans (Germany, 1497-1543)—Religious Paintings, Portraits, *The French Ambassadors*

_____ _____ Matisse, Henri (France, 1869-1954)—Painter: *Red Room*

_____ _____ Michelangelo (Italy, 1475-1564)—Sculptor, Painter: Sistine Chapel, *David, Creation of Adam, Last Judgment*

_____ _____ Miro, Joan (Spain, 1893-1983)—Surrealism/Fantasy: *Vegetable Garden With Donkey*

_____ _____ Mondrian, Piet (Holland, 1872-1944)—Abstract Artist: Neoplasticism, *Composition with Red, Yellow, and Blue*

_____ _____ Monet, Claude (France, 1840-1926)—Impressionistic Painter: *Haystacks*

_____ _____ Picasso, Pablo (Spain, 1881-1973)—Cubism, Costume Design, *Tete de Femme*

_____ _____ Raeburn, Sir Henry (Scotland, 1756-1823)—Water Color Miniatures, Oils, *The McNab*

_____ _____ Raphael (Italy, 1483-1520)—Painter: *Crucifixion, Holy Family, The Transfiguration*

_____ _____ Rembrandt van Rijn (Netherlands, 1606-1669)—Portraits, Oils, Drawings, *The Night Watch, Moses Smashing The Commandments*

_____ _____ Renoir, Auguste (France, 1841-1919)—Portraits, Impressionistic, *Jeanne Samary*

_____ _____ Rousseau, Henri (France, 1844-1910)—Portraits, Imaginary Landscapes, *Outskirts of the Forest of Fontaine Bleau*

_____ _____ Ruysdael, Jacob van (Holland, 1628-1682)—Landscapes: *Landscape With a Footbridge*

_____ _____ Seurat, Georges (France, 1859-1891)—Pointism: *A Sunday on La Grande Jatte*

_____ _____ Toulouse-Lautrec (France, 1864-1901)—Alcoholic Painter and Lithographer: Actors, Barmaids, *LaGoulou Entering the Moulin Rouge*

_____ _____ van Gogh, Vincent (Holland, 1853-1890)—Painter: Expressionism, *Wheatfield and Cypress Trees, In The Orchard*

_____ _____ _____

_____ _____ _____

_____ _____ _____

_____ _____ _____

_____ _____ _____

MUSIC & MUSIC HISTORY/APPRECIATION

Elem   Jr/Sr High

_____ _____ God's Purpose for Music (Heb. 13:15, Matt. 21:15-16, Col. 3:16)

_____ _____ Practical Uses of Music

_____ _____ Careers in Music

BASIC MUSIC KNOWLEDGE

_____ _____ Knows the Musical Scale (Do, Re, Mi, Fa, So, La, Ti, Do)

_____ _____ Sings in Choir, Praise and Worship Team, and/or Solo

_____ _____ Understands and Can Sing Melody and Harmony (2-,3-,4-Part Harmony)

_____ _____ Reads Music

_____ _____ Plays an Instrument in Band or Orchestra

_____ _____ Listens to Music of All Types (Music Should Glorify God, Encourage Godly Love, Behavior and/or Appreciation For God's Creation.)

_____ _____ _____

_____ _____ _____

_____ _____ _____

MUSIC FORMS

Elem	Jr/Sr High		Elem	Jr/Sr High	
___	___	Ballet	___	___	Opera
___	___	Canons	___	___	Orchestra
___	___	Cantata	___	___	Overture
___	___	Celtic	___	___	Rhapsody
___	___	Chamber Music	___	___	Scherzo
___	___	Chorale	___	___	Serenade
___	___	Concerto	___	___	Sonata
___	___	Etude	___	___	Suite
___	___	Folk Music	___	___	Symphony
___	___	Fugue	___	___	_____
___	___	Gregorian Chant	___	___	_____
___	___	Madrigal	___	___	_____
___	___	March			

MUSICAL INSTRUMENTS AND THEIR FAMILIES

_____ _____ Strings (Banjo, Cello, Guitar, Harp, Viola, Violin)

_____ _____ Percussion (Chimes, Cymbals, Drums, Fife, Gongs, Rattles, Tambourine, Timpani, Triangle, Xylophone)

_____ _____ Woodwinds (Bassoon, Clarinet, Flute, Oboe, Piccolo, Recorder, Saxophone,)

_____ _____ Brass (Cornet, French Horn, Trombone, Trumpet, Tuba)

_____ _____ Piano, Accordion, Organ

_____ _____ _____

_____ _____ _____

_____ _____ _____

MUSIC TERMS

____ ____	Acappela	____ ____ Rhythm
____ ____	Accent	____ ____ Scale
____ ____	Arpeggio	____ ____ Staff
____ ____	Bar	____ ____ Syncopation
____ ____	Chord	____ ____ Tempo
____ ____	Coda	____ ____ Third
____ ____	Downbeat	____ ____ Timbre
____ ____	Dynamics	____ ____ Time
____ ____	Expression	____ ____ Tone
____ ____	Fifth	____ ____ Treble
____ ____	Glissando	____ ____ Troubadours
____ ____	Harmony	____ ____ _____
____ ____	Improvise	____ ____ _____
____ ____	Interval	____ ____ _____
____ ____	Key	____ ____ _____
____ ____	Measure	____ ____ _____
____ ____	Melody	____ ____ _____
____ ____	Pitch	____ ____ _____

HISTORY OF MUSIC

____ ____ Music in the Bible
____ ____ Polyphonic Period (1200 to late 1500's)
____ ____ Baroque Period (late 1500's to middle 1700's)
____ ____ Classical Period (middle 1700's to early 1800's)
____ ____ Romantic Period (early 1800's to late 1800's)
____ ____ 20th Century (1900-2000)
____ ____ 21th Century (2000-)   –

____ ____ _____
____ ____ _____
____ ____ _____
____ ____ _____
____ ____ _____
____ ____ _____
____ ____ _____

AMERICAN COMPOSERS AND MUSICIANS

Study music in light of musician's relationship with God and how it affected his work.

_____	_____	Bates, Katharine Lee (?-d.1929)—Composer: America The Beautiful
_____	_____	Bennard, Rev. George (Ohio)—Hymn Writer: The Old Rugged Cross
_____	_____	Copland, Aaron (New York, 1900-1990)—Composer: Film Scores, Operas, Symphonies, Of Mice and Men, Our Town
_____	_____	Crosby, Fanny (New York, 1820-1915)—Hymn Writer: Saved by Grace, Safe in the Arms of Jesus
_____	_____	Foster, Stephen (Pennsylvania, 1826-1864)—Composer: Oh, Susanna, Beautiful Dreamer, Old Folks at Home
_____	_____	Gershwin, George (New York, 1898-1937)—Composer: Swanee, Rhapsody in Blue, Porgy and Bess
_____	_____	Key, Francis Scott (Maryland, 1779-1843)—Lawyer and Poet: Wrote The Star Spangled Banner (National Anthem)
_____	_____	Smith, Samuel Francis (Massachusetts, 1808-1895)—Composer: America
_____	_____	Sousa, John Philip (Washington D.C., 1854-1932)—Composer and U.S. Marine Bandmaster: The Stars and Stripes Forever, Semper Fidelis

COMPOSERS AND MUSICIANS OF THE WORLD

_____	_____	Bach, Johann Sebastian (Germany, 1685-1750)—Lutheran Organist and Composer: Cantatas, Polyphony, Baroque, Toccata and Fugue in D Minor
_____	_____	Beethoven, Ludwig van (Germany, 1770-1827)—Composer: Moonlight Sonata, Ode to Joy, Symphony No. 9
_____	_____	Bizet, Georges (France, 1838-1875)—Composer: Opera, Carmen
_____	_____	Brahms, Johannes (Germany, 1833-1897)—Conductor, Musician, and Composer: Piano, Hungarian Dance
_____	_____	Chopin, Frédéric (Poland, 1810-1849)—Composer and Pianist: Nocturnes
_____	_____	Debussy, Claude (France, 1862-1918)—Composer: Images and Préludes, LaMer
_____	_____	Dvořák, Antonin (Czech Republic, 1841-1904)—Composer: From the New World, Humoresque
_____	_____	Handel, Georg Frideric (Germany , 1685-1759)—Composer and Organist: Messiah, Water Music

_____ _____ Haydn, Franz Joseph (Austria, 1732-1809)—Composer: String Quartet, Classical Era, String Quartet 'Emperor' No. 62

_____ _____ Liszt, Franz (Hungary, 1811-1886)—Composer and Pianist: Hungarian Rhapsody No. 2

_____ _____ Luther, Martin (Germany, 1483-1546)—Religious Reformer, Bible Translator, and Hymn writer: Wittenberg, A Mighty Fortress is Our God

_____ _____ Mendelssohn, Felix (Germany, 1809-1847)—Composer: Midsummer Night's Dream, Wedding March

_____ _____ Mozart, Wolfgang Amadeus (Austria, 1756-1791)—Composer and Pianist: The Marriage of Figaro Symphony No. 80 in G Minor

_____ _____ Newton, John (England,1725 -1807)— Hymn Writer: Amazing Grace

_____ _____ Paganini, Niccolo (Italy, 1782-1840)—Violin Virtuoso

_____ _____ Puccini, Giacomo (Italy, 1858-1924)—Operatic Composer: Madame Butterfly, La Bohème

_____ _____ Rimsky-Korsakov, Nikolai (Russia, 1844-1908)—Composer: Scheherazade

_____ _____ Scarlatti, Alessandro (Italy, 1660-1725)—Composer: Piano Sonata in G Major

_____ _____ Schubert, Franz (Italy, 1797-1828)—Composer: Unfinished Symphony, Swan Song

_____ _____ Schumann, Robert (Germany, 1810-1856)—Composer: Carnival

_____ _____ Strauss, Richard (Germany, 1864-1949)—Composer: Don Juan, Alpine Symphony

_____ _____ Stravinsky, Igor (Russia/United States, 1882-1971)—Composer: Rite of Spring

_____ _____ Tchaikovsky (Russia, 1840-1893)—Composer: Swan Lake, The Sleeping Beauty Waltz, The Nutcracker, 1812 Overture

_____ _____ Verdi, Giuseppe (Italy, 1813-1901)—Composer: Dramatic Opera, La Traviata, Aida, Falstaff

_____ _____ Vivaldi, Antonio (Italy, 1678-1741)—Violinist and Composer: The Four Seasons

_____ _____ Wagner, Richard (Germany, 1813-1883)—Composer: Opera, The Flying Dutchman, Die Walkure

_____ _____ Watts, Isaac (England, 1674-1748) —Hymn Writer: When I Survey The Wondrous Cross

_____ _____ Wesley, Charles (England, 1707-1788)—Methodist Clergyman and Hymn Writer: Christ the Lord is Risen Today and Hark, the Herald Angels Sing

____ ____ _____

____ ____ _____

____ ____ _____

____ ____ _____

____ ____ _____

____ ____ _____

____ ____ _____

____ ____ _____

____ ____ _____

____ ____ _____

____ ____ _____

____ ____ _____

STATURE

Mature Physically and Chronologically

PHYSICAL DEVELOPMENT AND EXERCISE

Elem   Jr/Sr High

_____ _____ Small Motor Skills Developed
_____ _____ Large Motor Skills Developed
_____ _____ Eyesight Developed and Checked
_____ _____ Dental Care and Checkups
_____ _____ Immunizations as Needed (also see Disease and Immunity, page 154)
_____ _____ Physicals as Needed
_____ _____ Participates in Team Sports/Activities
_____ _____ Participates in Physical Fitness Program
_____ _____ Participates in Individual Sports/Activities
_____ _____ _____
_____ _____ _____
_____ _____ _____

CARE OF THE TEMPLE OF GOD

Elem   Jr/Sr High

_____ _____ Understand Good Health Habits
_____ _____ Safety (Home, Fire, Stranger Danger)
_____ _____ Driver's Education
_____ _____ Nutrition (also see Human Biology, page 154)
_____ _____ First Aid
_____ _____ Sex Education in Light of Scripture
_____ _____ Keeps Body Under Subjection to the Spirit
_____ _____ Abstinence in Drugs, Sex, Alcohol
_____ _____ _____
_____ _____ _____
_____ _____ _____

APPEARANCE

_____ _____ Clothes   _____ _____ Cleanliness
_____ _____ Cosmetics   _____ _____ _____
_____ _____ Skin Care   _____ _____ _____
_____ _____ Hair Care   _____ _____ _____

IN FAVOR WITH GOD—KNOWS GOD PERSONALLY

SPIRITUAL GROWTH

Elem   Jr/Sr High

_____ _____ Is Born Again

_____ _____ Personally Knows the Love of God (books by Philip Yancey such as *What's So Amazing About Grace* are highly recommended)

_____ _____ _____

_____ _____ _____

_____ _____ _____

_____ _____ _____

_____ _____ _____

_____ _____ _____

DOERS OF THE WORD

Elem   Jr/Sr High

_____ _____ Obedience—Obeys God's Word

_____ _____ Obedience—Obeys Parents and Follows Directions

_____ _____ Is Able to Lead Someone to Christ

_____ _____ Shares the Love of God With Others

_____ _____ _____

_____ _____ _____

_____ _____ _____

_____ _____ _____

_____ _____ _____

_____ _____ _____

_____ _____ _____

STEWARDSHIP

Elem   Jr/Sr High

_____ _____ Personal Property

_____ _____ Property of Others

_____ _____ Develops Gifts and Talents from God

_____ _____ Money (See Biblical Finances & Consumer Math, page 136)

_____ _____ Establish Healthy Boundaries and Respect the Boundaries of Others*

_____ _____ _____

_____ _____ _____

* I highly recommend the "Boundaries" series by Dr. Henry Cloud.

IN FAVOR WITH MAN

Be a Light and Example of Christ to the World. (I highly recommend that you and your children read the "Boundaries" series by Dr. Henry Cloud in order to keep this in perspective.)

SERVES THE BODY OF CHRIST

Elem   Jr/Sr High

CHARITY

_____ _____ Gives Financially to Those in Need—Offerings, Alms
_____ _____ Gives Time to Those in Need
_____ _____ _____
_____ _____ _____

CHURCH RESPONSIBILITY

_____ _____ Not Forsaking the Assembling—Attends Church Regularly
_____ _____ Members of Christ's Body—Volunteers in Church Ministries
_____ _____ Financial Responsibilities to Church
_____ _____ _____
_____ _____ _____

CHRISTIAN LOVE

_____ _____ Develops Compassion for Others
_____ _____ Loves Neighbor as Himself—Golden Rule
_____ _____ Edifies Each Other—Iron Sharpens Iron
_____ _____ Fruit of the Spirit Visible in His/Her Life
_____ _____ _____
_____ _____ _____

SERVES HIS OR HER FAMILY

Elem   Jr/Sr High

MARRIAGE PREPARATION

_____ _____ Dating and Courtship
_____ _____ Mate Selection
_____ _____ Marriage Commitment and Relationships
_____ _____ Sex Education (As Related to a Godly Marriage)
_____ _____ Child Training and Discipline
_____ _____ Roles of Father and Mother
_____ _____ Roles of Husband and Wife
_____ _____ _____
_____ _____ _____
_____ _____ _____

INDUSTRIAL ARTS

_____ _____	Auto Mechanics	_____ _____ _____
_____ _____	Carpentry	_____ _____ _____
_____ _____	Electricity	_____ _____ _____
_____ _____	Home Repair	_____ _____ _____
_____ _____	Plumbing	_____ _____ _____

HOME ECONOMICS

_____ _____	Comparison Shopping	_____ _____ _____
_____ _____	Cooking	_____ _____ _____
_____ _____	Decorating	_____ _____ _____
_____ _____	Gardening	_____ _____ _____
_____ _____	Housecleaning/Laundry	_____ _____ _____
_____ _____	Sewing	_____ _____ _____

CAREER PREPARATION AND SELF-EMPLOYMENT SKILLS
(Also see Biblical Finances and Consumer Math, page 136)

_____ _____	College Preparation
_____ _____	Internship, Apprenticeship
_____ _____	Advertising, Marketing
_____ _____	Management
_____ _____	Business Ethics

SERVES THE COMMUNITY AROUND HIM

Sociology—The Study of Society. Also See History, Geography, Geology

Elem	Jr/Sr High	
_____	_____	World Customs and Religions (In light of Missions)
_____	_____	Careers in Sociology/Social Work
_____	_____	Archaeology (See Archaeology and the Bible, page 22)
_____	_____	_____
_____	_____	_____
_____	_____	_____

FAMOUS MISSIONARIES AND BIBLE TEACHERS

_____	_____	Alfred the Great (849-899)—Christian King of Wessex
_____	_____	Brother Andrew (?, 1928-)—Ministry to the Communist World
_____	_____	Aylward, Gladys (Great Britain, 1903-1970)—Missionary to China
_____	_____	Booth, William (Great Britain, 1829-1912)—Founder of Salvation Army
_____	_____	Booth, Catherine (Great Britain, 1829-1890)—Mother of Salvation Army
_____	_____	Bunyan, John (Great Britain, 1628-1688)—Preacher and Author
_____	_____	Carey, William (Great Britain, 1761-1834)—Father of Modern Missions

_____ _____ Carmichael, Amy (Ireland, 1861-1951)—Missionary to India

_____ _____ Eliot, John (England, 1604-1690)—"Apostle to the Indians," translated Bible into Algonquin, 1st Bible translation in the U.S.

_____ _____ Elliot, Jim (Oregon, 1927-1956)—Missionary to Ecuador

_____ _____ Fry, Elizabeth (Great Britain, 1780-1845)—Prison Reformer

_____ _____ Graham, Billy (North Carolina, 1918-)—Evangelist and Christian Statesman

_____ _____ Judson, Adoniram (Massachusetts, 1788-1850)—Missionary to Burma

_____ _____ Kenyon, E.W. (d. 1948)—Minister and Bible Teacher

_____ _____ Lake, John G. (Canada, 1870-1935)—Minister

_____ _____ Liddell, Eric (Scotland, 1902-1945)—Evangelist, Missionary to China, and Famous Athlete: Chariots of Fire

_____ _____ Livingstone, David (Scotland, 1813-1873)—Explorer, Doctor, Author, Cartographer, and Missionary to Africa

_____ _____ Moody, Dwight L. (Massachusetts, 1837-1899)—American Evangelist, Children's Ministry, Moody Bible Institute, Hymn Book

_____ _____ Mother Teresa (Albania, 1910-1997)—Missionary to India

_____ _____ Müller, George (Prussia, 1805-1898)—Orphanages, Ashley Downs

_____ _____ Nee, Watchman (China, 1903-1972)—Chinese Pastor and Preacher

_____ _____ Palau, Luis (Argentina, 1934-)—Argentinian Evangelist

_____ _____ Scudder, Dr. Ida (United States, 1870-1960)—Founder of Vellore Medical College in India

_____ _____ Slessor, Mary (Scotland, 1848-1915)—Presbyterian Missionary to Calabar

_____ _____ Spurgeon, Charles (Great Britain, 1834-1892)—Minister

_____ _____ Taylor, Hudson (Great Britain, 1832-1905)—Founder of China Inland Mission

_____ _____ Ten Boom, Corrie (Holland, 1892-1983)—Ambassador for Christ, Holocaust

_____ _____ Wilberforce, William (Great Britain, 1759-1833)—Philanthropist and Reformer

_____ _____ _____

_____ _____ _____

_____ _____ _____

_____ _____ _____

_____ _____ _____

SOCIAL WORK

_____ _____ Witnesses, Shares the Gospel With Others (Jas. 5:20)

_____ _____ Hospitality

_____ _____ Outreach to the Community

_____ _____ _____

_____ _____ _____

_____ _____ _____

SOCIAL SKILLS

_____ _____ Etiquette/Manners

_____ _____ Leadership Training

_____ _____ _____

_____ _____ _____

Psychology—The Study of The Human Mind and Behavior

Elem   Jr/Sr High

_____ _____ Biblical Counseling, Compare Modern Psychology with God's Word
_____ _____ Careers in Psychology
_____ _____ Personality Differences
_____ _____ _____
_____ _____ _____
_____ _____ _____

CRISIS INTERVENTION

_____ _____ Abortion
_____ _____ Domestic Violence
_____ _____ Sexual Abuse
_____ _____ Substance Abuse

_____ _____ Suicide
_____ _____ _____
_____ _____ _____
_____ _____ _____

RESPECT FOR LIFE

_____ _____ Adoption
_____ _____ Eldercare
_____ _____ Euthanasia
_____ _____ Handicapped

_____ _____ Mental Illness
_____ _____ _____
_____ _____ _____
_____ _____ _____

FAMOUS PSYCHOLOGIST

_____ _____ Freud, Sigmund (Moravia, 1856-1939)—Psychologist, Beginning of Psychoanalysis, Oedipus Complex
_____ _____ Pavlov, Ivan (Russia, 1849-1936)—Physiologist, Pavlovian Conditioning
_____ _____ Adler, Alfred (Italy, 1870-1937)—Pioneer Psychologist, Inferiority Complex
_____ _____ Jung, Carl (Switzerland, 1875-1961)—Psychologist, Analytical Psychology, Extrovert, Introvert
_____ _____ _____
_____ _____ _____
_____ _____ _____
_____ _____ _____

Elem   Jr/Sr High

Yearly Planning Form

Name _____ Grade _____

WISDOM:

ART _____
_____
_____

BIBLE _____
_____
_____

COMPUTER _____
_____
_____

ECONOMICS _____
_____
_____

GEOGRAPHY _____
_____
_____

GOVERNMENT _____
_____
_____

HISTORY/SOCIAL STUDIES _____
_____
_____

MATH _____
_____
_____

MUSIC _____
_____
_____

ORAL COMMUNICATION _____
_____
_____

READING _____
_____
_____

RESEARCH SKILLS _____
_____
_____

SCIENCE _____
_____
_____

WRITTEN COMMUNICATION _____
_____
_____

STATURE:

HEALTH _____
_____
_____

PHYSICAL DEVELOPMENT _____
_____
_____

SAFETY _____
_____
_____

IN FAVOR WITH GOD:

SPIRITUAL GROWTH

_____
_____
_____

DOERS OF THE WORD

_____
_____
_____

STEWARDSHIP

_____
_____
_____

IN FAVOR WITH MAN:

ARCHAEOLOGY

_____
_____
_____

CHARITY

_____
_____
_____

CHURCH RESPONSIBILITY

_____
_____
_____

CHRISTIAN LOVE

_____
_____
_____

FOREIGN LANGUAGE

_____
_____
_____

HOME ECONOMICS

_____
_____
_____

INDUSTRIAL ARTS

_____
_____
_____

MARRIAGE PREPARATION

_____
_____
_____

MISSIONS/MISSIONARIES

_____
_____
_____

PSYCHOLOGY

_____
_____
_____

SOCIAL SKILLS

_____
_____
_____

SOCIAL WORK

_____
_____
_____

WORLD CUSTOMS

_____
_____
_____